Foodies

This important new and highly readable cultural analysis tells two stories about food. The first depicts good food as democratic. Foodies frequent "hole in the wall" ethnic eateries, appreciate the pie found in working-class truck-stops, and reject the snobbery of fancy French restaurants with formal table-service. The second story describes how food operates as a source of status and distinction for economic and cultural elites, indirectly maintaining and reproducing social inequality. While the first storyline insists that anybody can be a foodie, the second story asks foodies to look in the mirror and think about their relative social and economic privilege. By simultaneously considering *both* of these stories, and studying how they operate in tension, a delicious sociology of food becomes available, perfect for teaching a broad range of cultural sociology courses.

Josée Johnston is assistant professor of sociology at the University of Toronto. Her major area of research is the sociology of food. Her work ties together several research threads including globalization, political-ecology, culture, and consumerism.

Shyon Baumann is associate professor of sociology at the University of Toronto. He studies the sociology of culture, the arts, and the media. He is the author of *Hollywood Highbrow: From Entertainment to Art*, and is currently studying the production and content of television advertising.

Cultural Spaces Series

Edited by Sharon Zukin, *Brooklyn College and the City University Graduate Center*

Books Available in the Series

Buyways by Catherine Gudis
Silicon Alley by Michael Indergaard
Capitalism's Eye by Kevin Hetherington
After the World Trade Center edited by Michael Sorkin and Sharon Zukin
Branding New York by Miriam Greenberg
The Global Architect by Donald McNeill
The Diaspora Strikes Back by Juan Flores

Also of Interest from Routledge

Food and Culture, Second Edition edited by Carole Counihan and Penny Van Esterik
City Life from Jakarta to Dakar: Movements at the Crossroads by AbdouMaliq Simone
The Internet and Social Inequalities by James C. Witte and Susan E. Mannon
Common Ground?: Readings and Reflections on Public Space edited by Anthony Orum and Zachary Neal
The Gentrification Debates edited by Japonica Brown-Saracino
Military Legacies: A World Made by War by James A. Tyner

Foodies
Democracy and Distinction in the Gourmet Foodscape

Josée Johnston
University of Toronto

Shyon Baumann
University of Toronto

Routledge
Taylor & Francis Group

NEW YORK AND LONDON

First published 2010
by Routledge
270 Madison Avenue, New York, NY 10016

Simultaneously published in the UK
by Routledge
2 Park Square, Milton Park, Abingdon, Oxon OX14 4RN

Routledge is an imprint of the Taylor & Francis Group, an informa business

Typeset in Adobe Caslon and Copperplate Gothic by
RefineCatch Limited, Bungay, Suffolk
Printed and bound in the United States of America on acid-free paper by
Edwards Brothers, Inc.

Library of Congress Cataloging in Publication Data
Johnston, Josée.
Democracy and distinction in the gourmet foodscape / Josée Johnston,
Shyon Baumann.
p. cm. — (Cultural spaces series)
1. Food—Social aspects. 2. Food habits—Economic aspects.
3. Social status. 4. Gourmets. I. Baumann, Shyon, 1971–
II. Title.
GT2850.J64 2009
394.1—dc22
2009019768

ISBN10: 0–415–96538–1 (hbk)
ISBN10: 0–415–96537–3 (pbk)
ISBN10: 0–203–86864–1 (ebk)

ISBN13: 978–0–415–96538–5 (hbk)
ISBN13: 978–0–415–96537–8 (pbk)
ISBN13: 978–0–203–86864–5 (ebk)

DEDICATION

For Bram and Lucille—for whom we happily prepare gourmet hot
dogs and french fries.

TABLE OF CONTENTS – IN BRIEF

TABLE OF CONTENTS – IN DETAIL

SERIES FOREWORD

The *Cultural Spaces* series presents in-depth, sociological portraits and interpretations of people and places in constant change. Some authors look at the social forces that create cities, neighborhoods, districts like "Silicon Alley," and even buildings like New York's World Trade Center site. Other authors write about the social practices that develop around modern spaces—the "branding" of New York City in the 1960s and 1970s; the invention of highway billboards in the 1920s; and the way men and women looked at consumer goods in the late 19th century home, museum, and city. A recent book in the series examines the cultural space of "reverse remittances": changes in music, poetry, and performance that are brought back to their home countries by returning migrants, who experience more than their fair share of creative tensions between "home" and "away." The common element series authors share is a desire to document tensions between elite cultures and the cultures of the streets—between "high" and "low" culture, political domination and countercultural style, and conventional and innovative cultural forms.

Foodies appears at a moment of great contradiction in consumer culture. Though large-scale farming and advanced technology make available a vast variety of foods in almost limitless supply, the simple act of choosing among these foods—or even choosing whether to eat at all—plunges us into deep anxiety. Ubiquitous fast-food restaurants make nourishment widely available and, at least in the United States, relatively cheap—but the prevalence of fat, animal products, and corn syrup in their menus is connected with problems of obesity, diabetes, and depletion of natural resources. An apparently bottomless craving for fast-food staples such as cheeseburgers and chicken nuggets does not solve real problems of physical hunger—but it risks eroding traditional standards of good eating in countries around the world. At the same time as fast food has become a universal norm, however, a widespread culture of fine eating, identified with local produce, slow cooking, and careful consideration of the aesthetics of cuisine, has grown.

Josée Johnston and Shyon Baumann show us how the apparently deviant standpoint of "foodies" has developed a powerful influence over consumer culture. In contrast to elitist gourmets of the past, foodies praise both the high culture of great restaurant chefs and the low culture of street vendors. They travel far and wide to forage for humble products and unknown preparations. They worship the peasant cook, the local specialty, and anything that suggests an authentic experience that can penetrate through the standardization of modern life to the essence of "good taste." Foodies are, in short, omnivorous consumers in pursuit of perfection wherever they can find it.

This appetite for everything conceals a crucial contradiction. Johnston and Baumann take the idea of omnivorousness that has been developed by the sociologist Richard Peterson and others, and reveal how the apparently democratic support of both high and low cultures really creates subtle means of social differentiation. A fetish for peasant foods, especially in the Global South; a new Orientalism that finds value in exotic foods and places; and continued support for "European" food producers suggest that omnivores shape consumer discourse in a way that deepens rather than diminishes inequalities of social status.

Reading *Foodies*, then, we enter into two hotly contested debates: What makes food good? (what we could call the social production of taste) and Who has the social power to determine these standards? (that is, the social production of taste communities). Johnston and Baumann challenge the idea that the democratization of tastes in recent years has created a more democratic society. They inspire us to think critically about consumer culture.

Sharon Zukin
Series Editor

PREFACE

There are at least two stories to tell about food. The first narrative depicts good food as democratic. This view emphasizes how foodies frequent "hole in the wall" ethnic eateries, appreciate the pie found in working-class truck-stops, and reject the snobbery of fancy French restaurants with formal table-service. The second story describes how food operates as a source of status and distinction for economic and cultural elites, indirectly maintaining and reproducing social inequality. While the first storyline insists that anybody can be a foodie, the second story asks foodies to look in the mirror and think about their relative social and economic privilege. In this book, we insist that foodies cannot be fully understood by either story told on its own. Instead, it is only by simultaneously considering *both* of these stories, and studying how they operate in tension, that we can fully develop a sociology of foodies.

In our personal lives, we continually observe the tension between the two storylines of democracy and distinction. We have seen how knowledge of foodie phenomena like molecular gastronomy, sous-vide cooking, "undiscovered" ethnic cuisines, and single-origin chocolate can be cultural capital, even in recessionary times. In the neighborhood where we live, a food journalist recently reported that "foodie children" are the hot new accessory, and described overhearing parents proudly boasting that their children ate pig intestines at local Korean restaurants. At the same time food serves as fuel generating cultural status, foodie culture valorizes foods outside of the traditional culinary canon eaten outside of formal dining rooms—foods like Vietnamese bánh mì, South Indian dhosas, and Hakka take-out. Not only is the foodie repertoire wide-reaching, but we have also observed how food can mobilize social and environmental critique. We live in a city, Toronto, that is known in food circles not just for its fine dining and innovative chefs, but for its vibrant food activist scene and municipal food policy council. This city is home to various projects seeking to connect eaters with high-quality, sustainably-produced foods. In conditions of economic recession, these food projects take on increased importance, while conspicuous culinary consumption can appear excessive and grotesque. In tough times, food writing becomes more sensitive to gastronomic excess, and more "of the people"—publishing comfort food recipes and travel articles about cheap eats in Paris and London (even though the criterion for affordable usually means over $100 for a meal).

As we write this preface, the United States is experiencing a wide-scale economic crisis. Is this the right moment, one might ask, to write a book about something as frivolous as food, and even worse, *foodies*—people who obsess about hand-crafting the perfect meatball and then uploading a meatball photo to their blog? We wondered this ourselves as the economic crisis deepened, and we read staggering statistics about homelessness, job losses, home foreclosures and bankruptcies. Would the burgeoning interest in good food retrench in hard times? While grocery budgets and share prices of Whole Foods Market have been impacted by the economic downturn, it appears that interest in fine food is far from disappearing. While some restaurants and consumers have tightened their belts, an April 2009 article in *Gourmet* reported that newly-opened high-end restaurants in New York City (featuring $45 entrées and $125 tasting menus) are doing very well—so well that it is hard to get a reservation. One of the reviewed restaurants, Bouley, features opulent surroundings, a foyer decorated with thousands of apples, and a dress code, while the other restaurant, the John Dory, is a casual seafood restaurant with a kitschy fish-themed décor. The juxtaposition of these two successful restaurants speaks to the central tension we identify and elaborate in this book between ideologies of distinction and democracy in the foodscape.

If we accept that economic recession has not killed off foodies, it is worth asking a basic question that animates our food research. Why do foodies care about food so much? Why are they (we) so obsessed? These kinds of "why" questions are not the central concerns of this book, which is focused on *how* foodies make the decisions they do about what foods to value, and what criteria they use to determine high-quality food. However, after several years of research on the topic, we have some speculations about the myriad factors underlying foodie obsessions, as well as our own interest in food and food research. First, and perhaps most obviously, the contemporary gourmet foodscape offers incredible pleasures. Discovering hand-crafted, artisan-produced cheeses can be more interesting than mass-produced Parmesan, even if there is no independent aesthetic criterion to verify this point. When you read foodie blogs, what is immediately apparent is the incredible satisfaction people derive from being a food producer—making your own sourdough bread, hand-crafting sausages on the weekend, churning ice-cream in the summer-time—as opposed to simply being a food consumer. The writing of philosopher Albert Borgman on focal practices aptly illustrates the importance of actively engaging with a *practice*, like cooking, rather than passively consuming a *thing*. More tangibly, in our personal lives we take tremendous joy and pleasure in the daily rituals of food preparation. Even in our most time-crunched, harried state, we anticipate what food will punctuate the end of our workday.

Another factor underlying foodie passions is concern about the industrial food system, and its implication in health problems, ecological devastation, and social injustices. As the environmental and health risks associated with industrial agriculture become more apparent in the public sphere, making different kinds of food choices becomes a way for foodies to protest environmental degradation and injustice, as well as a way to protect their health. Ethical consumer politics can also prove more alluring than conventional political channels, particularly in a political climate where many people feel disenfranchised from traditional political processes and institutions. In terms of the rhythms of daily life, it is often easier to express one's politics through a food purchase, than it is to find the time to write a letter, attend a protest, or participate in social movement politics. We realize that fair-trade coffee or organic tofu themselves won't change the world, but consuming these products seems like an achievable gesture, especially when time constraints militate against more substantive action.

An additional factor behind foodie obsessions is globalization processes. With heightened transnational migration and increased cross-border travel, food culture has changed accordingly, becoming more cosmopolitan. We have been engaged with the food cultures of our multicultural, downtown neighborhood, and have been influenced by the foods we have consumed while traveling. In addition, the explosion of food media, particularly food television and Internet resources, undoubtedly plays an important role fueling the foodie fire. While both of our mothers had an interest in cooking when we grew up, the information available to them in the 1970s pales in comparison to our current access to online recipes, food television programming, and foodie blogs. After eating the famous Poilâne bread in Paris, we consulted with myriad web resources to produce a reasonable facsimile in our home kitchen. Watching a food television program often leads to an Internet search, which, in turn, leads to a culinary experiment.

While we cannot deny, and do not wish to deny, the pleasures and possibilities of foodie culture, nor the increased availability of information about food and foodie culture, our research also emphasizes food's role perpetuating social hierarchy and inequality. In this book we cast a cultural light on social stratification, demonstrating how foodie culture operates as a form of cultural capital that enables and legitimates social inequality. Participating in foodie culture not only is a tremendous privilege, reliant on the possession of adequate economic and cultural capital, but also represents a kind of cultural hegemony. Hegemony can be understood as a kind of collective common sense that legitimizes elite control of a disproportionate share of resources; in the case of contemporary United States politics, this refers to global resources, rather than simply national resources. As we write these words, a newsletter in our community food box arrives, reminding us that 80 percent of the food in the world is consumed by just 17 percent of the world's population, while 57 percent of the world's population can access only 2 percent of the world's food.

The scale of global food inequality is undeniably grotesque, yet often imperceptible in the gourmet foodscape. Analytically, it is important for scholars to avoid a functionalist view of how this inequality is culturally legitimized and rendered invisible. As Gramsci himself imagined, hegemony is a fluid process, where common sense must be continually constructed, and remains vulnerable to challenges. While we believe that overall, foodie culture reinforces and legitimizes a positive association between wealth and good food, counter-hegemonic challenges are significant. The most prominent challenges are environmental, as evident in the increased attention to local eating, the expansion of organics, the growth of farmers' markets, and the expanded public consciousness of concepts like food miles. While "green" challenges have increased, "red" challenges of social justice have been less significant in the gourmet foodscape, although even there, we find surprises. The April 2009 issue of *Gourmet* featured a remarkably candid article on the processed commodity foods eaten on a native American reservation in South Dakota, while the March issue featured an equally surprising exposé of the extreme labor exploitation in the Florida tomato industry. So while cultural hegemony is a theme in this book, we emphasize that cultural domination is not monolithic and guaranteed, but must be continually recreated. Critiques can be taken up by the dominant food industry players, a process which blurs the boundaries between mainstream and "alternative" food. This makes for an incredibly complex foodscape, but suggests that now is an exciting time for food scholarship, and the perfect moment for sociologists to take food seriously as a subject of inquiry.

In terms of food scholarship, our ambition is to make clear that the gourmet foodscape cannot be interpreted in simple binary terms: as good or bad, egalitarian or elitist, politically progressive or bourgeois piggery. Transcending these binaries, and instead studying the tension between these polarities, allows us to generate new insights into the cultural underpinnings and political implications of the foodie phenomenon. Analytically, a study of these tensions renews the legacy of French sociologist Pierre Bourdieu, whose seminal scholarship revealed the nuanced connections between taste and social class; while our taste in food continues to speak to our class position, this is not a simple correspondence between rarefied "fancy" food for high-class people, but a more complex, omnivorous affair. Foodies are clearly omnivores—not in the sense of eating all things, but in the sense of carefully selecting from a wide array of genres. Politically, we study the tensions of foodie omnivorousness and hold on to narratives both of democracy and of distinction in order to develop a perspective of normative critique and hopefulness. Our work is intended to make clear the immense privilege of using food as an art form, leisure pursuit, and source of social status, but at the same time, we believe that food can serve as a sort of window into the soul of the capitalist food system, generating awareness of the ecological devastation and social inequality that underpin most of our meals.

ACKNOWLEDGMENTS

As foodies, we love our subject matter and enjoyed immersing ourselves into the gourmet foodscape. As enjoyable as the topic is for us, it was still an enormous amount of work to write this book. Luckily, we had help along the way.

Kate Cairns worked as a research assistant throughout the project. Simply put, she is an academic star who has a bright future. We are extremely fortunate that we were able to draw on her skills and talent. This project also benefited from the excellent research assistance of Devani Singh and Mercedes Lee, who helped with the research that we incorporated into the Introduction and Chapter 1.

Several years ago Neil McLaughlin asked a question that inspired this collaboration, and which encouraged us to cross boundaries between the sociology of culture and food scholarship; we are grateful to him for providing that important initial spark, as for his intellectual support over the years. Of course, we are also grateful to the many people who commented on various versions of these chapters, both in written form and in conference presentations. Thanks, in particular, to the anonymous reviewers at the *American Journal of Sociology*, the anonymous reviewers who reviewed the manuscript for Routledge, the exceptional support provided by Steve Rutter, the important suggestions and insights of series editor, Sharon Zukin, and also for helpful comments provided by Elaine Powers, Bonnie Erickson, and Richard Peterson.

The Social Science and Humanities Research Council of Canada provided research funding that facilitated this project. This funding allowed us to hire research assistants and to collect the data. We are grateful that this funding agency believes in the value of this research.

We would also like to thank the interviewees who gave so generously of their time and who provided such rich depictions of how they think and feel about food.

Besides intellectual support, we are grateful for all of those who fed us while we were laboring on this project, especially Leonore Johnston and Ronit Dinovitzer. And we want to acknowledge our children, who were very patiently born during the writing process and continued to patiently tolerate our preoccupation with completing this project.

INTRODUCTION
ENTERING THE DELICIOUS WORLD OF FOODIES

We begin this book with a confession: We have never really considered ourselves foodies. Yes, we bake our own bread with a sourdough culture that we vigorously tend to like a beloved pet, religiously adding filtered water and organic flour to sustain its bubbly natural yeasts. And yes, our idea of a good time on New Year's Eve is not a raucous night on the town, but staying home with friends to make (and eat) home-made gnocchi. We'll admit, we do follow the aspiring culinary stars on the Bravo Network show Top Chef, and are inspired to cook things after flipping through the pages of glossy food magazines like *Gourmet* or *Saveur*. After watching Bobby Flay's show, *Throwdown*, we were thrilled—even touched—when friends flew home from Boston illegally transporting six sticky buns from the bakery ("Flour") that whooped Chef Flay's celebrity behind. The sight of the "hello-kitty" cake pops and "14 layer cake" on the food blog "bakerella" both inspires us and makes us laugh out loud. We know the names of our city's most acclaimed chefs, and read many of their reviews, even though the demands of having young children (and professors' salaries) means we rarely eat their food.

At the same time we unconsciously acquire knowledge of high-end food establishments, we frequent an extensive roster of lower-cost eateries selling foods like bi bim bop, lamb roti, and barbeque brisket. We try to eat organic and local foods as frequently as possible, but we are not above tucking into food court french fries, or using the occasional bribe of fast food to obtain compliance in our children. We enjoy the challenge of learning how to make unusual food items at home, like marshmallows or osso buco, but we frequently fall back on homey staples like rice pudding, roast chicken, and cinnamon buns. Perhaps because both of us were raised in remote outposts where jello salads and hamburger helper were culinary mainstays, we are acutely conscious of how "fancy" food can mark you as a snob and an outsider. While we tend to reject many of the packaged foods of our rural food culture (e.g., a neighbor's chocolate fudge made with Velveeta cheese), we genuinely love eating many dishes prepared from rural community cookbooks[1]—even though we know that a "sophisticated" palate provides ease and comfort in many settings, like high-end restaurants and fancy university functions.

Given our obvious affection for foods of various varieties and genres—high and low, fast and slow—doesn't this make us foodies? We hope this book will shed light on both the contested term "foodie," and the phenomenon that surrounds the label: the food television, the obsession with celebrity chefs, the glossy food-porn, the food blogs, and the general obsession with culinary pursuits. We can't hope to provide all the answers, or all of the information on the foodie world—especially since we ourselves discover new foods, cookbook authors, restaurants, and food blogs on a regular basis—but we do hope to outline some of its defining features and contradictions. In particular, we focus on the contradiction between foodies' democratic openness to exploring new food cultures, alongside the continued existence of exclusion, inequality, and exploitation in the gourmet foodscape. Put differently, we explore the world of foodies to discover what they can teach us not only about eating, but also about the cultural politics of belonging, exclusion, and status. We use the gourmet American foodscape as a lens to explore the complexities and contradictions of elite cultural consumption, particularly as it evolves in a cultural context that endorses democratic ideals and rejects overt snobbery.

Before proceeding, it is worth clarifying what we mean by the term "foodscape." Drawing from geographic and sociological literature on landscape (e.g., Mitchell 2002; Zukin 1991), we use the concept of

"foodscape" to describe the cultural spaces of gourmet food. We understand the foodscape as a dynamic social construction that relates food
to specific places, people, and meanings. Just as a landscape painting has
a mediated, indirect relationship to place, a foodscape may variously
capture or obscure the ecological origins and social implications of food
production and consumption. The advantage of the term "foodscape" is
twofold: First, it recognizes that our understandings of food and the
food system are mediated through social mores and cultural institutions
like the mass media; second, it suggests the interrelationship between
culture, taste, and physical landscape, or ecology. Our focus in this book
is on the foodscape occupied by foodies, what we call the "gourmet
foodscape" (mainly because of the obvious problems with the term
"foodie foodscape"), but we will provide a brief overview of the broader
American foodscape below.

In the field of cultural sociology today, it is widely recognized that
cultural elites—including gourmets—have exited a period of straightforward cultural snobbery and entered an "omnivorous" era (Peterson
2005) where the traditional divide between highbrow and lowbrow
has eroded. (Omnivorousness is explored more in Chapter 1.) In this
context, terms like "foodie" have emerged as a counterpoint to the
cloistered world of high-culture food snobs. While American gourmets
are interested in a diversity of cuisines, this does not mean that any and
every food is now appropriate for gourmet connoisseurship. This book
documents and explores how new markers of high-status food have
emerged: Quality, rarity, locality, organic, hand-made, creativity, and
simplicity all work to signify specific foods as a source of distinction
for those with cultural and economic capital. Clearly, food snobs have
not disappeared from the cultural landscape. Instead, we document
the existence of a culinary tension in the American foodscape between
democratic inclusion (the foodie who declares a willingness to eat
anything), and status-based exclusion and cultural distinction (the
foodie who declares the only Mexican food worth eating is hand-made
by peasants in Mexico).

We have two major goals in this book. Our first goal is to investigate food's continuing role establishing symbolic boundaries and status

distinctions. Despite the apparent openness of foodies to consuming *anything*, our research reveals that foodies shape their world—the gourmet foodscape—around distinctions between "good" and "bad" foods. We argue that the drawing of these boundaries between good and bad foods reveals how people think about cultural consumption more broadly. At the same time that they genuinely enjoy food, foodies engage in identity politics and status distinctions through their eating practices. In making our argument, we also document the particular qualities of food that are used to draw the boundaries between worthy and unworthy culture. These qualities—particularly authenticity and exoticism— tell us a great deal about how cultural consumption functions to produce status in the contemporary United States.

Our second goal is to use foodie culture as a lens for investigating the political dimensions of food practices. The rise of food politics in the current decade creates an opportunity for food journalism and for foodies to integrate environmental issues, labor rights, animal welfare, and health concerns within discussions of gourmet food. We find that, although there is growing awareness of these issues within the gourmet foodscape, not all these concerns receive attention. Moreover, the attention they do receive frequently takes on a particular form, one that privileges an individualized stance on personal consumer ethics over a collectivist approach to solving social problems through food policies and collective action.

To study the culture and politics of the gourmet foodscape, we juxtapose the omnipresent need for cultural distinction with the potential for democratization that stands alongside the politicization of food choices. We find productive analytic possibilities by exploring the democracy/distinction tension, and resist the tendency to either extol or denounce foodie culture. While our writing is focused on American gourmet culture, it is important to situate the gastronomic field within a larger context of globalized food production and all its attendant inequities, social anxieties, and ecological risks. For instance, while the demand for organic food represents a critique of conventional agricultural practices, it also embodies the inequalities of the global system; 98% of organic food in Mexico is grown for export (Lotter 2005)—a pattern that holds true for many developing-country agricultural producers. While gourmet food culture is inextricably implicated in inequitable global commodity chains, gourmet food culture may create transformative cultural spaces—spaces where food journalists emerge as public intellectuals, and some foodies attempt to express their social and environmental commitments through grocery shopping.

To fully understand the significance of an omnivorous foodie era where food choices are more open and politicized, we need to see how gourmet culture evolved from a snobbish era where French cuisine dominated the culinary hierarchy. In the following section, we briefly describe the long-term shift in the United States away from a focus on French food as the primary high-status cuisine. We follow that description with a look at some key foodie phenomena, providing information about current food trends that give the gourmet foodscape some of its color and flavor.

The Fall of the French: A Historical Perspective

Prior to the 1960s, America's gourmet food culture was the terrain of an elite minority. America's oldest culinary magazine, *Gourmet*, had been launched in 1941, and had a small, loyal, and elite following. In the first years of its publication, *Gourmet*'s most popular feature was a column about "the help"; "Clémentine in the Kitchen" was an account of an American family and the French country girl they hired to be their cook (Kamp 2006: 39). Other regular features included "Specialités de la Maison," "*Gourmet*'s LIVES", and "Kitchen Mechanics." A few early cooking shows, such as James Beard's fifteen-minute segment "I Love to Eat!", drew small audiences of middle-class housewives seeking tips for daily food preparation (Fussell 2005: 34). Despite these early glimmers of food media, epicurean food culture was a relatively elite affair and the average American consumer considered eating a mundane feature of daily living.

While not having a mass following, gourmet culture was alive and well for a certain sector of society. A historical perspective on the gourmet in the United States begins with French food. While the French reference point for haute cuisine waxed and waned throughout the 19th century,

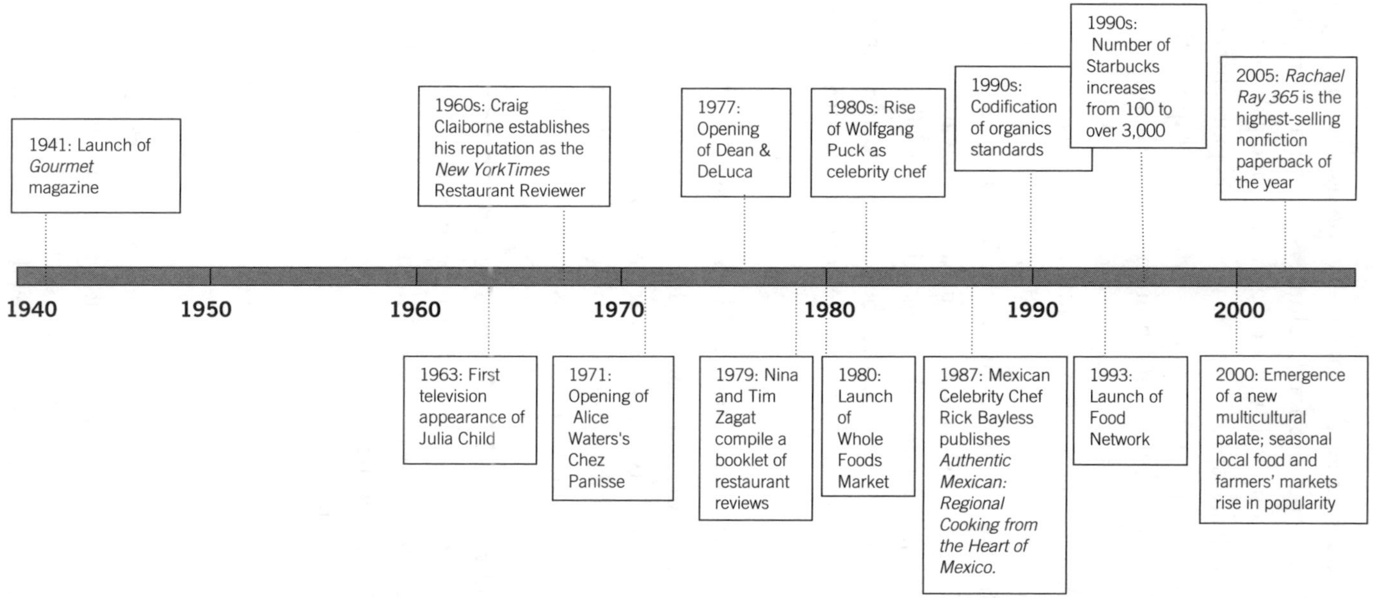

Figure 0.1 Major events in recent American culinary history

1940   1950   1960   1970   1980   1990   2000

1941: Launch of *Gourmet* magazine

1960s: Craig Claiborne establishes his reputation as the *New York Times* Restaurant Reviewer

1963: First television appearance of Julia Child

1971: Opening of Alice Waters's Chez Panisse

1977: Opening of Dean & DeLuca

1979: Nina and Tim Zagat compile a booklet of restaurant reviews

1980s: Rise of Wolfgang Puck as celebrity chef

1980: Launch of Whole Foods Market

1987: Mexican Celebrity Chef Rick Bayless publishes *Authentic Mexican: Regional Cooking from the Heart of Mexico.*

1990s: Codification of organics standards

1990s: Number of Starbucks increases from 100 to over 3,000

1993: Launch of Food Network

2005: *Rachael Ray 365* is the highest-selling nonfiction paperback of the year

2000: Emergence of a new multicultural palate; seasonal local food and farmers' markets rise in popularity

elite American food culture was dominated by French haute cuisine at the turn of the 20th century (Mennell 1996: 134). Prestigious hotel restaurants like the Ritz-Carlton and Waldorf-Astoria were run by French chefs such as Auguste Escoffier, and in the early post-World War II period, the 1941 opening of Le Pavillon both exemplified and perpetuated the high-status of French cuisine amongst American elites. Run by French immigrant Henri Soulé, Le Pavillon emphasized the subtleties of refined French food as well as "le standing"—an anglicized term referring to the class of elites who gained access to the elevated dining experience (Kuh 2001: 12–17; 32–33; Levenstein 1989: 71, 78; Kamp 2006: 39). The elevation of French haute cuisine through restaurants like Le Pavillon represented a form of culinary "sacralization"—a North American cultural phenomenon that prioritizes 'Old World' knowledge, values professional cultural producers over amateurs, and valorizes a singular model of legitimate Culture, or in this case, Cuisine (L. Levine 1988: 139, 168).

While sacralization was a key characteristic of restaurants like Le Pavillon, this trend began to unwind in the post-war period. The de-sacralization of haute cuisine was perhaps best symbolized with the opening of the Four Seasons restaurant in the Seagrams building in New York in 1959 (Kuh 2001: 58). A new 'modern' menu was overseen by James Beard—an emerging culinary giant who dared to include 'genuine' American food items such as Amish ham steak with prune knoedel, and showed a shocking insouciance toward French culinary classics (Jacobs 2002: 262; Kuh 2001: 60–70; Kamp 2006: 64).[2] The de-centering of French haute cuisine was not limited to New York's gastronomic elites, but signaled an emerging culinary curiosity about exotic foods like curry as well as interest in defining American cuisine—a broadening trend that slowly but surely knocked French haute cuisine off its high pedestal.[3]

While elite restaurants broadened their menus beyond the French culinary canon, interest in French food expanded amongst the middle class.[4] As French food became more accessible, its role as an exclusive, almost mystical culinary reference point and status symbol diminished (Levenstein 1989: 80–81). The year 1962 marks the year of a highly celebrated event in this process of de-sacralizing French food: The first television appearance of spirited media personality, Julia Child. Child's bestselling text, *Mastering the Art of French Cooking*, and television show introduced French menus to the middle-class host and hostess. In Child's own words, "[w]hat I was trying to do was to break down the snob appeal" (cited in Levenstein 1993: 143). With her candid performances on "The French Chef," Child welcomed viewers into the realm of sophisticated cuisine, and made it accessible to middle-class viewers. In the words of Betty Fussell, Child "changed we happy few to we happy millions by taking the la-dee-dah out of and putting the hee-haw-ho into French cooking" (2005: 47). Her appeal was broad: In November of 1966, Child was featured on the cover of *Time* magazine, with the title "Our Lady of the Ladle" (Civitello 2007: 336). Over the years, Child has been revered as perhaps the most significant American figure in the democratization of gourmet food. According to biographer Laura Shapiro, "Julia attracted love, torrents of it, a steady outpouring of delighted love that began with the first pilot episode of *The French Chef* in 1962 and continued through and beyond her death in 2004" (2007: xiv). After Child died, she was remembered in glowing tributes offered by many major media outlets, including PBS, CNN, and the Food Network, each celebrating her life's work. Each tribute interpreted Child's contribution "as opening a *lumpen* land up to sophistication in a way that it could stomach" (Miller 2007: 135).

Not only did television broaden the knowledge of gourmet cuisine, but food writing also worked to broaden middle-class knowledge of the elite food world. Besides Julia Child, another key food figure in this development in the 1960s was Craig Claiborne. Working as the restaurant reviewer at the *New York Times*, Claiborne "turned food writing into a bona fide arm of journalism and invented the make-or-break starred restaurant review" (Kamp 2006: xv). As the "first man to hold the title of food editor in the country" (Davis 2004: 14), Claiborne took seriously his duty as restaurant reviewer; he insisted on maintaining professional standards and provided consumers with critical assessments that departed from the tradition of more superficial, generally flattering accounts (Zukin 2004). Each restaurant review functioned as a lesson in culinary education for the average American newspaper reader. In the words of Betty Fussell, Claiborne was "the first to system-atically let us in on the secrets of famous chefs, to take us behind the scenes of restaurants we'd never dreamed of visiting, to tease us into sampling exotica like Nuoc Mam Sauce that we could cook before we could pronounce" (2005: 40). Modeling the refined tastes of a discern-ing consumer, Claiborne's reviews quickly gained "cultural currency" among *Times* readers, and restaurant-goers came to rely upon his culinary expertise (Davis 2004: 64).

French haute cuisine was further "de-sacralized" as a singular culinary model in the American context through its transmogrification into the relaxed, pluralistic cooking style of California cuisine.[5] Of particu-lar influence here was the celebrated Chez Panisse, Alice Waters's renowned Berkeley restaurant that drew from French culinary classics, but bucked convention to emphasize the importance of seasonal, local ingredients—perhaps best symbolized by the salad of fresh baby greens accompanied with a round of warm goat cheese that they popu-larized. Alice Waters was one of the first chefs to openly recognize the political consequences of personal eating habits. Her restaurant, Chez Panisse, which opened in 1971, featured seasonably-available California foods, and has been credited with inspiring interest in local ingredients and direct connections with farmers (McNamee 2007). Elizabeth David's literary works on working-class and peasant cooking in the Mediterranean, Italy, and France (1998a, 1998b, 1998c) inspired the chefs at Chez Panisse, who tended to lack formal culinary training but possessed university degrees and the political acumen of the Berkeley counterculture. Influenced by the countercultural influences of the late 1960s, the gastronomic emphasis was on the "revolutionary" spirit, not a stuffy, rule-bound nod to haute cuisine formal conventions, and less a statement on the status of those who dined in elite restaurants.

The broad counterculture movement that developed throughout the 1960s decade raised difficult questions about consumption practices (Belasco 1989), and furthered the de-sacralization trend of gourmet food. After the groundbreaking release of Rachel Carson's *Silent Spring* in 1962, the discourse of ecology circulated widely (Binkley 2007), and some politically-minded individuals "began eating with a consciousness about the environmental consequences of where their food came from and how it was produced" (Civitello 2007: 338). The counterculture movement also provided a forum for vegetarianism, popularized through publications such as Frances Moore Lappé's *Diet for a Small Planet* (1971), as well as the 1973 launch of the Moosewood Restaurant. Embodying this seeming politicization and democratic opening of gourmet culture, the then *New York Times* food critic, Ruth Reichl (2005: 228), who herself emerged from the 1960s Berkeley counterculture, rebutted the charge that gourmet cuisine was about "restaurants where rich people get to remind themselves that they are different from you and me," and claimed that although eating in good American restaurants in prior decades had a cultural resemblance to opera attendance, it had more recently become both casual and accessible.

The 1960s and 1970s also saw an increasing interest in ethnic foods.[6] One factor driving these changes to American food culture was shifting immigration patterns. More migrants from Latin and Central America and Asia were granted entry into the United States after the 1965 Immigration Act which put an end to national quotas that favored British migrants over those from other regions; these migrants brought ingredients and cooking styles that were new to the American foodscape. New ethnic cuisines were picked up by the counterculture (Belasco 1989), but eventually many of these new tastes and flavors made their way into the mouths of gourmets and food critics. In a culinary walking tour of New York, writer Calvin Trillin declared the Immigration Act of 1965 a major turning point in the history of American cuisine, and remarked of the pre-1965 immigration policies, "I guess the idea was that people who like bland food make good citizens," adding, "In food terms, it wasn't a good policy" (Farmer 2008).

In the 1970s, food became a central component of a stylish lifestyle, and the American gastronomic field matured in important ways. Food writer Douglas Kamp notes that the emergence of the term "lifestyle" signaled the broadening of stylish living beyond the aristocratic class, as style advice was pitched to those seeking upward mobility through food choice (2006: 211). This cultural shift paved the way for successful specialty food stores such as Dean & DeLuca in 1977, and Whole Foods Market in 1980.[7] American chefs also gained substantial legitimacy as professionals in the 1970s. The American Culinary Federation successfully lobbied for their status as professionals in 1976 (in the U.S. Department of Labor's *Dictionary of Official Titles*), and this status was publicly affirmed at the first anniversary party for *Food & Wine* magazine in 1979, which marked the "first gastronomic event anywhere to present American chefs . . . on the same footing with recognized stars of France and Italy's nouvelle kitchens" (Batterbury and Batterbury 1999: 341). Also in 1979, food criticism began to take a more democratic flavor, as Nina and Tim Zagat put together a short booklet of restaurant reviews derived from a survey they had circulated among friends. (A decade later, the couple would leave their jobs as lawyers to devote themselves fulltime to the annual release of the Zagat Guide, which today represents the voices of over 140,000 reviewers worldwide [Zukin 2004: 194].)

Gourmet culture in the 1980s was actively shaped by the decade's conspicuous consumption trend, a trend fueled by a new class of consumers—the "Yuppies" in everyday parlance—who were thought to cultivate dining experiences as a source of status. Binkley describes this cohort as "a new class of aspiring, urban young people who had abandoned social conscience for the pursuit of social prestige and career success, yet had brought with them all the personal and cultural assets of the countercultural lifestyle experience, centered on individual choice and personal authenticity" (2007: 70). While these status-oriented diners sought "taste sensations [and] exotic new foods" (Lovegren 1995: 57), a nascent movement for local cuisine arose emphasizing the virtues of American ingredients and flavors, such as Cajun and Creole. Prominent chef personalities clearly existed in earlier decades (e.g., James Beard), yet an increasing number of celebrity chefs rose to prominence in the 1980s. Rick Bayless promoted the virtues of Mexican cooking through both his cooking show and 1987 cookbook, *Authentic Mexican: Regional Cooking from the Heart of Mexico*. Wolfgang Puck gained public attention with the opening of Spago in Los Angeles in 1982, an A-List restaurant that foreshadowed the omnivorous trend by marrying upscale culinary credentials and gourmet ingredients on a casual, but exotic, gourmet pizza menu.

In the years that followed, the gourmet foodscape developed more star chefs, more star-chef restaurant empires, more gourmet food branding, and more capital. Throughout the 1990s, the number of Starbucks expanded from under 100 to more than 3,000 (P. James 2002: 1); this not only increased the availability of gourmet coffee, but also promoted a national interest in techniques and sourcing of beans to make beverages previously associated only with European coffee culture. Star chefs like Emeril Lagasse achieved celebrity status and media omnipresence, a trend that was in large part facilitated by the 1993 launch of the Food Network, a cable television channel devoted entirely to food. Restaurant giants like chefs Thomas Keller (*French Laundry*, and *Per Se*) and Charlie Trotter came of age during this decade. The 1990s also saw the growth of demand for organic food, along with the institutionalization of the organics movement. The United States Department of Agriculture (USDA) developed uniform national standards for organic crop production in 1990, and many of the original organic brands were purchased in the subsequent wave of corporate mergers and acquisitions (Fromartz 2006; Goodman and Goodman 2001: 101).

Foodie tastes came to veer not just towards "natural" and "organic" foods, but also towards the "exotic." Throughout the 1990s, an increasing range of consumers welcomed new "ethnic" cuisines, a world of tastes cultivated by heightened processes of globalization and the diversifying cultural make-up of the population. According to United States Census Bureau data, the white, non-Hispanic proportion of the United States population shrank from 75.6% in 1990 (itself a drop from 79.6% in 1980) (Gibson and Jung 2002) to 69.1% in 2000 (Grieco and Cassidy 2001). Over the same decade, the foreign-born population in the United States grew in size by 57%, from 19.8 million to 31.1 million, with growth occurring in all regions of the country (Malone et al. 2003). Members of the foreign-born population come from every continent, though some countries and global regions are represented more heavily than others, such as Mexico, Latin America generally, China, the Philippines, and India. The increasing racial and ethnic diversity of the United States is undoubtedly a key social change that has been driving changes in American food practices, specifically the increased interest in "exotic" ethnic foods. This interest has grown not just at the level of *national* cuisines, but also at the level of foreign *regions* (e.g., Szechuan rather than Chinese). It also stands to reason that Americans' increased exposure to cuisine around the globe has contributed to the same process. In continuation of a long-standing trend of growth, over the 1990s international travel by Americans increased considerably, from fewer than 16 million trips overseas in 1990 (excluding Canada and Mexico) (International Trade Administration 1998) to 26,853,000 overseas trips in 2000 (International Trade Administration 2001). These processes of growing ethnic diversity and awareness of elements of cultures from around the globe continue, of course, in the current decade, contributing to greater awareness of "exotic" cuisines.

In sum, the realm of gourmet food evolved from a relatively narrow, elite focus on French food, towards a more complex terrain with greater mass appeal. As gourmet cuisine became more prominent in the public eye and Emeril became a household name, new modes of making status distinctions emerged. Exemplifying the continuing importance of hierarchy and exclusion in the culinary field, Chef Charlie Trotter noted that "sometimes it's better for me to take care of those who really understand [my] type of dining and not to worry about trying to satisfy everybody. We have deliberately, definitively cut off more and more segments of our customer base" (Kamp 2006: 328). While stratification persisted, foodie culture took up values of ecological sustainability, ethnicity, and authenticity and served them to the broad audience watching food television and buying celebrity chef cookbooks. The de-sacralization path described by food historians and scholars brings us to the contemporary gourmet foodscape—a space where food's authentic and exotic qualities appear paramount relative to formal markers of snobbery, and where the relationship to social status and distinction must be carefully analyzed to reveal its latent content. Revealing this complex, and implicit, relationship between cuisine, class, and social distinction, Ruth Reichl later wrote that her *New York Times* defense of elite dining as broadly accessible was "a cop-out," and that "deep down I knew that there was something basically dishonest about what I had written" (2005: 229).

The Contemporary Gourmet Foodscape

While it is clear that more and more people are now interested in food, the gourmet foodscape is a large and complex entity. While there is a democratic notion that everybody should have access to good food, and that "anybody can be a foodie," the most highly valued foods and food experiences—the foods that provide maximum distinction— are far from universally available. Non-elites may have knowledge about gourmet foods, and may desire things like cappuccinos, organic produce, and meals at celebrity chef restaurant destinations, yet such knowledge and desires are restricted by economic capital. The American food system is a highly segregated terrain where what you eat depends heavily not just on your income, but where you live. Food deserts, understood as large geographic areas without access to healthy and affordable foods, plague the American foodscape, and typically have a racial and class dimension (Raja et al. 2008). Having access to good food is not simply a matter of convenience or pleasure, but is strongly associated with health outcomes (Gallagher 2008; Cook et al. 2004; Stuff et al. 2007). Food security remains a significant national issue, affecting an estimated 11.9% of households (38 million people) in 2004 (American Dietetic Association 2006: 448). The food banks and pantries that appeared in the 1980s as temporary stopgap measures have not disappeared, but have only expanded and become more deeply institutionalized (Daponte and Bade 2006), while participation in the food stamp program has increased alongside poverty rates (American Dietetic Association 2006: 447).

While there is growing interest in organic foods and local foods, as evident in the surge of interest in farmers' markets that have enjoyed unprecedented sales in urban settings (Porjes 2005), most Americans do not consume a diet comprised primarily of fresh, locally-grown produce. Americans' consumption of fruits and vegetables rarely lives

up to health recommendations,[8] and significantly, is highest amongst
the college-educated, affluent population (CDC 2005). At the same
time more Americans have become aware of epicurean indulgences
like truffle oil, mascarpone, and foie gras, there has been a collective
panic about fast food and the obesity "epidemic" thought to plague
the country's working- and lower-middle-class population, as well as
certain ethnic minority groups.[9] The high rates of obesity among children are a major concern for some culinary icons, most notably Alice
Waters. In an interview Waters remarked that obesity is "really a moral
issue. We're killing our children here" (*School Library Journal* 2008).

Related to these concerns about the food system and public health,
the American food system has also been critiqued for the influence of
large corporations on food policy and population nutrition (e.g., Nestle
2003). Food corporations have reacted to these critiques by adopting
health-promoting and environmentally-friendly discourses, and have
become heavily invested in the organic sector and frequently employ
a discourse of "local" food (Johnston, Biro, and MacKendrick 2009).
Besides adopting new nutritional claims (e.g., margarine with Omega
3s, and transfat-free Oreos), they have also sought out culinary personalities to endorse their products.[10] Chef Rick Bayless's endorsement of
a low-calorie Burger King meal in 2003 resulted in a flurry of contro-
versy in the foodie world, as well as an email rebuke from Alice Waters.
While the idea of a top chef endorsing a fast food chicken sandwich
offended culinary purists, Bayless defended himself as being a realist
who was more connected to what the mass public was actually eating
(Garber 2003). Indeed, as Eric Schlosser's *Fast Food Nation* documented, Americans spend half of their food money eating out, and a
quarter of Americans buy fast food every day (spending $110 billion in
2000—more than was spent on personal computers, new cars, or higher
education) (Schlosser 2001: 3).

These general critiques of the broader American foodscape—on
grounds of health, sustainability, equity, and corporate dominance—
remind us that the rarified world of foodies is a relatively exclusive, and
segregated terrain. This exclusivity has a discursive dimension: despite
the embrace of "multicultural" cuisine within an expanding gourmet

foodscape, dominant foodie culture in the United States continues to feature a particular demographic—namely, white and relatively affluent—as the normative ideal. A quick scan of the glossy photos of celebrity chefs on Food Network.com or a perusal through the pages of *Gourmet* magazine is likely to reveal a sea of predominantly white faces along with the occasional person of color. Indeed, the launch of the Food Network's first program featuring African-American hosts in February 2008 sparked heated debate on the foodie blogosphere. While some bloggers were optimistic that "Down Home with the Neelys" signaled a trend toward more diverse representation of culinary icons (We Are Never Full 2008), many viewed the program as a superficial gesture that relied upon troubling racial stereotypes. One critical viewer commented that "[f]rom the very first episode, Pat and Gina Neely were basically bouncing off the walls with catch-phrases and Southern twang." The critique continued: "The show was met with high ratings, but at what cost to the countless viewers in the South who decry this type of characterization for the network's first show hosted by an African American couple, especially considering Food Network was nearly 100% white for so long" (Food Network Addict 2008).

In a related post entitled "Is the Food Network the Whitest of Cable Stations?", another blogger observes that the program launch happened to coincide with Black History Month, and points to how racial tokenism restricts non-white chefs to stereotypical personas:

> Yes, it seems Food Network is very behind the times here. All the white cooks can do all kinds of different ethnic foods. Ingrid Hoffman only gets to cook Latin-inspired dishes since she's Latina. And since Giada and Mario identify with their Italian heritages so they must cook everything Italian. Guess the philosophy of Food Network is if you want the freedom to cook whatever you want and cross those ethnic boundaries, don't let it be known what your racial or ethnic heritage is—or you'll be forever segregated into a cooking ghetto.
>
> (Racialicious 2008)

These bloggers' critiques add important nuances to the general observation that the American foodscape is becoming more diverse and interested in ethnic, exotic cuisine. Yet bloggers are not the only people to highlight the significance of race within foodie culture, nor is the Food Network the sole site where these dynamics are apparent. Recently, a handful of food scholars have examined how whiteness operates within alternative food practices in the US. Julie Guthman's research on Community Supported Agriculture (CSA) and farmers' markets in California finds that "these institutions disproportionately serve white and middle to upper income populations," even in racially diverse communities (2008b: 392). Analyzing participant narratives within a range of alternative food projects, Guthman argues that "the alternative movement has been animated by a set of discourses that derive from whitened cultural histories, which, in turn, have inflected the spaces of alternative food provision" (2008a: 435). Similarly, Rachel Slocum critiques the absence of anti-racist practices within community food movements, which she characterizes as "a predominantly liberal, white, middle class social change effort" (2006: 331). Slocum argues that it is not simply a matter of coincidence or individual preference that leads to the predominance of white consumers in alternative food spaces, but rather the product of "a culture of food that has been made white" (2007: 526). She writes:

> How this food is produced, packaged, promoted and sold—engages with a white middle class consumer base that tends to be interested in personal health and perhaps in environmental integrity. White, wealthier bodies tend to be the ones in Whole Foods, at co-ops (e.g. in Syracuse's Real Food Co-op, the Wedge in Minneapolis), the people attending CFSC conferences, those making certain purchases at the St. Paul Farmers' Market and the leaders of community food nonprofits.
>
> (Slocum 2007: 526)

Slocum and Guthman both clarify that their analyses should not be read as implying that *only* white people shop at farmers' markets or

Whole Foods Market, or use CSAs, since that is clearly not the case. Rather, these studies draw attention to how race continues to structure the American foodscape such that particular spaces are normatively coded as white.

These scholars' observations on race make clear that the foodie quest for culinary diversity and exoticism exists within a highly inequitable foodscape—a dualism that reflects the underlying tension between democracy and distinction we explore throughout this book. In our analysis, particularly in Chapter 3's discussion of exoticism, a primary focus is the reference point of the Euro-American foodie, since that is the dominant perspective represented in the larger foodie discourse. (In addition, the majority of the foodies we interviewed were white, despite attempts to make the sample more inclusive.) This focus is not intended to deny the complexity of a foodscape where inter-ethnic consumption, cultural appropriation, and discrimination occur, nor do we want to perpetuate the centrality of a white Western perspective (Kadi 1996; Narayan 1997: 183–184, 187). Rather, our objective is influenced by the anti-racism imperative to theorize hegemonic ideals, like "whiteness," in the foodscape and to unpack the seemingly neutral, Euro-American vantage point used to construct a sense of the culinary core (versus the exotic periphery). Despite foodies' interest in broadening the culinary canon, we want to show how race and social class remain a key part of the gourmet foodscape.

Clearly, important questions must be asked about who has legitimate access to "gourmet" status and foodie culture. While the food system remains highly segregated on multiple levels, the appeal of gourmet food culture has undeniably broadened to reach a larger segment of the general population. Daily, American newspapers feature numerous stories on our more obsessive, and more intimate, relationship with gourmet food. One article declared 2006 "the year the people took back the food," as "the Food Network edged aside chefs like Mario Batali to make room for home-cooking queens like Paula Deen, Sandra Lee and Rachael Ray" (Moskin 2006: F3). Food bloggers work around the clock to meet the needs of "diners hungry for the next, the newest, the best, and with no patience to wait for the annual Zagat Guide"

(Salkin 2007: 9). A booming business has emerged to serve the sophisticated palates of growing young foodies, as children's cooking classes reach record enrollment across the country (Denitto 2008: WE1). Even babies can be identified as foodies with relevant reading material (Colman 2008), and themed onesies heralding slogans like "sippee cup sommelier," and "aspiring foodie" (http://www.elliesparty.com/). These stories join a chorus of commentaries by leading journalists, culinary experts, academics, and market research firms that remark upon Americans' "near-obsession" with food (Adema 2000: 114). According to these gastronomic authorities, consumers continue to refine their "sophisticated palates" (Porjes 2005: 10), and increasingly feature food-related activities centrally in their daily living (Granastein 1999: 50).

To understand the cultural transformation that gourmet food has undergone in recent decades, we can look to culinary indicators that include (among others) the rise of culinary tourism driven by a growing appetite for global cuisines, the appeal of local, organic, and sustainable foods along with concern over ethical consumption, the widespread popularity of gourmet foods and specialty ingredients, the enormous success of food television, anchored in the popular icon of the celebrity chef, and the proliferation of media discourses about food and the establishment of food journalism as a valid profession. While these changes suggest a democratization of food culture, as more Americans devote more time, money, and attention to food, we remain sensitive to persistent divisions within the gourmet foodscape.

In the following section we draw from food industry data to give an overview of primary consumption traits in the American foodscape. Our goal is not to supply an exhaustive account of every element of the gourmet foodscape and its associated industries—a task that exceeds the confines of any one book, let alone an introductory chapter—but to provide material details that give color and flavor to the foodie story we develop in the rest of this book. These details are not focussed on the discursive dimension of foodie culture, but are instead directed at its material dimensions, thereby providing a context for succeeding chapters examining the discursive justifications for defining good food.

Even a casual glance at a trendy restaurant menu or food magazine reveals a few standout traits: an increased interest in eating locally and seasonally and a hunger for exploring ethnic cuisines. A 2007 National Restaurant Association survey of over 1,100 members of the American Culinary Federation (ACF) offers a snapshot of the hottest food trends, and confirms these findings. Close to 80% of ACF chefs indicated that "seasonal availability of foods is exerting great influence on how and what diners consume," making this the most universally-cited trend (Kruse 2007: 50). As well, over two-thirds of participants agreed that "ethnic cuisines continue to have a significant impact on menu trends," and said that chefs are experimenting with foreign dishes by "marrying the exotic with the familiar" (Kruse 2007: 50). The food industry data we consulted confirm the impressions of ACF chefs, and suggest that while the culinary marketplace is vast and complex, the prevailing patterns in tastes involve three overlapping trends described below: (1) enthusiasm for local and organic foods, reflecting consumers' interest in authentic food and concern with ethical consumption; (2) the growing popularity of "ethnic" cuisines, linked to Americans' developing "global palate"; and (3) widespread consumption of specialty and premium ingredients, often as a means to satisfy the two previously mentioned trends. Describing these trends, we aim to provide some rudimentary details about how food has become more prominent in the lives of Americans, while simultaneously exploring how ideologies of distinction and material inequalities continue to segregate the broader American foodscape.

Local, Organic, Seasonal

Eating locally is a very old concept, describing how many people ate before the advent of mass refrigeration and modern transportation systems. What is new, however, is "locavorism"—a culinary and political ideal that values eating locally and seasonally as much as possible, and perhaps even forsaking long-distance fare. While the parameters of locality are debated by locavores and food system activists, the term generally refers to food that travels hundreds (rather than thousands) of miles from farm to fork; these are foods that can be transported to market within a few hours of truck transport, rather than a few days of transnational air-transport supply chains (see Halweil 2005). Understanding locavorism as an ideal helps make clear that the practice of locavorism can vary considerably—from one foodie who makes sure to bake something with the seasonal bounty of apples, to another foodie's commitment to avoid all imported produce. While the implementation of locavore principles varies, its accolades are uniformly positive. Eating locally was named the "hottest trend in food" in 2006 by the *San Francisco Chronicle* (Ness 2006: F1), and many food system activists consider "local" food to be the new organic, particularly with the corporate-takeover of large sections of the organics sector (Johnston, Biro, and MacKendrick 2009).[11] DuPuis and Goodman write: "local has become 'beautiful', just as small was beautiful in the 1970s, and organic was de rigueur in the 1990s" (2005: 359). As evidence of this trend, "locavore" was declared the 2007 word of the year by the *New Oxford American Dictionary* (Zelman 2008).

Locally-grown foods constituted a $5 billion market in 2007, up a full billion dollars from five years previous (Porjes 2007a: 5). According to the National Restaurant Association's 2008 Restaurant Industry Fact Sheet, 86% of fine-dining restaurants in the United States serve locally-sourced food items (National Restaurant Association 2008). In a 2006 survey conducted by Technomic Information Services, 39% of respondents said the availability of local foods would affect their impression of a restaurant, making this concern second only to diners' desire for more trans fat-free options (Sloan 2007a: 35).

In the search for local foods, more and more consumers are forgoing the disconnected shopping routine of the traditional supermarket in favor of market experiences that facilitate a firsthand connection with food producers. According to the USDA's Agricultural Marketing Service (AMS), the number of farmers' markets in the United States reached 4,685 in August 2008, an increase of 3,000 nationwide since the AMS began tracking farmers' markets in 1994 (Shaffer 2008). In addition to shopping at farmers' markets, many Americans are becoming members of Community Supported Agriculture (CSA) programs. According to LocalHarvest.Inc., there are now over 2,000 CSAs in the

United States, up from an estimated 50 in 1990 (LocalHarvest 2008). While local foods have a broader appeal, it is important to recognize that this is by no means universal. In a study of consumer preferences for shopping location, only 30% of respondents expressed a desire to always buy from local producers and 20% reported no preference for local sources (Keeling Bond, Thilmany, and Bond 2006).

Farmers' markets appeal not only to those in search of locally-produced foods, but also those seeking organic goods. While locavorism may have surpassed organic's ethical appeal, the appeal of organic food remains strong, and is associated both with healthfulness and ecological sustainability. Between 2002 (when national organic standards were implemented) and 2005, the acreage of certified organic farmland doubled in the United States (Porjes 2007a: 8), and the terms, " 'natural' and 'organic' lead the ethical claims on new products launched in 2006" (Porjes 2007b: 26). Sales records suggest that "natural" and "organic" labels have an influence on purchasing behavior, as individuals respond to cultural pressures to exercise their social and environmental responsibility through conscientious consumption. A study conducted in 2006 found that consumers were willing to pay an additional 37 cents on each dollar for organic foods and 27 cents for natural foods (Sherwood B. Smith 2006). An article in *Restaurant Business* notes the growing popularity of "hot dogs for the haute-and-healthy," as "organic, natural, grass-fed and nitrite- and nitrate-free" dogs find a willing market (Tanyeri 2006: 28). Even infants are seen as deserving of natural and organic goodness, as evidenced by the popularity of all-natural baby foods (Sloan 2007a: 31). Industry giant Sysco (the nation's largest food service provider for restaurants and institutions like hospitals) revealed a new logo in 2009 featuring a green leaf sprouting from the "y," and boasted that it can provide restaurants with "grass-fed, antibiotic-free, and humanely raised animals," as well as "seasonal and organic produce" (Sen 2009: 46).

Culinary and food marketing experts suggest that the attraction toward ethically-infused food descriptors like "local" and "organic" as well as "fair-trade" or "free-range" is not simply a passing fad, but a more fundamental shift in the way that shoppers engage with food, and a challenge to the apolitical dining of an earlier gourmet era. The magnitude of this shift can be seen in *Food & Wine* magazine's August 2006 issue, devoted entirely to "How to be an Ecoepicurean," or in *Gourmet* magazine, which began featuring magazine articles and web content under the heading "Politics of the Plate" in 2006. By 2008 *Bon Appétit* was running a regular feature on the "conscious cook consumer" on its website and also published a special "ways to eat green" issue in February of 2008.

While the issues surrounding ethical, sustainable foods are developed further in Chapter 4 (Foodie Politics), it is worth briefly noting here that the appeal of fresh, local, and organic foods cannot be interpreted solely as evidence of a developing American foodie conscience, but that the industry also understands these labels as connected to consumers' desire for products which are "real" or "authentic" (explored further in Chapter 2). As chef Patrick O'Connell states, "the consumer is tired of chasing 'the next big thing'. They want realness" (quoted in Lang 2007: 2). One way to achieve a sense of realness and authenticity is by buying local, seasonal foods, and developing personal connections with local growers and producers. Beyond the local realm, consumers can identify culinary authenticity by a food's regional specificity, as identified in the *Culinary Trend Mapping Report* by the Center for Culinary Development (2007): "The current trend in Mexican cuisine is regionalization. This indicates a growing awareness that will soon equal greater demand for more sophisticated, subtly flavored foods from South of the border" (12). The center's business development manager, Rachel Koryl, explains further: "We see Mexican food evolving to include a wide range of Latin American cuisines, including Oaxacan, Guatemalan, Cuban, Argentinean, and Peruvian fare" (quoted in Arnott 2003c: 18). Similarly, "it's not just Chinese anymore, with Szechwan, Shanghai, and Mandarin cuisines becoming more desired and sought out by consumers" (Arnott 2003c: 18). In expressing preference for these regionally specific cuisines, consumers are demonstrating a more sophisticated knowledge of exotic fare, and this pattern leads us to the second major food trend: the growing popularity of ethnic cuisines.

Ethnic Foods, Exotic Flavors

Another pattern noted universally throughout the food industry literature is the burgeoning interest in exotic cuisine. Compared to a previous gourmet era when fancy food was equated with French food, Americans "have become more adventurous in their tastes" (CCD 2007: 6). This trend is not limited to a narrow epicurean elite, but rather, "the craving for adventure and intense flavors is pushing mainstream consumers to explore ethnic cuisines" (Arnott 2003b: 31). Perhaps unsurprisingly, the appeal for adventurous foods is highest among younger consumers. A 2003 study found that "25-to-34-year-olds showed the greatest enthusiasm for ethnic foods. Fully 50.4% of them agreed to some extent that they 'enjoy eating authentic foreign foods,' compared with 46.4% of 35-to-44-year-olds, the group with the next-highest percentage" (Arnott 2003c: 6). Age is not the only factor segmenting the foreign foods market. Class position is also a distinguishing feature, as "more educated, more highly paid professionals are more inclined to like spicy food than lower-income individuals" (CCD 2007: 16). The National Restaurant Association's "Ethnic Cuisines II" study found the greatest preference for foreign flavors among "young professionals living predominantly in major metropolitan areas" (Arnott 2003b: 23).

Complicating these findings is the fact that popular understanding of what is "ethnic" food varies across time and space. The previously cited study conducted by the National Restaurant Association found that Cantonese and Chinese cuisine have become "so ingrained in American culture that [they are] no longer considered ethnic," and are now integrated into the American palate alongside Italian and Mexican cuisines (quoted in Arnott, 2003b: 18), while sushi "is largely considered 'sooo 1980s'" (Purcell 2008). This normalizing tendency highlights how "ethnic" identifications are constituted through historically situated understandings of the foreign and exotic. As further evidence of these shifts, when Turkish food was highlighted at the Culinary Institute of America's Worlds of Flavor conference in 2005, this emerging cuisine was described as "where Indian was ten years ago" (Cobe 2006: 59). According to gourmet food entrepreneur Laxmi Hiremath, "these days, spices that used to be viewed as exotic are commonplace" (CCD 2007: 60). Tim Tsao, vice president of marketing at Kahiki Foods, notes that even supermarkets are working to provide a wider availability of "ethnic" foods in stock. In Tsao's words, major grocery chains are "recognizing that customers have a more worldly palate, and they're allowing them to satisfy that craving in minutes" (quoted in Wray 2007: 80).

Exotic appeal is not limited to unknown foreign cuisines, but can also refer to unconventional or unusual culinary combinations. A recent report tracking "Emerging Food Concept Trends in Foodservice" offers the following dish descriptions:

> Boursin stuffed kangaroo nachos with roasted avocado corn salad and huckleberry habanero demi-glace. Chocolate-covered caramel topped with Welsh smoked sea salt. Hanger tartare, pickled Asian pear, amaro, Béarnaise ice cream. Roasted red pepper with goat cheese Kettle chips. Has it really all come to this? These actual foods that you can actually order off a menu or buy in a store are emblematic of several of today's food trend innovations.
>
> (Lang 2007: 1)

Exotic combinations may not be available in mainstream eateries or chain restaurants, but can instead be understood as charting new horizons of gourmet cuisine. In a report on "The United States Market for Emerging Ethnic Foods," industry readers learn about "products and cuisines that have not yet reached mainstream or even trendy status among ethnic foods," but which "have begun to attract a following among 'foodies' and food professionals" (Arnott 2003c: 1). Much like a fashion cycle (Simmel 1957), elite food professionals and food enthusiasts constantly push the boundaries of what is considered daring, bold, and exotic; some (but not all) of these trends slowly filter down to mainstream eaters, and are then reclassified as bland or passé by the food avant-garde.

Another way that food with exotic appeal is created is through the creative hybrids constructed when chefs take a novel approach to familiar dishes. These creations range from the lobster and white truffle mac'n cheese at CIRCA in San Francisco (Lang 2007: 4) to Chicago-based Alinea's unconventional flavor pairings in its tasting menu (e.g., butterscotch, apple, thyme and bacon, or bubble-gum, long pepper, hibiscus and crème fraîche) (http://www.alinea-restaurant.com/pages/menus_top.html). While not all economic elites consume such adventuresome fare, it is important to note that these unconventional taste hybrids are primarily available to high-end consumers who can afford to pay the price of exotic distinction. While a standard hamburger remains a fixture of many low-income diets, a high-end hamburger of Kobe beef, foie gras and truffle can sell for as much as $175 (*New York Times*, 4 June 2008: F8), while a 24-course dining "tour" at Alinea costs $225 per guest.

Gourmet, Specialty, Artisanal Ingredients

Related to the quest for ethnic and exotic flavors, as well as the desire for authentic and ecologically-friendly foods, is the growing American demand for gourmet and specialty food products such as artisan cheeses, gourmet coffees and single-source dark chocolate. This market draws on foodies' search for ever more rare, exotic ingredients (Sloan 2007b), at the same time it reflects the broadening interest in gourmet foods. In 2004, total retail sales of gourmet foods and beverages reached $41.2 billion in the United States, representing a growth of 9.8% over the previous year's sales, compared with a 1.4% annual growth rate in the overall food and beverage market (Porjes 2005: 6). Industry reports note that specialty products serve a typical shopper who is affluent, with an income exceeding $100,000 (Purcell 2008), yet gourmet foods also appeal to younger, less affluent consumers with a strong interest in gourmet trends (Sloan 2007b: 59). Having grown up with greater exposure to gourmet goods, this discerning group of young food consumers "frequents restaurants regularly and is accustomed to everyday luxuries such as a $4 latte" (Purcell 2008).

While most gourmet foods and specialty beverages are associated with small businesses and artisans, large food conglomerates represent a growing presence in the specialty foods market, and illustrate the populist dimension of foodie culture: Mass markets are taking up more "gourmet" elements, at the same time specialty products seek to broaden their market-share. A 2005 report on *The United States Market for Gourmet and Specialty Foods and Beverages* notes that consumers come across more specialty, gourmet products than ever before, "even at the fast-food level, with chains like Dunkin' Donuts offering fresh-brewed espresso and Subway and McDonald's incorporating artisan breads and fancy salad greens into their new menus" (Porjes 2005: 12). At the same time mass-market eateries work to add a more gourmet, artisanal dimension to their menus, specialty food producers proliferate and seek to broaden their appeal. An article in *Specialty Food Magazine* offers advice on "Taking the 'Fancy' Out of 'Fancy' Food"; noting that "for many potential customers, the terms 'gourmet' or 'specialty' food still conjure up outdated notions of a fancy, elite and exotic world that is expensive, exclusive and filled with jargon-loving foodies and chefs," the article provides tips on how to "shift away from that white-tablecloth-and-fine-china perception" in order to attract main-stream consumers (Shoukas 2008). Specialty food suppliers are also using innovative marketing techniques, like the Etsy model of online handicraft sales (etsy.com). The website foodzie (http://foodzie.com/) describes itself as "a marketplace to discover and buy food directly from small passionate producers and growers," and offers a wide array of specialty items ranging from "thyme walnut and cherry butter crunch" candy ($17 for 2 ounces) to jerky made from organic, grass-fed bison ($11 for 3.5 ounces), to a slab of marshmallow you can cut into chick shapes with cookie cutters ($13.50 for a 9" × 6" slab).

The immense success of Starbucks is frequently cited as an indicator of the broadened appeal for gourmet products. In the words of one writer, "Starbucks . . . nails a magical American success formula: Its core product is both elitist in appeal and also altogether massified, even inescapable" (Collins 2007). Another good example can be found in the case of chocolate, the high-end market for which is growing rapidly and the taste for which can serve as "a sign of a discriminating palate" (Buford 2007: 69). The market research firm, Packaged Facts, comments that "the increased availability of such products is fueling what is being called the 'democratization of luxury' as lower- and middle-income consumers aspire to buy products that once were the purview of the very rich" (Porjes 2005: 14). While the aspirational quality of gourmet food is an important dimension of foodie culture, and fits within a larger consumer context characterized by upscale emulation (see Schor 1998), it is also critical to recall that the typical consumer for specialty foods is somebody with a six-figure salary (Purcell 2008), and that many Americans cannot afford a $4 or $5 daily coffee habit, or the $15 single-malt scotch chocolate bars that foodzie.com makes available.

The popularity of Whole Foods Market (WFM) symbolizes this tension between democratic accessibility and high prices, as well as what some experts have dubbed a "synergy" between gourmet food and natural food genres. Since it opened as a single store in Austin, Texas, in 1980, Whole Foods Market has grown exponentially to become the world's largest supermarket specializing in natural and organic foods, but also selling a wide range of gourmet items like exotic cheeses and artisan olive oils. In an interview with *The Wall Street Journal* in 2006, John Mackey, Whole Foods' co-founder and CEO, commented on how the natural and organic food movement was "penetrating into the mainstream" (Gray, 4 Dec. 2006: B1). While WFM may attract consumers from across the socioeconomic spectrum,[12] regular shopping for its specialty, organic and natural items requires the possession of cultural capital as well as economic resources (see Johnston 2008). For instance, a journalist comparing a basket of monthly food goods (based on a minimal, USDA-recommended "low-cost food plan") required to feed a small family calculated that the basket would cost $232 plus sales tax at WalMart, and $564 at Whole Foods Market (using only the lowest price foods in each category, and excluding the store's popular luxury items) (Cox 2006).[13]

Industry analysts predict a growth in the market for specialty, "artisan foods," which encompass "a combination of emphasis on the uniqueness and quality of each ingredient, traditional craftsmanship and artistry, the place where the products are made or grown, and the passion and personality of the producer" (Porjes 2005: 25). This forecast highlights the interrelated discourses of craftsmanship, authenticity, and exoticism that define the current culinary vogue. While mass market firms attempt to incorporate some dimensions of these trends—offering more specialty items and greener product lines—not all of these items are broadly accessible, and will remain restricted to those with sufficient cultural capital to seek out these items, and the economic capital required to purchase them.

Chapter Overview

We lay a foundation for our argument in Chapter 1, where we discuss the analytic tools anchoring the book: discourse, omnivorousness, and the concept of the "foodie." In Chapters 2 and 3, we discuss the nature of foodie discourse through in-depth explorations of the two main frames used to distinguish worthy food: Authenticity and exoticism. Chapter 2 explores the role that authenticity plays in the evaluation of food. Based on an analysis of food journalism from a wide variety of sources as well as our interviews with foodies, the chapter identifies the rhetorical devices that foodies employ to justify select foods as authentic. We also situate the importance of authenticity in food within a broader idealization of authenticity in contemporary culture. Chapter 3 accomplishes the same task with regard to the second frame, exoticism. For both frames, we show how worthy foods are identified through discussions of the contexts in which food is produced and consumed. Although the characteristics of food are naturally significant to its evaluation, we find that foodies present the social context of food more prominently to justify its worth.

In Chapter 4 we address the political dimensions of food preferences and choices, relying again on both food journalism and the interviews with foodies. We find that although the political implications of the food system are more visible to foodies than ever before, they take a backseat to more traditional foodie concerns with deliciousness and food adventurousness. In addition, to the extent that food politics influence foodies' preferences, they take the form of individualized ethical stances, primarily on the environment, rather than encouraging a collective approach to solving the serious social problems stemming from the food system. In Chapter 5, we again bring together information from both food journalism and the interviews to discuss the role of food in generating social status and in class politics. We show how foodie culture embodies a larger cultural tension in American society between an inclusive democratic ethos and a tendency for food consumption to serve as a means by which people demonstrate cultural sophistication and signal high status.

1

FOODIES, OMNIVORES, AND DISCOURSE

We are, of course, interested in what foodies eat. As scholars who are personally interested in eating, we think a lot about the texture, flavor, aroma, freshness, and general deliciousness of foods. We admire the skills involved with finely dicing an onion into perfectly uniform pieces, creating a flavorful fish stock, or piping perfect *macarons*. However, as sociologists studying food, we need to go beyond the specific details of the food itself, to investigate the social conditions of food's production and consumption. Food scholar and historian, Warren Belasco, identifies a "food studies axiom": "what we think about food may have little to do with the actual material properties of the food itself" (2002: 13). This means that we are interested in not just what foodies eat, but how foodies talk about food, write about food, use food in public culture, and how food operates as a source of status and distinction. In this chapter, our goal is threefold: (1) to briefly situate our study within a larger literature on the sociological study of food, culture, and taste; (2) to demonstrate food's connection to discourse, or, put differently, the significance of how foodies think, write, and talk about food; and (3) to outline some of the debate surrounding the term "foodies," including the thoughts of those that we interviewed. By fulfilling these goals, we will provide an overview of key concepts that we use throughout the book.

An Introduction to the Study of Food and Taste

This section presents an overview of the realm of food studies as it relates to questions of meaning and identity, as well as concerns of social status and distinction. In general, it is worth noting that food is a subject that has traditionally not received a great deal of scholarly attention. In part, this stems from the Western intellectual dualism that prioritizes cognition over embodiment, and denigrates the material and practical nature of human life (Curtin and Heldke 1992: 6–7). This denigration has a gendered dimension: While food can be made significant when it resides in the domain of men, markets, and production, the realm of everyday eating and sustenance has been linked with the private, seemingly less important world of women. Anthropologist Sidney Mintz (2002: 26) presents this as a conundrum: Food is essential as sustenance and a form of group membership, yet it is frequently taken for granted. Sociologists Priscilla Parkhurst Ferguson and Sharon Zukin echoed Mintz's sentiment in a 1995 review article—despite the immense popular interest in food, "few sociologists have analyzed food in terms of systems of production or consumption, cultural products or cultural words, or social context" (1995: 194). While anthropologists have paid attention to how closed societies feed themselves (Mintz 2002: 24), sociologists have traditionally neglected the realm of food (Warde and Martens 2000: 1), with some important exceptions (e.g., Mennell 1996; Goody 1982; Elias [1982] 2000). The French sociologist, Claude Fischler, for example, drew broadly from physiology, psychology, and sociology to illuminate contemporary food culture, or what he termed "gastro-anomie," in his influential work, *L'Homnivore* (1990).

Despite historic neglect, sociologists have increasingly come to understand the importance of food in social life, shedding light on how food plays a vital role in the creation of meaning and the construction of bonds of solidarity and attachment (e.g., Ferguson 2004; Warde 1997; Wood 1995). As Priscilla Ferguson's 2005 review of food scholarship suggests, an increasing number of scholars have come to appreciate "just how good food is to think with" (2005: 681). Sociologist Gary Alan Fine writes: "[t]he connection between identity and consumption gives food a central role in the creation of community, and we use our diet to convey images of public identity" (1996: 1). Who eats what can speak volumes about who belongs, and who is excluded from communities at a local and national level. Belasco argues that "to eat is to distinguish and discriminate, include and exclude. Food choices establish boundaries and borders" (2002: 2). Scholars have weighed in on how food is used to constitute boundaries of belonging to cities, nations and diasporas, particularly in light of transnational flows of capital and people (Gabaccia 1998; Penfold 2008; Wilk 2002; Appadurai 1988; Hauck-Lawson and Deutsch 2009), while other scholars have made important connections between food, empire, and globalization processes (Mintz 1985; Wilk 2006; Barndt 2007; Ritzer 2000). The link between food and gender identities has also been explored, along with the connections between food, race, and ethnicity (e.g., Ray 2004; Williams-Forson 2006; Parasecoli 2007, 2005; Bentley 2005; Inness 2001), as well as the role of food in popular culture (e.g., Parasecoli 2008; Ferry 2003).

These contributions to our collective understanding of food have been multi-disciplinary and interdisciplinary, but another more specific contribution that we draw upon in this book has been made through the sociology of culture and its study of taste. While the sociology of culture has not been centrally concerned with food, it can help us understand how taste and culture evolve across time, and how a sense of "good taste" is linked to social status. Bourdieu's seminal work in this area, *Distinction* (1984), drew on surveys with French citizens to investigate how tastes related to social class, and how aesthetic preferences operated to bolster and reproduce class inequality. For Bourdieu, the consecration of certain cultural preferences as part of "good taste" is not a random phenomenon, but reflects the ability of dominant class fractions to legitimate their tastes as superior. Further, Bourdieu argued that it is difficult for those born outside of a privileged socio-economic milieu to develop this "good taste"—or to put it differently, to acquire the cultural capital required to appreciate cultural artifacts associated with good taste.

Bourdieu's work has inspired a plethora of cultural analyses examining how access to cultural capital facilitates the construction of class identities and maintenance of social hierarchy. Most studies of cultural consumption that have examined the constitution of cultural capital have been concerned with the arts—music, the performing arts, museum-going, etc.—and as a result, research on cultural capital has tended to neglect the banal concerns of everyday life, like eating and drinking.[14] This is somewhat puzzling since *Distinction* opens with a call to conceptualize culture broadly, moving beyond an understanding of culture as synonymous with ballet and theater and instead connecting culture with the "elementary taste for the flavours of food" (Bourdieu 1984: 1). For us, looking at Bourdieu's work suggests the need to examine the ways cultural capital operates in the intimate realm of social reproduction to bolster the legitimacy of the cultural preferences of dominant groups.

In the decades following the publication of Bourdieu's *Distinction*, sociologists have also debated the extent to which aesthetic preferences are correlated with socio-economic hierarchies. As Alan Warde puts it, "Does taste still serve power?" (2008). Scholars have also questioned to what extent Bourdieu's work is relevant outside of France (Vander Stichele and Laermans 2006), and raised questions about the connection between class rule and aesthetic preferences, particularly in an era when overt snobbery is frowned upon. With haute cuisine in decline, and a greater interest in rustic, authentic foods, and filling, hearty fare associated with working people (Bourdieu 1984: 194–195), it might appear that the age of food snobbery and status-seeking is in retreat. While contemporary taste hierarchies are not simple or straightforward affairs, we believe that there is still an important relationship between social class, power, and aesthetic preferences as they relate to food. In this book, it is our contention that the everyday life concerns of eating can say a great deal about the relationship between taste, class, and power. When read carefully, gourmet culture can serve to affirm and elaborate Bourdieu's key assertion on the importance of everyday cultural forms—like food—for understanding the creation and maintenance of social status and distinction (see Johnston and Baumann 2007).

Part of the complexity of contemporary culinary trends lies in their "omnivorous" nature. Because our analysis will rely heavily on recent sociological work on omnivorousness—since we argue that foodies are omnivores—here we provide an introduction to the central ideas of this vein of research. While the term "omnivore" has an intuitive meaning as somebody who eats many things, in this context, the term "omnivorous" does not simply refer to a species' openness to eating various plants and animals. Sociologists of culture (e.g., Richard Peterson), have used the term "omnivorousness" to posit a general trend away from snobbish exclusion towards cultural eclecticism by high-status cultural groups (Peterson 2005; Peterson 1997a; Peterson and Kern 1996; Peterson and Simkus 1992; Lawrence W. Levine 1988: 243).[15] In the omnivorous era, cultural consumption marking high status through a reliance on a few highbrow genres of culture, like opera, is a less effective signal of social status. In place of the traditional high/low divide as a status marker, high status is signaled by selectively drawing on multiple cultural forms from across the cultural hierarchy. With musical tastes, for instance, high status in past decades was signaled through one's appreciation of classical music. More recently, however, high status can be effectively signaled through knowledge of a wide variety of musical genres ranging, for example, from Appalachian blue-grass to Cuban music from the 1930s, in addition to knowledge about chamber music and Wagnerian opera.

While past sociological work on cultural omnivorousness has mainly focused on musical tastes (van Eijck 2001; Peterson and Kern 1996; Peterson and Simkus 1992), reading (Zavisca 2005) or a variety of types of arts consumption (DiMaggio and Mukhtar 2004; Fisher and Preece 2003; López Sintas and García Álvarez 2004; Vander Stichele and Laermans 2006), in this book we examine omnivorousness in American gourmet food culture. In taking the term of omnivorousness back to a concern with comestibles, we argue that, like arts consumption in general, cuisine is a cultural realm where individuals can effectively engage in status displays. Some might object that because food is fundamental to human existence, it belongs in a different category of analysis than cultural products like film or movies. While food consumption does indeed contain an element of necessity not possessed by other cultural realms (e.g., not everybody listens to music, but everybody must eat), food choices cannot be adequately understood as purely functional.

Food scholars have persuasively demonstrated cuisine's significance as a socio-cultural realm ripe with meaning, symbols, myths, and latent messages about gender, class, race, and social standing (for examples, see Korsmeyer 2005; Ferguson 2005).

The omnivorousness era appears to support a more inclusive and democratic notion of what counts as good or prestigious culture, and to do away with the arbitrary and discriminatory standards of the traditional cultural hierarchy. However, as Peterson and Kern (1996) and others (Bryson 1996; Emmison 2003; Johnston and Baumann 2007) have noted, omnivorousness does not indicate the end of social status distinctions, but seems to function as an alternative strategy for generating status. Omnivores are not necessarily less status-seeking, but status is sought out in newly selective ways. A large number of studies within various national contexts have effectively demonstrated that high-status cultural consumption is "becoming increasingly diversified, inclusive, or omnivorous" (Peterson 2005: 261). At the same time, the research emphasizes that omnivorous consumption "does not imply that people are equally apt to like everything" (van Eijck 2001: 1180). A key question then arises: Which cultural choices are selected by omnivores and how are these selections legitimated?

Sociological research has brought some useful speculation to bear about why snobbish exclusion is in decline, and omnivorous cultural hierarchies are on the rise (van Eijck and Bargeman 2004: 442).[16] Peterson and Kern, for example, suggest that "omnivorous inclusion seems better adapted to an increasingly global world managed by those who make their way, in part, by showing respect for the cultural expressions of others" (1996: 906). Other authors (Bryson 1996; van Eijck 2001) have examined patterns of cultural consumption in survey data to produce excellent studies of the nature of omnivorous tastes. However, the data they employ force them to infer, rather than observe, underlying logics for omnivorousness, and these accounts cannot explain why certain cultural products are preferred by omnivores. In this book, we hope to illuminate the principles at work in omnivorous culinary consumption to distinguish legitimate from illegitimate cultural options. In chapters 2 and 3, we argue that food is legitimized for omnivorous foodies when it can be framed as authentic or exotic. We argue that through these two frames, cultural consumption allows foodies to negotiate a fundamental ideological tension between democracy and distinction—a tension that resurfaces in the book's various chapters. On the one hand, the decline in the legitimacy of snobbism and the rise of meritocracy (whether imagined or real) encourages an inclusive cultural ethos. Not only is open snobbism frowned upon, but down-home charm and lack of pretentiousness are qualities that are highly valued in our cultural leaders and culinary icons. Both authenticity and exoticism are reasonable and potentially egalitarian criteria— not snobbish—for cultural consumption, and suggest that cultural forms outside the dominant Western cultural canon can be appreciated on an equal footing. On the other hand, authenticity and exoticism can work to validate a relatively narrow range of foods—despite coming from disparate culinary traditions—that require considerable cultural and/or economic capital on the part of individuals. As a result, frames of authenticity and exoticism contain elements of democratic inclusivity, while they simultaneously work to legitimize and reproduce status distinctions.

It is important to acknowledge that the culinary tension between democratic inclusiveness and class distinction is by no means new. In his study of 19th-century gastronomy, Stephen Mennell (1996: 266) noted precisely this tension between the democratizing and status-affirming function of gastronomy, and suggested that over the last two centuries, the codification of gastronomic principles democratized taste by making standards more broadly accessible to the public.[17] We do not dispute Mennell's argument, and recognize the importance of democracy as an organizing ideology that has emerged over decades, and, indeed, centuries. However, recent omnivorousness trends warrant critical interrogation, since democratic ideology appears to obscure the simultaneous persistence of status distinction and displays of cultural capital in gourmet culture. Certainly the mass media may have made it easier for non-elites to learn about new food fashions and high-status cuisines, but this does not stop the status wheel of fashion and distinction from rolling on. To be clear, we *do not* think that an omnivorous food culture is a straightforwardly democratic food culture. Instead, our argument is that within foodie discourse, democratic ideology operates in tension with ideologies of status and distinction, suggesting that foodie culture cannot be dismissed as simple snobbery re-packaged, or unequivocally praised as indicating a new era of cultural democracy.

Discourse, Democracy, and Distinction

As noted above, our focus in this book is not simply on particular culinary practices (e.g., who cooks what and what cooking techniques are employed), but engages fundamentally with the constitution of culinary *discourse*—how food is talked about, discussed, and understood in the public realm and what this means. Discourse can be understood as an institutionalized system of knowledge and thought that organizes populations. Critically-oriented discourse analysis is not simply interested in how social reality is discursively constituted, but has a particular focus on how discursive activities create, sustain, and legitimate relationships of power and privilege (Fairclough 1992: 67; Fairclough and Wodack 1997; Phillips and Hardy 2002: 25; Carroll 2004: 226). Coming from this perspective, we are interested in how foodie discourse shapes how social agents do (and do not) respond to social injustices and ecological degradation in the food system, since discourse constructs normative boundaries of accountability and responsibility for these issues (Dryzek 2005; Mick Smith 1997).

The discourse produced by gourmet food writers, authors, and culinary personalities is an ideal access point for understanding the contours of the contemporary culinary field, and for illuminating how cultural capital operates in the era of omnivorousness. To access food discourse, we systematically studied textual sources of food discourse produced by food experts, such as gourmet magazines and the dining sections of major American newspapers like the *New York Times*. We also examined how foodie discourse was articulated by foodies themselves, using data produced through 30 in-depth interviews with foodie men and women from across the United States.[18] Foodie discourse generates an ideal data source for several reasons. First, a number of highly regarded discursive sources exist that are widely-

circulated, are influential amongst foodies and allow them to commu-
nicate across spatial boundaries (Lamont 1992: 108). Food magazines,
for instance, operate as legitimating institutions with the cultural
authority to bestow symbolic capital and target the tastes of upper-
middle and upper-class audiences—the same audiences who are
found in prior research to practice omnivorous cultural consumption
(Ambrozas 2004; Fisher and Preece 2003; Emmison 2003). Second, a
major role of foodie discourse is to spot culinary trends and to identify
particular dishes and foods as being worthy food choices. The selection
function of foodie discourse defines a repertoire of desirable food
choices, while excluding other available foods. This is an omnivorous
cultural consumption strategy that stays open to include a wide number
of food "genres," but is not indiscriminate about which genres and
particular foods are considered high-status. Third, foodie discourse not
only identifies certain foods as worthy, but also extensively contextualizes the meanings and motivations underlying food fashions. In the
extensive process of justifying why certain food choices are more interesting, authentic, and legitimate than others, the discursive legitimation
of omnivorous choices is rendered transparent.

As Ferguson (1998, 2004) argues, gastronomy, and indeed all cultural
fields, is textually constituted.[19] Like others in the field of discourse
analysis, we understand text to not simply include words written on
a page, but to also include visuals, images, and speech patterns.[20]
Gastronomy must be understood not simply as a fixed set of culinary
practices, but as a fluid discursive field where the legitimacy of food
production and consumption methods is negotiated: "texts of culinary
discourse" translate individual culinary activity into a "collective enter-
prise" that constitutes a taste community (Ferguson 2004: 17). In his
work on French and English culinary history, Mennell distinguishes
gastronomy and the gastronome through the element of public
discourse: "the gastronome is more than a gourmet—he [*sic*] is also a
theorist and propagandist about culinary taste" (1996: 267). In other
words, gastronomy is interested in more than personal culinary pleasure and refined tastes. Through writing and talking about food and
taste, the gastronome hopes to cultivate and elevate the taste of social

groups (Mennell 1996: 267). While not all foodies are gastronomes, foodie discourse is gastronomic, meaning that it involves a communicative public-sphere dimension specifying what foods and food trends are interesting, relevant, and high status for foodies.

To analyze how foodie discourse is produced through gourmet food writing, we employ the analytic tools of *ideology* and *frame*. These concepts have been used to study social movements, and we employ them here to provide analytic clarity and nuance to our study of foodie discourse. The concept of frames has been used rather loosely by social movement scholarship, but recent debates provide greater precision, and clarify the relationship between frames, discourse, and ideology (Oliver and Johnston 1999; Benford and Snow 2000; Ferree and Merrill 2000). Ferree and Merrill usefully suggest the visual metaphor of an inverted pyramid to describe the relationship of discourse, ideology, and frames, with each respective term connoting a more coherent ideational concept at the level of content and specificity (2000: 455). At the top of this inverted pyramid is discourse, understood as an inherently conflictual ideational realm that "links concepts together in a web of relationships" (Ferree and Merrill 2000: 455). Beneath discourse fall ideologies, conceptualized as coherent systems of related ideas that combine explanation with normative prescription (Ferree and Merrill 2000: 455–456; Oliver and Johnston 1999).[21] At the bottom of this inverted pyramid are frames, which draw from the supporting ideas and norms of ideologies, but are more specific cognitive structures that shape understanding of specific issues (Oliver and Johnston 1999).

Within the larger discourse of gourmet food, framing is an activity that shows foodies how to derive a "correct" understanding of foods, and provides an understanding that legitimates certain foods as high-status. To be convincing, framing must draw from ideologies, which contain values and ideals that resonate with popular culture. In this book, we argue that there are two primary frames employed in the omnivorous era: *Authenticity* (Chapter 2) and *exoticism* (Chapter 3). We argue that these frames draw from two competing ideologies at play in the field of omnivorous culinary discourse, and help explain its contradictory inclusionary and exclusionary tendencies. First, there is the ideology of democratic inclusivity and equality, an ideology that is overtly displayed in gourmet food writing, and helps explain the ideational underpinnings of cultural omnivorousness more generally.[22] Democratic ideology is organized around normative liberal principles of human equality and meritocracy. These ideals have a long history at the national scale of American politics, but have been reinvigorated with the increasing prominence of a globalization discourse supporting a normative belief in the equality of all people regardless of race, ethnicity, and nationality (Gould 2004). More specific to the American context, democratic ideology is connected to normative conceptions and populist ideals of the United States as a classless, multicultural society, where immigrants of multiple races and ethnicities have equal opportunities for socio-economic and cultural advancement, at least in theory (Stern 1952; Lamont 1992). Democratic ideology is also associated with market culture and consumerism (see Lipovetsky 1994). As Zukin writes, "we persist in believing that shopping is a realm of freedom from work and politics—a form of democracy open to all" (2004: 34). More specific to foodie discourse, democratic ideology fuels the omnivorous notion that arbitrary standards of distinction based on a single, elite French notion of cuisine are unacceptable, and that multiple immigrant ethnicities and working-class cuisines possess their own intrinsic value.

The second primary ideology in culinary discourse is the more covertly displayed ideology of status and cultural distinction. Operating in a dialectical tension with democratic ideology, an ideology of status and distinction operates implicitly to suggest that only certain individuals can appreciate and understand "quality" culture or have "good taste." This ideology recalls the hierarchy of old-fashioned snobbism, but is reformulated in individualistic, meritocratic language for a democratic era. As it becomes less socially acceptable to overtly declare high status based on wealth, social position, or ethnic/racial superiority, the status attained through cultural appreciation is framed as a matter of individual tastes and lifestyles, which are posited as sophisticated, savvy, and cosmopolitan (Bourdieu 1984; Lamont 1992: 107).[23] Because the focus is on the autonomy of individual tastes and lifestyles, the collective underpinnings of high-status cultural forms are not readily transparent or discussed, which is why we describe the ideology of distinction as operating primarily at a covert level, particularly in the United States context where democratic populism has such strong currency. Rather than a genuine populism that advocates for the interest of working-class and middle-class people, an ideological process of faux populism suggests a democratic connection across classes, while minimizing the existence of socio-economic inequality (see Frank 2000).[24] Faux populism reflects the fact that the overt ideals of liberal democracy operate in dialectical tension with a covert ideology of status and cultural distinction. Reflecting this tension, a belief in equality of opportunity that emphasizes cultural openness (e.g., anyone can potentially make a reservation at a hot new restaurant), is commonly accompanied with minimal awareness of the power relations, class inequality, and ethnic hierarchies that shape cultural choices (e.g., only a select few have the economic capital and cultural capital to frequent elite restaurants). Like democratic ideology, the ideology of status and distinction is learned through education and socialization in the habitus (Bourdieu 1984), so that certain cultural selections and choices are presented as natural elements of sophisticated (or unrefined) taste.

More specific to the realm of omnivorous foodie discourse, ideologies of democracy and distinction provide an analytic tension emphasizing cultural openness to multiple ethnic and class cuisines, while simultaneously constructing criteria for identifying "high-quality" foods and high-status ways of eating. Acknowledging this dialectic tension helps avoid deterministic accounts that see cultural distinction as producing inevitable, hermetically-closed hierarchies, and can also account for American cultural repertoires that appreciate diversity (Lamont 1992: 82). The challenge is to document the balance between these competing ideologies in foodie discourse and to explain how they inform the frames of authenticity and exoticism used to legitimize omnivorous choices.

Now that we have clarified what we mean when we say we are studying foodie "discourse," we can provide some details of the substance of this discourse. While food will always retain an inescapable material dimension, contemporary food culture is deeply discursive. We don't simply *eat* food—we think about, talk about, dream about, and philosophize about food. Food is not just "what's for dinner," but is the subject of numerous television shows, magazines, cookbooks, chefs' memoirs, websites and blogs. In the words of *Gourmet* Editor in Chief, Ruth Reichl, "food has become a part of popular culture in the way film or theatre is" (quoted in Brown 2004: 51). Numerous media outlets produce food-related features, and food public intellectuals take up prominent space in popular culture more generally. Oprah Winfrey invites British chef Jamie Oliver to cook on her show, while Emeril Lagasse's signature phrase, "Bam!", is declared one of "the 100 greatest catchphrases in TV" ("A Phrase Right out of History" 2006). Chef Mario Batali goes on a Spanish road trip with celebrity and actress Gwyneth Paltrow for a primetime television show and tie-in cookbook. Celebrity chefs not only dominate cookbook sales, but many of these cookbooks are national bestsellers. Food-related articles are among the *New York Times* most emailed features ("The L Magazine" 10 Jan. 2008), and finding recipes is one of the main online activities for women (Tedeschi 2007). We cannot hope to document the full panoply of foodie discourse in the space below, and our aim is more modest: To outline the expansion of food journalism, food television, and food cookbooks in the gourmet foodscape, while staying attentive to how these discursive domains are shaped by material inequalities and status distinctions.

Food Writing

It is hard not to pick up a mainstream American newspaper without finding a food-related article or section. Food writing is wide-ranging, and covers restaurant evaluations, lessons on how to prepare (as well as buy) your own food, in addition to travelogues and interviews with culinary celebrities. Fifty years ago there were about 25 food-related magazines, and by 2002 there were 145 (Miller 2007: 118). A 2004 article in the *American Journalism Review* relates the remarkable success story of the food news genre: "Food journalism, once a throwaway compendium of recipes and 'what's hot' articles, has gone upscale. Newspapers and magazines are dedicating top talent to the food beat, and they are hungry for sophisticated stories with timely angles" (Brown 2004: 50). This brief excerpt conveys food journalism's current position of distinction; it is not simply that culinary media has grown more popular, but that it has become "upscale" and "sophisticated," and represents a domain of "top talent" in journalism. This represents a significant shift from the peripheral position traditionally held by food writing, often considered a lower-status women's issue buried in the "food ghetto" of a publication's final pages (Adams 1996). In the words of Stephen Proctor, deputy managing editor for news at the *San Francisco Chronicle*, "[Food] has become much more of an essential focus of our life. A newspaper usually reflects what the culture is doing, and I think that's why you're seeing so much more devotion to food journalism" (quoted in Brown 2004: 52).

When Craig Claiborne began his weekly restaurant reviews at the *New York Times* in 1963, food received little coverage in the news. Indeed, Davis (2004: 62) notes that "the very term 'food writer' would have been meaningless at the time." First launched as the "Directory to Dining," and eventually securing the title of "Restaurant Reviews," Claiborne's column gradually achieved newsworthy, "must-read" status, rather than being "an element of household management to be buried on the 'women's page'" (Zukin 2004: 181). Claiborne's success represented the beginning of a wave of prominent food writing that offered culinary critiques within the news genre, while simultaneously facilitating a "new sensibility" among culturally savvy consumers (Zukin 2004: 181). Even today, the *New York Times* Dining and Wine section remains the "gold standard of newspaper food sections" (Brown 2004: 53), and was widely read by the sample of foodies we interviewed for this book, regardless of where they lived in the United States.

While the *New York Times* remains an incredibly influential source of information for foodies, the success of the Zagat Guide complicates the prevailing image of restaurant reviewer as established culinary authority. The annual booklet, first published in 1979, now shares the collective reviews of over 350,000 international reviewers (Zagat 2008). By providing restaurant goers with the assessments of common patrons, rather than simply extending the expert testimony of a seasoned critic, diner-led guides, like Zagat, stand as a significant piece of evidence of the democratization ideology within foodie discourse. Beyond the Zagat Guide, eaters now turn online to find a multiplicity of everyday food reviewers posting on personal blogs, or updating e-communities like Chowhound and eGullet. Professional knowledge producers have had to adapt to this democratization trend. For example, the *New York Times* Dining and Wine section now features regular blogs as well as the popular "minimalist" column by Mark Bittman focused on gourmet accessibility and featuring how-to video clips.[25]

Epicurean magazines also have to walk the line between presenting themselves as culinary authorities, and providing an accessible, chummy, more populist approach to food culture that resonates with a broad readership. *Gourmet, Bon Appétit,* and *Food & Wine* lead the market for epicurean magazines. As America's oldest and "most esteemed" (Case 2007) culinary magazine, *Gourmet* maintains a position of distinction among gastronomes as well as advertisers seeking to connect with its affluent readership.[26] The self-described "Magazine of Good Living" shares "the pleasures of dining, entertaining and travel with an affluent and active audience of 5.5 million passionate readers each month" (Travel Industry Association 2007). At a time when many magazines are struggling to compete with new media, *Gourmet* is enjoying record sales: "Single-copy sales for the second half of 2006 were up 11.1% over the previous year, according to the Audit Bureau of Circulations. And overall circulation—including subscriptions, which account for most of the magazine's sales—is at an all-time high, with 994,951 copies" (Beem 2007).

Many credit Gourmet's recent successes to current Editor in Chief, Ruth Reichl, who left her post as *New York Times* restaurant critic in 1999 to take the lead at *Gourmet*. In the years since Reichl arrived, the magazine won "its first-ever National Magazine Award, for General Excellence, from the American Society of Magazine Editors" in 2004 (Beem 2007), as well as "a dozen James Beard Awards" (Case 2007). In 2006, Reichl was honored by *Adweek Magazine* as Editor of the Year, "in recognition of her award-winning transformation of the

66-year-old *Gourmet*" (Case 2007). According to Ed Levine, founder and overseer of the food blog, *Serious Eats*, Reichl "has succeeded in making a formerly stodgy magazine utterly contemporary without losing its gravitas and relevance" (Levine 2007). When asked to account for the magazine's resounding success under her reign, Reichl points, in part, to a particular historical juncture. At the end of the 20th century, she says, "Food came into the culture and it became not something that just a few foodies cared about, and not just something that people who were cooks cared about, but something that is really on the national agenda. People are understanding that food is a prism for everything" (quoted in Case 2007). More important, though, Reichl approached *Gourmet* with an explicit agenda, determined to "democratize it" (quoted in Granastein 1999: 50). She explains: "*Gourmet* saw itself as being extremely useful, but now I'm asking it to be more accessible and friendlier, as well as being the authority" (Reichl, quoted in Granastein 1999: 50). While this approach has apparently gained favor with a broader base of readers, the magazine has not completely abandoned its role as purveyor of good taste and high-status lifestyles. As one journalist remarked, "*Gourmet*, being an upscale lifestyle magazine chock-full of luxury advertisers the likes of Rolex, Chanel and Mercedes-Benz, can still be about fancy, complicated and exotic cuisine. It is called *Gourmet*, and recent recipes include an ambitious vegetable-stuffed loin of veal with sweetbreads (prep and cooking time: 19 hours)" (Case 2007). The contradictory aims of developing a more accessible, yet high-status, magazine reflect the prevailing tensions between ideologies of democracy and distinction that now inform much of the gourmet foodscape.

Saveur,[27] another of the leading foodie glossies, also seeks to balance competing ideologies of democracy and distinction. *Saveur* aspires to be an authoritative source for foodies seeking out exceptionally detailed food knowledge (e.g., How do you make your own ricotta? How do you use the fermented fish and rice condiment, pa dek?). One of the magazine's founders, Dorothy Kalins, explains, "*Saveur* gave journalists who were interested in food a place where they could 'go deep' " (quoted in Brown 2004: 54). At the same time as the magazine provides information for foodies and supplies ample material to use as a food-related source of cultural capital, *Saveur* seeks to pay homage to the everyday foods people eat, particularly those eaten outside of elite restaurants. Says one writer, "The articles exhaust their subjects. They tend toward the celebratory, or even the evangelical" (Brown 2004: 53). Editor in Chief, Colman Andrews, shares *Saveur's* founding philosophy—a philosophy that resonates with the democratization impulse to connect with "real" people:

> From the beginning we wanted to present food in context, to say this isn't just a disembodied recipe we made up in our test kitchen, but something that people have been cooking for hundreds of years . . . The joke was that we wouldn't write about the hot young chef in Seattle or Chicago, but we might want to write about his grandmother, because she probably gave him his love of cooking.
> (Quoted in Brown 2004: 54)

While *Saveur* does seek to provide information on the "real food" made by grandmothers, it is worth noting that the intended audience for this magazine is not your average grandmother. The average *Saveur* is a well-educated professional whose head-of-household makes over $127,000 a year (Mendelsohn Media Research 2005).

Food Television and Celebrity Chefs

Food television has been an important part of the democratization of gourmet culture, at the same time it serves up a menu of culinary authority figures. As mentioned above, television pioneer, Julia Child, deliberately set herself the agenda of making French food more accessible to the home cook. The advent of the Food Network has pushed this demystification process even further, and has given rise to a new generation of food experts—celebrity chefs and cooks who offer a voice of culinary authority to the viewing public.

Today, celebrity chefs "routinely sell more than 100,000 copies of their cookbooks and people like Lagasse, Puck, Bobby Flay, Charlie Trotter, and Daniel Boulud are raking in millions in annual revenues on products that have nothing to do with restaurants" (Cohen 2001). Many, if not most, of today's popular cooking personalities have the Food Network to thank for their impressive celebrity status. The Food Network was started in 1993 by Reese Schenfield, founding president of CNN. Early programming featured a typical instructional format of traditional cooking shows, and drew small audiences. This prompted some critics to scoff at the notion that an around-the-clock food channel could sustain the interest of an adequate number of viewers. However, the network took off in 1996 when then-new CEO Erica Gruen "eliminated the 'talking-head-behind-the-stove' model and replaced it with chefs who could entertain while cooking" (Adema 2000: 114). Since this period of reinvention, the network now features "a bifurcation between daytime shows, which are still fairly didactic, and prime-time ones, which stress glamour and expense" (Miller 2007: 131). After adding "nine hundred and fifty new hours of programming" in 2001, ratings increased by 25%. They continued to climb at a steady rate of about 20% annually over the next few years, and by 2004, the network boasted prime-time numbers of 681,000 viewers (Miller 2007: 131). In 2007, the website announced that the Food Network is "distributed to more than 90 million United States households and averages more than seven million Web site users monthly" (Food Network 2007).

Tracking trends in culinary bestsellers reveals the salience of the celebrity chefs popularized by television programming. When we chart bestsellers from 1982 to 2006 (see Figure 1.1), we find a gradual shift from health- and diet-related cookbooks towards celebrity chefs, particularly those affiliated with the Food Network.[28] These numbers seem to suggest that the network has found a formula for commercial success, and for influencing an impressive segment of the population interested in food.[29] The consistent exposure of a celebrity often translates to cookbook success. In 2004, the network's focus on a single celebrity for one weekend day was consistently accompanied by " 'a huge spike' in sales of related titles the following Monday" (Danford 2005). Some experts predict that it is "possible that cookbook authors without television shows may be unable to find major publishers in a few years" (Danford 2005).

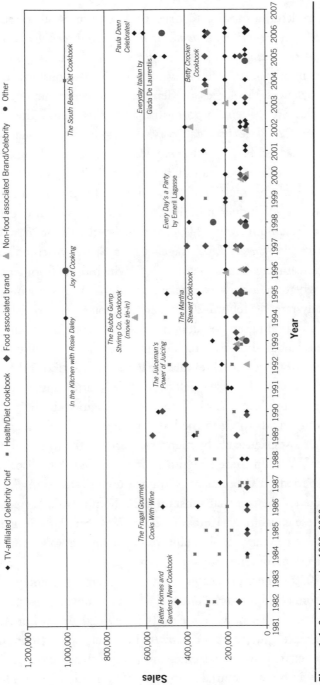

Figure 1.1 Cookbook sales 1982–2006

Legend:
◆ TV-affiliated Celebrity Chef   ▪ Health/Diet Cookbook   ▲ Non-food associated Brand/Celebrity   ● Other
◆ Food associated brand

Labels within chart:
The South Beach Diet Cookbook
Paula Deen Celebrates!
Everyday Italian by Giada De Laurentiis
In the Kitchen with Rosie Daley
Joy of Cooking
The Bubba Gump Shrimp Co. Cookbook (movie tie-in)
The Juiceman's Power of Juicing
The Martha Stewart Cookbook
Every Day's a Party by Emeril Lagasse
Betty Crocker Cookbook
The Frugal Gourmet Cooks With Wine
Better Homes and Gardens New Cookbook

Axis labels:
Sales: 0, 200,000, 400,000, 600,000, 800,000, 1,000,000, 1,200,000
Year: 1981 1982 1983 1984 1985 1986 1987 1988 1989 1990 1991 1992 1993 1994 1995 1996 1997 1998 1999 2000 2001 2002 2003 2004 2005 2006 2007

Ketchum describes four categories of programming featured on the Food Network—"*traditional domestic instructional cooking; personality-driven domestic cooking; food travel programs; and the avant-garde*" (2005: 223, italics in original)—which reveal a great deal about how the Food Network balances ideologies of democracy and distinction, and the "tensions that are evident in promoting elite cuisine to a diverse audience" (2005: 22). The first category, domestic instructional cooking shows, like Rachael Ray's *30 Minute Meals*, are designed to be broadly accessible, but still contain significant, yet implicit, class messages. The kitchen sets look "normal," but also stylish, well crafted, and expensive, "indicating a solidly upper-middle-class space achieved through careful purchases" (Ketchum 2005: 244). Personality-driven or "new domestic" cooking, like *Emeril Live*, stages a more "party-oriented" cooking experience featuring "charismatic males," which draw from a gendered tradition where men cook on special occasions, and women cook less special daily fare (Ketchum 2005: 226) Although Emeril is regarded as the icon of egalitarian cooking, his emphasis on high-quality ingredients and labour-intensive recipes (e.g., extra-virgin olive oil and home-made fromage blanc) reveals the ways that cultural and economic capital are connected to even relatively democratic culinary programming (Ketchum 2005: 226). The third category, food and travel programming, tends to air in the late afternoon and early evening, and is hosted almost exclusively by men who perform the role of the daring adventurer.[30] Within these programs, "it is implied that all people can equally experience the fantasies of the featured destinations," yet what goes unstated is the fact that substantial economic capital is required to recreate these adventures (Ketchum 2005: 229). Similar critiques point out that these culinary utopian fantasies obscure the ways in which the wealthy food production system exploits cheap labor and resources (Meister 2000). The fourth category of programming, avant-garde food shows, is connected through "unusual aesthetic conventions" (Ketchum 2005: 229), as in the show, *Iron Chef* (Civitello 2007: 350) or Anthony Bourdain's travelogue, *A Cook's Tour*. As in travel shows, Bourdain goes in search of exoticism and extremes in a format that could not be easily replicated without substantial amounts of economic capital. However, in an appeal to the humble and the authentic dimension of food culture, Bourdain often appears unpolished, caught smoking or swearing on camera. This lack of refinement grants the host a special degree of democratic accessibility in his performances, as Bourdain represents "both a 'regular guy' who viewers could relate to and an exciting adventurer they could vicariously emulate" (Ketchum 2005: 229).

The challenge of reconciling broad appeal with high-status cuisine is not easy to execute. The case of Emeril Lagasse is an interesting case in point. As one writer comments, "with his over-the-top, loud, and decidedly unpretentious approach to cooking, Lagasse has managed to appeal to a broader audience than anyone in the food industry could have dreamed" (Cohen 2001). Indeed, his enormous stardom is conveyed in the opening line of one of his shows: "In case you just landed from another planet, I'm Emeril Lagasse" (quoted in Adema 2000: 113). His signature exclamations of "Bam!" and "Let's kick it up a notch!" never fail to induce the cheers of enthusiastic audiences, and have become common elements of the popular cultural lexicon (Chan 2003). In 1998, Lagasse was *GQ* magazine's "Chef of the Year," as well as one of *Time*'s 25 most intriguing people (Adema 2000: 116). Yet the greater the reach of Emeril's populist appeal, the less he invokes legitimacy as a figure of culinary status and distinction. As Kamp (2006: 247) explains, "even as he raked in the dough and the Nielsen numbers, his credibility with the intelligentsia eroded." In a scathing *New York Times* review, Amanda Hesser (1998) quoted Michael Batterberry, editor of *Food Arts* magazines, saying that *Emeril Live* "smacks a little bit of the wrestling ring or the roller derby." Reflecting on similar shots offered at Bobby Flay, Kamp comments, "therein lies the (seven-spice) rub of commercial food television. In its zeal to entertain and find formats that will elicit good ratings, it often obscures the culinary gifts of its stars" (2006: 349). As Lagasse, Flay, and other top chefs have won public hearts with over-the-top TV personas, they have suffered a loss of culinary credibility among elite gourmands.

Home-based female personalities like Rachael Ray and Paula Deen are the subject of even greater derision, even though neither figure has staked her reputation on her professional training, with both insisting that they are "cooks" rather than "chefs." Named "TV's kitchen queen" (Hamm and Tauber 2007), Rachael Ray explicitly flaunts her lack of culinary training, stating, "Not only am I not a chef, I'm not a better cook than my own husband" (quoted in Hamm and Tauber 2007). Despite her lack of professional credentials, the animated host of *30 Minute Meals* boasts "four hit Food Network shows, 12 million copies of her 13 bestselling cookbooks in print . . . a self-titled monthly magazine and even her own brand of olive oil" (Hamm and Tauber 2007). Ray's 2005 cookbook *Rachael Ray 365* was the highest selling nonfiction paperback for that year, with annual sales exceeding one million copies (the Bowker Annual 2006). While it seems that there is space for amateur foodies in the public realm, she is frequently castigated for her lack of food knowledge. In the words of one food blogger:

> [Rachael Ray] is not serious about food. To the contrary, she's at the core of the dumbing down of the Food Network. As an investor, I have no objection to profit maximization. As a foodie, however, I don't want to be entertained. Cooking as a hobby consists of the skilful preparation of high quality or exotic foods during free time and for pleasure. The true food hobbyist thus is always looking to get past the mall food court version to the real thing. The Food Network used to be about food hobbyists making serious food. Now it's about making hamburgers and hot dogs.
>
> (ProfessorBainbridgeOnWine.com 2008;
> see: http://www.professorbainbridgeonwine.com/
> wineandfood/comments/the_case_against_rachael_ray/)

In sum, as with other elements of foodie culture, food television is constituted by a complex and delicate balance of democracy and distinction. While food television is broadly accessible to anybody who accesses cable television, a close reading of the programming reveals that these shows continue to embody significant elements of cultural and economic capital. At the same time, the Food Network is frequently credited for expanding American's knowledge of a wide range of cuisines, and popularizing the world of gourmet food to a wider demographic. Director of marketing for the Cultural Access Group describes the Food Network as a "remarkable tool" that has "done a great deal to expose people to new foods and cuisines" (quoted in Arnott 2003c: 21; see also King 2004). At the same time the television programming in the Food Network is a significant part of the democratization of foodie culture, television's food celebrities have been critiqued for their populist appeal, thereby reducing the basis for distinction, and rendering them less potent symbols of foodie status.

What is a "Foodie"?

In this final section, we discuss the meaning of "foodie" and its contested status. The meaning of the term "foodie" is hotly debated, and this debate reflects the ongoing tensions within the gourmet food-scape. Drawing from public discussions of "foodieism," we first sketch out what it means to be a foodie, and describe some of the nuances that make the term controversial. Finally, we describe our interviews with foodies, and present some of their key characteristics, as well as some of their thoughts on foodie terminology.

The original usage of the term "foodie" is commonly attributed to the British authors Paul Levy and Ann Bar. In their book, *The Official Foodie Handbook (Be Modern—Worship Food)*, Levy and Bar give credit for the term to New York food critic Gael Green, as well as a 1982 article in *Harpers & Queen* (1984: 7). While the *Foodie Handbook* is over 20 years old, its message strikes a chord with contemporary foodie discourse, touching on themes like the abysmal quality of mainstream food (e.g., "cheese in plastic-wrapped portions"), the appeal of foodie accoutrements like chefs' knives and gas stoves, as well as the impor-tance of thinking and talking about food (as opposed to just eating well—"pigs can eat well") (1984: 6–7). Levy and Bar define the term foodie simply, as "a person who is very very very interested in food," and who "consider[s] food to be an art, on a level with painting or drama" (1984: 6). They note that foodies physically look "like anybody else," and are not distinguished by "fatness" (1984: 6). Like Bourdieu, Levy and Bar connect class and food, arguing that foodies are "from the ambitious classes, who know about exercise and bran" (1984: 6).

Instead, understanding the significance of discourse is key to identifying a foodie: "the way to tell a foodie is by listening. The mouth will declare its passion . . . Food talk is the *staple* diet of social intercourse now" (Levy and Bar 1984: 6).

Discussions of foodie terminology usually mention that there are no good alternatives to the term "foodie." Words like gastronome or epicure are considered too stuffy, gluttonous, or old-fashioned (Slashfood 2006). Gourmet is too snobby, and is associated with an older era of wealthy, male food snobs (Levy and Bar 1984: 7). Others use terms like "food lover," "food obsessed," or "food enthusiast," while some reject labels altogether (e.g., the blog entitled iamnotafoodie.com, with the tagline, "I just like food"). When the term foodie is employed, it is often used in a relative sense when people compare themselves to someone who is more, or less, of a "foodie" than themselves. Even when the foodie term is not used, foodie discourse typically involves some form of distance and distinction from the non-foodie—people who eat anything, people who eat fast food, people who eat processed food, or people who lack a developed food palate. One foodie blogger distinguishes foodies (and herself) from "food slobs," which she describes as having "lackadaisical and indiscriminate eating habits . . . They can appreciate the difference between a BMW and a Chevrolet, but not iceberg and radicchio" (Feuillet 2007). While this foodie insists that good food can be simple, a clear distinction is made between foodie simplicity and "food slob" simplicity: "In the time it takes the Food Slob to toast frozen waffles a Foodie can soft boil the perfect egg, butter toast, and call it a meal" (Feuillet 2007).

While foodie status is frequently defended as being universally accessible, interestingly, one of the primary reasons that the term foodie is rejected is because it is associated with snobbery and the faddish trend-setting of elites. Some associate the foodie label with a preference for patronizing expensive, stuffy, or formal restaurants. For example, the popular online food community, "Chowhound", (whose website tagline reads: "Food. Drink. Fun") rejects the term foodie as elitist, staid, and faddish. In their description of their mission statement, the Chowhound manifesto boldly proclaims, "We're not talking about foodies. Foodies eat where they're told. Chowhounds blaze trails. They comb through neighborhoods for culinary treasure. They despise hype. And while they appreciate ambiance and service, they can't be fooled by flash" (Chowhound 2008). While elitism is one of the major negative connotations associated with the term "foodie," the Chowhound manifesto makes clear that the term is also associated with the pursuit of food fads in the absence of a deep or meaningful connection to food.

Despite these negative connotations, others embrace (or reluctantly accept) the term "foodie" precisely because it is thought to avoid the snobbish associations of terms like "gourmet," "gourmand" or "epicurean" (e.g., Feuillet 2007). This presents an interesting situation where both people who self-identify as foodies, and those who reject the term, do so on the ground that they are not food elitists or snobs. This ironic commonality speaks to the democratic ideology that is a central theme in foodie discourse. For those who accept the term, "foodie" is seen as a relatively democratic category, and held in contrast to a former era where good food was reserved for highbrow gourmets who dined on truffles in expensive restaurants. As Nicole Weston writes on the blog "Slashfood," "anyone can be a foodie" (Slashfood 2006). Not only is the foodie world seen as having an open door policy for new recruits, but the kind of foods that are eligible for consumption are also perceived as inclusive. On the "Serious Eats" blog, one foodie posts: "When I say 'foodie,' my boyfriend translates that as 'snob.' I've never considered myself a food snob, I'll try anything, eat anything or eat anywhere. I actually love discovering new hole in the walls joints, especially when they serve ethnic food" (Serious Eats A. 2008).

When the term "foodie" is taken on as a marker of identity, it is thought to describe a category of people that love good food, and want to learn about good food. It is understood as being about "loving food" more than the average person. A self-described foodie articulates this sense of joy and passion and rejection of gourmet pretentiousness in a post to "Serious Eats":

> I am a foodie, and dang proud to be one. I love shopping for ingredients, I love putting them all together to make a fantastic meal, I

don't care if the wine doesn't match. My favorite room in my house is my teeny tiny kitchen. I'm the girl my friends and family call for cooking advice and tips about new and/or different restaurants. My favorite restaurants are little hole in the walls. I'm constantly teaching myself how to be a better cook. I made my own cheese once! I love to bake bread. I make my own stock. I read restaurant reviews religiously and menus that I look up on-line. I've been known to curl up with a good cookbook and read it for hours. My hero is Julia Child. I just have a passion for food and want to learn everything about all of it. If all of that makes me a foodie, count me in.

(Serious Eats B. 2008)

Another self-described foodie echoes this sentiment, and makes explicit a willingness to cross lowbrow and highbrow boundaries, at the same time they distance themselves from processed industrial foods:

I'll call myself a foodie. I purchase and prepare quality natural (not processed crap) ingredients. I love to cook for my friends, whether it's mac and cheese or a standing rib roast and all the sides [side-dishes] for the holidays. I love to try new things and serve them to my hungry friends. I can enjoy a decadent ribeye with all the fixin's in Midtown or a quick supper at a hole-in-the-wall up here in Westchester. What matters is what goes into the prep. In fact, holes-in-the-wall are my favorite places. Saturday night my fiancé and I ended up at an Asian joint in a strip mall in Armonk; we were both raving about the food and have sworn to go back again. Yeah, food(ie) is good, it's all about love.

(Serious Eats C. 2008)

Foodie-ism, whether the term is accepted or rejected, is also strongly associated with food knowledge. For those who reject the term, "foodie" can be a derogatory label they apply to those who pretend to know food. In the words of one poster on eGullet, "I typically interpret 'I am a foodie' to mean 'I am now going to pretend to know something about

food and will proceed to parrot something I heard on Food Network' "
(eGullet 2008). For those who accept the term, "foodie" can refer to
somebody who wants to learn about food, irrespective of their precise
knowledge of specific foods. To belong you don't need to know about
all the latest food trends, but you must be interested in acquiring more
food knowledge. As the Chowhound manifesto states, "You needn't be
an expert to participate. If you're less food-obsessed than the rest of us,
but have a yen for egg creams, gazpacho, or Quisp Cereal, let the resident hounds guide you to the best stuff" (Chowhound 2008). A food
blogger makes a similar point about the centrality of the acquisition of
food knowledge:

> To be a foodie is not only to like food, but to be interested in it.
> Just as a good student will have a thirst for knowledge, a foodie
> wants to learn about food . . . Do you have to know the difference
> between a beefsteak tomato and an heirloom tomato? No, but you
> might be interested to find out what it is. Do you have to only
> shop at farmers' markets? No, but you still look for good, fresh
> produce . . . Just like food, learn about food and, most importantly,
> eat food.
>
> (Slashfood 2006)

To put it somewhat differently, what seems to matter in foodie
discourse (for both those who accept and those who reject the term) is
not necessarily the precise list of food that one consumes or the restaurants one dines at, but the disposition one brings to food—as a subject
for study, aesthetic appreciation and knowledge acquisition. This is
significant, because it relates to an important observation by cultural
theorists that patterns of status and distinction are created and repro-
duced not simply by *the content* of cultural products, but the manner
in which one consumes culture. Peterson and Kern write: "criteria of
distinction, of which omnivorousness is one expression, must center not
on *what* one consumes, but on the way items of consumption are understood" (1996: 904). Bourdieu (1984: 54) described this as an "aesthetic
disposition," which referred to the attitude of approaching everyday

objects, like food, in a way that de-emphasizes functional utility (e.g., food as the fuel needed to sustain life), and instead views everyday objects through an aesthetic lens of cultural appreciation and knowledge acquisition (e.g., seeing food as a serious hobby, or conceptualizing a meal as a work of art). To belong in the foodie world is not simply a matter of what one eats, or where one eats, but the manner in which one approaches food—as a topic for serious aesthetic consideration, deliberation, and appreciation.

The emphasis on knowledge acquisition within foodie discourse makes clear that there are still lines of status and distinction in the foodie community, even if they are not rigid and unchanging. While some insist that anybody can be a foodie, many food discussions involve discussions about the culinary "Other," suggesting that symbolic boundaries are frequently drawn between who belongs and who does not belong—often on the basis of food knowledge. These boundaries can be drawn explicitly or implicitly. For example, to belong to the food message board, eGullet (which is frequented not only by professional chefs, but also by food stars like Ruth Reichl and Anthony Bourdain), one must formally apply—a process that includes writing a short piece on why one is passionate about food. A more implicit process of drawing boundaries between true food lovers, versus superficial poseurs, also frequently occurs. In response to an online article entitled "Why Foodies Give me Indigestion," one post defends true foodies by distinguishing between those who mobilize their foodie status as "an excuse to try to act superior or fashionable," and those who "are passionate about learning and trying new things . . . [and] see food as a way of appreciating life, understanding other cultures, and spending time with others" (The Daily Beast 2008). While demarcating who does and does not belong in the foodie community usually involves the construction of symbolic boundaries, these boundaries are both fluid and contested. For example, there is a debate on the website Serious Eats about whether you have to reject "junk food" (e.g., chain restaurants, processed food) to be a real foodie. This website displays a general consensus that you can be a foodie and have your guilty food pleasures (e.g., KFC popcorn chicken), although the idea is also expressed that if you just wolf it down (like a "fattie"), then you are not really a foodie (Serious Eats D. 2008).

While much of foodie discourse displays little awareness of privilege and social status, foodies display varying degrees of reflexivity. Indeed, a significant segment of the debate surrounding the term "foodie" involves reflection about the issues of culinary elitism and the food world. For example, some foodies are conscious of the negative connotations surrounding the term "foodie," but suggest re-appropriating the term nonetheless:

> I'm a foodie, too. It's a shame that a perfectly good word has become a stigma. Like liberal. Or gay. I read on Chowhound that the hounds are definitely not foodies. What the heck are they then? They spend all day chiming in to every possible thread, ranting about everything from holes-in-the-wall to El Bulli. They're foodies. Take back the word. Foodies unite!
>
> (Serious Eats E. 2008)

Other foodies think critically and reflexively about their own participation in food culture, and how it relates to larger structures of class and material privilege. In our reading of food media, these instances were relatively uncommon, but their presence is significant. For example, commenting on the contradictory implications of organic farming, one blogger advises fellow foodies to "think about the side-effects of seemingly well-intentioned food choices" (The Frugal Foodie 2006).

Interviews with Foodies

Our interviews with foodies make clear that they are aware of the complications around the term "foodie," and are ambivalent about how well the term applies to themselves. Nevertheless, our questions, "What does the term foodie mean to you?" and "Do you consider yourself a foodie?" yielded an intriguing set of responses that allow us to draw a broad picture of how foodies see themselves.

Regarding the term itself, our interviewees varied greatly in their willingness to apply the term "foodie" to themselves. While some readily adopted it, others reported that that they would call themselves foodies only because they didn't have a better term in mind, and were familiar with its various negative connotations. One interviewee who was reluctant to self-identify as a foodie, Norman Arbus, a 56-year-old lawyer from New York, thought it was more appropriately applied to food bloggers whom he saw as obsessed with food: "I think that those people are much more obsessive, or compulsive, or possessed than I am. Um, I wouldn't go to the ends of the earth for the best morel . . . I accept the [foodie] label, but I'm not sure I wear it comfortably." Among those who were reluctant or who rejected the term "foodie," most were wary of the snobbish connotations of the term, and wanted to distance themselves from that particular aspect of it. Others rejected the connotations of faddishness, reporting that they were not simply interested in the latest food trends or restaurant personalities, but instead their commitment to food was deeper and more enduring than the term foodie implied. As Norman later remarked, he understood a typical foodie as "someone who's obsessive about finding this year's first white truffle . . . or has to go to every new restaurant five minutes after they open, be the first one there."

Among the other terms that some interviewees offered as an alternative to "foodie" were "epicure," "food sensualist," and "food enthusiast." What is notable is that, for the most part, the self-descriptions and distinctions between worthy and unworthy food that our interviewees provided were largely similar, regardless of whether they used the label "foodie" to describe themselves. The interviewees who refused the term outright tended to display more knowledge about the food world than was typical in our sample, which suggests that the individuals who are most heavily invested in a gastronomical identity eschew a label that is commonly applied to "average" members of the gourmet food scene.

Overall, however, we feel justified in describing all of our interviewees as foodies because our conceptualization of the term is centered on its inherent ambiguities. It bears repeating that the term "foodie" emerged as an alternative to the snobbish connotations of gourmet, even though it has, in turn, come to connote elitism. This is no accident, since the term "foodie" has emerged at the crux of an ideological tension between two competing poles: A democratic pole that eschews elite cultural standards and valorizes the cultural products of "everyday" non-elite people, and a pole of distinction that continues to valorize standards that are rare, economically inaccessible, and representing significant amounts of cultural capital. Embodying this tension, foodies commonly seek out the food of common people, at the same time they frequently idealize foods, meals, and restaurants (e.g., the molecular gastronomy destination in Spain, El Bulli) that are inaccessible for the majority of the population with less cultural and economic capital.

While we conceptualize the term foodie as embodying the tension between democracy and distinction, when conducting this interview research we used a minimalist working definition of foodie as somebody with a strong interest in learning about and eating good food who is not directly employed in the food industry. Not surprisingly, the most salient characteristic cited by our interviewees is that they possess a strong interest in food. This enthusiasm was indicated through words like "obsession," and "passion," saying that food is "meaningful," and that foodies "live to eat rather than eat to live." In the words of Fiona Callworth, a 54-year-old mother and wife in Boston: "I became obsessed [laughs] in some ways, with cooking. I love cooking, I love to cook. I think about cooking as I'm going to sleep at night, I think about what I'm going to cook the next day." Nancy Light, a 51-year-old working in marketing in Oakland, similarly expressed the centrality of food to the daily rituals of her life: "I'm sure there's a poetic way to put it, but you know, when my kids are sick, when somebody's had a bad day, when someone's had a good day, when you want to celebrate, I mean it's all about food." Natalie Underhill, a 55-year-old administrative assistant in Pennsylvania, also identified food as a central passion: "I just love talking about it, I love reading about it, I love watching shows about it . . . just to read and learn about and be sort of obsessed with food." Of course, what is interesting about foodies' self-perceptions are the ways that this interest in food manifests and the kinds of foods that interest them. Foodies see their interest in food as going far beyond simply liking to eat, and they demonstrate their interest most frequently and intensively in the following four ways: Education, identity, exploration, and evaluation.

The educational dimension of being a foodie connects food and knowledge. In our interviews, foodies frequently reported that their interest in food leads them to continually gather information about food's qualities, history, and conditions of production and consumption, including highly specific technical information. Verifying what we observed in foodie discourse more generally, the interviewees suggest that a foodie should be familiar with, or interested in, learning about the dishes and ingredients associated with a very wide range of cuisines. Sarah Driscoll, a graduate student in Berkeley, California, identifies the importance of a foodie's being "inquisitive." In her words:

> So if something interests you, I'm going to be very general here, but let's say that you're interested in whole grains. That could, that could lead you to an interest in, you know, millet, which could then lead you to finding out about teff, and finding out about teff could lead you to going out to an Ethiopian restaurant for the first time, or something. I think it's sort of one little thing leads to another. And I think being a foodie is, I would hope, implies a curiosity . . . you're always sort of seeking information and there's sort of a flood of it in the United States.

A foodie should also possess or pursue knowledge about where to acquire the best ingredients. The interviewees commonly described shopping at many different stores, markets, online shopping, or acquiring fish "right off the boats" at a 4:30 a.m. wholesale market. When asked about her shopping habits, Nancy Light replied, "My shopping is insane. I go about six places in the course of a week!" The same is true for knowing good restaurants; being knowledgeable about truly "good" restaurants, and not simply the trendiest restaurants, is often cited by the interviewees as important to being a foodie. Knowing where to dine and to shop presupposes knowing what constitutes good ingredients (produce, meats, spices, etc.) and good cooked food. And while some interviewees mention that a foodie can simply appreciate well-crafted dishes without being able to cook himself or herself, others answer the question about the definition of a foodie by stating that a foodie must know a lot about cooking techniques, and some even say that a foodie must practice these techniques. Criticizing the Food Network show, "*Semi-Homemade Cooking with Sandra Lee*," Ted Darby, a retired lobbyist in Washington, DC, notes, "I mean the essence of foodies is that it's cooking from scratch."[31]

The knowledge dimension of being a foodie is at the forefront of interviewees' understanding of the nature of a foodie. Concomitant with this understanding is the expectation that foodies seek out this information. When asked about where they learned about food, the most common source cited by our interviewees was the *New York Times* (regardless of their state of residence), followed by a range of food magazines, other newspapers such as the *Washington Post*, the *Los Angeles Times*, and the *San Francisco Chronicle*, food blogs and other Internet resources, cookbooks, cooking classes, and, for some of our interviewees, the Food Network.[32] Specific chefs and cooking shows were also seen as a source of knowledge. For example, Nathaniel Snider, a 38-year-old engineer from the Bay Area, admired Rick Bayless, for his "commitment to the history of Mexico and the authentic cuisine, and his, kind of his investigatorial [*sic*] nature," and Sarah Driscoll praised Elton Brown as somebody "who teaches me new information." Just as common as learning about food through the media or through culinary personalities, the interviewees reported learning about food through their social networks. A common response to the question of the meaning of the term "foodie" was that foodies are people who talk about food, restaurants, the food industry, food regulations, and food politics, as well as the sensory characteristics of food and the sensual pleasures it brings. This talk of food implies that the learning that foodies do is frequently a social activity that involves sharing information, either online or in person. The term "foodie" can be useful this way, since it serves as a "short cut you would use because it's a fast way to tell somebody that you're interested in good food," said Nancy.

The notion of the social aspect of being a foodie brings us to the second way in which foodies' interest in food is manifested: As an identity. The interviewees frequently stated that foodies are people who make their interest in food a central part of who they really are. They are all about food, meaning that this particular interest is a leading dimension of their self-identification. Part of what defines foodies, then, is that their orientation toward food is as important a facet of themselves as virtually any other dimension of their identity, and often connects with other facets of their identity. One interviewee, Nancy Light, who describes herself as "a food fanatic," a "food sensualist," and "obsessed with food and wine," recounts how her interest in food is central to the way she views the world, and intimately rooted in her familial socialization: "I have always been interested in food. My father was French and I grew up on great food all my life. My father was also an artist and an oenophile as long as I can remember, and a great critic, we were asked to notice the nuance in things . . . so I sort of grew up being discerning about flavor." In response to the question of how she became interested in food, Sarah Driscoll answered similarly, noting its centrality to her life and her family's interests: "[Food is] really the center of my family. But not just from a consumption standpoint. My family is incredibly curious and interested in learning, and it happens to be something we're really passionate about. So we, it's really how we experience life . . . I mean there really isn't anything that doesn't interest my family regarding food."

Besides linking their foodie identities to their core identities and family socialization, foodies discuss how food is central to how they relate to others. Several of our interviewees mentioned that to be a foodie one must frequently talk about food or participate in group activities that are centered on food, and many other interviewees reported that food conversations and group activities were routine in their own lives. This self-presentation as food-obsessed is an important marker of who is a foodie and also explains how being a foodie is most often understood as a social, rather than solitary, activity.

The interviewees also stressed exploration as an essential component of being a foodie. This exploration can occur in many forms. Foodies explore new and unusual foods, and they are willing to consume new individual foods or dishes that are frequently foods from unfamiliar cuisines. Neil Taverna, a 25-year-old working in the media and living in Brooklyn, reports that "I'm very big on trying new recipes and don't cook things twice a lot." He identified himself as feeling "pretty bold about food and will try, you know, sweetbreads and tripe," and also described in detail a meal at a Japanese restaurant in New York where everything on the menu was made out of pigs' feet. Pedro Maradona, a 22-year-old working as a marketing coordinator in Manhattan, also positively described eating brain at St John's restaurant in London, and noted that he thought of himself as being interested in trying "different dishes that you won't find other places." Timothy Bauer, a retired lawyer in Los Angeles, mentioned a joke he has with his wife that he will always order the unfamiliar thing on the menu: "Sometimes it gets me into trouble and I think, 'Oh God, that really was disgusting!' But I'm very adventuresome and I always like to try something new." Besides trying new and unusual foods, foodies are also willing to explore new places to get the foods that they are already familiar with. This entails exploring new restaurants and new stores or markets, but it can also mean traveling to acquire variations on or perfected versions of foods. A preference to explore or to experiment, rather than to enjoy only familiar foods or familiar settings for the consumption of food, is a key distinction that sets foodies apart, in our interviewees' perceptions. The importance of exploration generates interest in online forums that discuss where to get new kinds of food and discover new types of restaurants. Besides cooking and ordering unusual foods, Timothy Bauer described his active participation publicizing these culinary explorations on Chowhound, stating: "I wrote a lot about food for [Chowhound Los Angeles board] and would share, you know, every little new restaurant that I discovered in the Los Angeles area." While foodie exploration has its limits (as we explore in our discussion of Exoticism in Chapter 3), it appears vital to gaining new knowledge about food, living a food-focused lifestyle, and signifying a commitment to eating the best possible foods, sometimes requiring great effort, resources, or ingenuity.

Finally, for foodies, enjoyment of food is synonymous with evaluation of food. Foodies are partly defined by their application of standards to all of the food they consume. Each meal or individual food is an opportunity to assess the quality of what is about to be eaten, and this quality of foodies also fuels their participation in online forums and blogs that serve as vehicles for food assessment. Some of this evaluation connects food to political issues. One interviewee, Nathaniel Snider, posted blog entries on topics like the United States Farm Bill and genetic engineering. However, the majority of foodie evaluation is focused on aesthetic criteria, as in online discussions about how to get the best crust on sourdough bread. Again describing his participation in Chowhound, Timothy Bauer noted: "I think one time I counted and I have over twenty-five hundred posts on Chowhound. And I became sort of infamous particularly for my knowledge of sushi, which I do know an awful lot about." Later in the interview, when describing the difference between different kinds of watercress, Timothy aptly demonstrates the importance of evaluation to foodie pursuits, as well as the interconnections between evaluation, knowledge, and exploration of different foods not available in conventional supermarkets:

> The watercress that you buy at the supermarkets, including Whole Foods by the way, is grown, what they call hydroponically. Ah, and, it just doesn't have any taste. Watercress should have a real bite to it, a sharp, very sharp taste, and a high acid content. And when I go to the farmers' markets, one of the great farmers' markets of Southern California is in Santa Monica, California, and if you go to, their big market day is Wednesday but they also have one on Saturday morning. But they have a woman there who has, you know, wild watercress that she grows on a creek bed, along a creek bed and stuff like that. And it's just, the quality is just amazing. Plus you can buy things like arugula flowers, not just the arugula, but arugula flowers, and a wonderful thing that I love to cook with called green garlic, which is the little baby garlics before they turn into the big clove, and they look almost like spring onions. And you just can't buy those things in supermarkets.

There was variation in the extent to which our interviewees reported being willing to relax their evaluation standards. In our interviews with foodies, over half of interviewees made an explicit reference to their dislike for chain restaurants, like the Olive Garden and Denny's, even though we did not have a specific question about chain restaurants in our interview guide. While some reported being vigilant about never eating low-quality food, others reported being willing to temporarily suspend their evaluations. One good example of this was an interviewee who explained that he would agree to eat Doritos when his aunt offered them to him. Another interviewee, Ted Darby, after describing his delight at a 33-course molecular gastronomy tasting menu, admitted that he liked McDonald's, and in his defense, offered a textbook articulation of omnivorousness: "I avoid restaurants that I know to be mediocre. You know. But I love McDonald's. I mean, my daughters are just aghast that I like McDonald's. [Laughs.] *I have, not indiscriminate tastes, but I have wide-ranging tastes*" (emphasis ours).

While standards among our interviewees differed, what was clear, though, was that evaluation—or what Bourdieu referred to as an "aesthetic disposition"—was an ongoing and essential part of being a foodie. Differences amongst foodies lay in the vigilance behind the enforcement of aesthetic standards, but the existence of these standards was a constant presence with them. The interviewees in general saw the upholding of principles of good food as an essential foodie characteristic. While some labeled this "food snobbery," these respondents also maintained an emphasis on eating good quality food, making clear that expensive food was not necessarily synonymous with good food, in their opinions. This tension between quality and expense is significant to our analysis of the boundaries that foodies draw between worthy and unworthy food, but it is important to note that the vast majority of foodies we interviewed do not explicitly base their self-perceptions as foodies on an ability or a willingness to spend a lot of money on food. Developing standards and the willingness to apply them to the daily diet were frequently conceptualized as separate from questions of finances.

In sum, the foodies that we interviewed perceived themselves as well-informed, discovery-minded, discerning consumers (and most often food producers as well) who lead food-focused lives and present themselves to others as uncommonly passionate about food. They see themselves as well positioned to talk about and distinguish worthy food from unworthy food, and as we saw in our interviews, they are loquacious and articulate about this topic that is so important to them. In this chapter we have sought to review important prior research that we draw on and contribute to, as well as to review major concepts that inform our analysis of democracy and distinction in foodie discourse. In the next two chapters we draw from food journalism as well as our interviews with foodies to substantiate our argument that worthy food is framed in foodie discourse as having two central qualities: Authenticity and exoticism.

2

EATING AUTHENTICITY

What is "real" Texas barbecue, how is it different from other barbecues, and why does it matter? To speak of the "real" versions of things is to invoke the concept of authenticity. Barbecue styles are just one example of countless foods that are evaluated and valued by foodies on the basis of their authenticity. But what is "authentic" food, and why does it figure so largely in foodies' evaluation of food? And is "authentic" food really better than "inauthentic" food?

In this chapter we argue that authenticity is a key element of how foodies evaluate and legitimate food choices, and explore some of the nuances of this important, and complex, concept. Our argument about authenticity in foodie discourse is built "from the ground up," meaning that we closely examine a large sample of foodie discourse to identify the particular rhetorical claims that foodies use to mark food as authentic or inauthentic. We also draw from our interviews with foodies to see how they articulate the elements of authenticity we identify in foodie discourse.

The chapter has two goals. The first goal is to explore the ways in which foods are understood as authentic or inauthentic and how the boundary is drawn between the two. An important premise in our argument is that authenticity is socially constructed, and is not inherent to particular foods—it is not a simple case of either you have it or you don't. Instead, we understand the concept of authenticity as both socially constructed and relational. Authenticity is not inherent, but is *constructed* through the perceptions of food producers and consumers. People understand food as being authentic if it can be characterized in certain ways *in relation to* other foods, particularly inauthentic foods. To foreshadow our argument, food is understood as authentic when it has geographic specificity, is "simple," has a personal connection, can be linked to a historical tradition, or has "ethnic" connections. The nuances of these categories and examples of them constitute the first part of this chapter.

The second goal of this chapter is to discuss the meaning of authenticity in cuisine and explore what this tells us about the importance of authenticity in our culture more generally. Why is authenticity so valued? How does it work for diners and cultural consumers more generally to provide them with the kind of aesthetic experience they enjoy? The conclusion of this chapter will focus on a discussion of authenticity's place in cultural consumption and the particular role it plays in contemporary class politics.

Unpacking Authenticity

Before delving into a presentation of how food is construed as authentic, it is useful to take stock of how authenticity has been understood in other research in order to more fully appreciate its meaning. There is general agreement that authenticity is a modern value (Appadurai 1986; Erik Cohen 1988; Fine 2003). Being authentic is commonly linked with the existential idea of being "true" to one's self, and is thought to be based on modern ideals like individualism, uniqueness, sincerity, self-determination, and personal choice (Trilling 1972). Philosopher Charles Taylor (1992) argues that our modern cultural understanding of authenticity has been corrupted through a narcissistic focus—understanding authenticity exclusively as being true to one's self—and contends that authenticity must be reconnected to a larger social context, or "horizons of significance." Taylor examines personal actions and argues that they can be considered authentic when they are freely chosen *and* when they register on socially defined "horizons of significance" (1992: 39).

Choices and experiences are authentic because they matter to others and are socially recognized as significant. Taylor's work is sociologically significant to our analysis of culinary authenticity because it bolsters the notion that authenticity must be evaluated not through an exclusively individual lens (e.g., what one particular eater views as an authentic tamale) but within a broader social context.

Sociologists studying the authenticity of cultural objects focus on the processes through which authenticity is socially constructed (e.g., Fine 2003; Grazian 2003; Peterson 1997b). As Ram (2007: 466) notes, there is a broad scholarly consensus that authenticity is not an intrinsic quality of cultural artifacts, but is instead part of how people perceive and understand these artifacts: "nothing is 'really' authentic; everything is socially constructed."[33] In discussing the authenticity of shopping areas, Zukin (2008: 728) puts it succinctly: "We can only see spaces as authentic from outside them." Put differently, authenticity is generated through perceptions of how a cultural object negotiates a set of standards and values, instead of emerging from a cultural object's qualities. Crucially, these standards and values differ from time to time and from place to place. In his book *Creating Country Music: Fabricating Authenticity*, Richard Peterson (1997b) shows how authenticity in country music is constructed around particular singers and styles in different ways over time. Authenticity is produced not only by a singer's genuineness and uniqueness, but also by his or her relationship to a tradition within country music. Singers must express themselves in ways that resonate with and acknowledge values within the country music tradition, at the same time they must also be seen as unique. Authenticity, then, is generated through the evaluation of a singer's originality within the "horizons of significance" (to draw a parallel with Taylor's analysis) that are set out by the conventions of country music. Authenticity in the case of country music, therefore, is not simply about a musician's self-expression, but is cultivated through a negotiation between the artist's personal creativity and his or her engagement with musical tradition.

While Peterson's work demonstrates how authenticity is negotiated through a dialogue between creativity and tradition, David Grazian's

(2003: 17) study of the Chicago blues scene explains how actors operate within an elaborate "symbolic economy of authenticity" that varies in different cultural scenes. Within a blues club, there is "a specific network of commodified signs, social relations, and meaning, a world of human experience and subjectivity" that is the basis for evaluating and appreciating the blues musicians' authenticity. Different cultural scenes have their own signifiers of authenticity. Those who are immersed in a scene get a feel for its specific meanings and signs, and are able to evaluate authenticity within it. While individuals gain an intuitive sense of authenticity so that they can recognize it quickly, these impressions rely on the social evaluations of the performances, performers, and settings that produce authenticity. Grazian's analysis helps make clear that authentic cultural products—like blues music—are social products constructed in scenes that are continually evolving, and not about the timeless, or essential, qualities of a cultural genre or artist.

Drawing from cultural sociological work on authenticity, we can move to discuss the symbolic economy of authenticity in foodie discourse. Food scholarship has done some important work on the topic of culinary authenticity, and has tended to emphasize the connection between authenticity, specific geographic context, and the ethnicity of food producers. Noted food scholar and anthropologist, Sidney Mintz, famously argued that an authentic national cuisine is not possible in the United States, but instead defended the possibility of authentic regional cuisines which have more specific, local roots that resist long-distance travel and transmogrification (1996: 106, 114–115). Global flows of food resources, eaters, and food producers muddy the analytic waters of geographically-based authenticity, making it difficult to determine exactly how authentic food is being constructed, conserved, or conceptualized in an age of global cultural homogenization and creolization (James 2005). Food scholars have raised questions about what groups take responsibility for conferring "authentic" status on ethnic cuisines, and the power dynamics involved in this process (Heldke 2005; Abarca 2004). Philosopher Lisa Heldke focuses on understandings of cross-cultural culinary authenticity, and links authenticity with food adventurers' understanding of an exotic Other (e.g., authentic Thai cuisine)

(2005: 43–44). Heldke's work supports Grazian's argument that authenticity comes to be understood intuitively by those in a cultural scene: "for the most part, we [food adventurers] know just what we mean by the word authentic" (2005: 24). Rather than take this assumption on face-value, Heldke deconstructs unproblematized foodie notions of culinary authenticity—including "authentic" dishes designed to replicate their original incarnations, or understandings of authentic cuisine connected to a specific locale. Heldke's writing reveals that foodies' understandings of ethnic authenticity are complex, confusing, confused, and frequently work in the service of colonial relationships (2005: 29–43, 194), a point we explore more in Chapter 3.

While food scholars like Heldke have shed light on the complex and problematic links between ethnic identities and authenticity, what remains unclear are the precise qualities that confer culinary authenticity in foodie discourse. While exoticism and geographic specificity are clearly linked to culinary authenticity, we argue that authenticity cannot be equated with exotic Otherness, and believe it is important to parcel out and make explicit the various dimensions of authenticity. The rest of this chapter is devoted to this task, and to describing the qualities of food that promote evaluations of authenticity in the foodie discourse we examined. At the same time as we build on scholarly work on authenticity, we are going a step further to provide a set of categories meant to apply to evaluations of authenticity more broadly to realms outside of food. So while we provide a detailed picture of authenticity in gourmet food, we also want to make a statement about cultural authenticity in general. While it is true that signifiers of authenticity vary between scenes or cultural realms (the texture of an authentic New York bagel has no parallel in music, literature, film, etc.), the *categories* of signifiers of authenticity that we identify (*geographic specificity*, "*simplicity*," *personal connection*, *history and tradition*, and *ethnic connection*) do have such parallels. While these qualities clearly work together to construct a food's authenticity, they are separated for analytic clarity, and we discuss them in turn. At the end of this chapter, we come back to the question of why authenticity is valued so highly: What does it provide for cultural consumers and what are its social functions?

Dimensions of Authentic Food

Geographic Specificity

The connection between a food and a specific place is central to determining a food's authenticity. This connection is so common that it comes to be built into the names of certain foods, as in Parmigiano-Reggiano (Parmesan) cheese from Parma, Italy (not from a green Kraft shaker!), or Roquefort cheese aged near the town of Roquefort, France.[34] But even when geographic specificity is not built into a food's name, that connection remains a central component for evaluating food's authenticity. Foodies value foods prepared and consumed in specific locations (e.g., Chinese food from Shenzhen, or pulled pork barbecue from Charlotte, North Carolina), and confer less status on placeless foods that are found everywhere and come from nowhere special or specific.

In foodie discourse, geographic referents can occur at varying levels of specificity, with greater specificity tending to correlate with stronger assertions of food's authenticity. The most general associations are at the geographic scale of continents, such as "Asian" food or "South American" flavors. When employing these general terms, foodies are obviously aware of the variations in cuisines within a continent, and they use these terms as shorthand to refer to some of a continent's most common ingredients or flavors. Such vague continental references are relatively rare in foodie discourse. Broad geographic references are more often regionally-based, such as the Middle East, the Mediterranean, or Eastern Europe. National linkages are common, such as French food, Taiwanese food, Argentine food, or Vietnamese food, but so are the specification of regions within a country, such as the southeastern United States, northern Mexico, the Côte d'Azur, or Tuscany.

Foodie discourse is remarkable, however, for the frequency of geographic references to highly specific places, cities, or towns such as Bologna, Italy; New Iberia, Louisiana; Lucknow, India; Mesa, Arizona; New York, New York; Cape Town, South Africa; or Siglufjördhur, Iceland. Such precise geographic specificity signals authenticity by indicating that this food is valuable in part because of restrictions on its production and consumption, and these restrictions set it apart from more generic versions. We know that place-specific food is both different from versions available elsewhere, and true to traditions that are perfected and best known in that place alone. That is why the oysters from a particular spot on the Atlantic coast of France are like no others and are therefore authentic. That is also why we accept the authenticity of a local fish sauce from Phu Quoc, an island 30 miles off the coast of southwest Vietnam, where the fish sauce is sophisticated, nuanced, delicate, and unlike any other fish sauce commercially available. How do we know whether we are eating authentic tamales? First we need to establish whether we should be evaluating the tamales as Oaxacan or Salvadorean or Chiapaneco.

One of our interviewees, Timothy Bauer, a retired lawyer from Los Angeles, aptly articulates how authenticity is connected to a high degree of geographic specificity in describing a favorite restaurant, which is

> a Thai restaurant and the chef there is a female chef and her name is Saipin Chutima . . . and she's from northern Thailand so she has a lot of dishes that you don't find in a typical Thai restaurant. Most Thai restaurants, number one, are very dumbed down for Americans . . . So she has food that is from North, sort of Northwest Thailand, which is not very spicy but has sort of a Burmese and Southern Chinese influence. And then she has also food from Northeastern Thailand, which is called Isaan cooking, which is very spicy. And so she has some stuff that's really unusual, very authentic, totally delicious, and inexpensive.

Another interviewee, Dennis Nolan, a software engineer living in North Carolina, shows a similar degree of attention to geographic specificity in describing his favorite restaurant "called The Barbecue Joint," which has "a big chalkboard . . . which basically lists, you know, that you can get the North Carolina style, actually technically central North Carolina style pulled pork barbecue."

A connection to place is perhaps the central orienting feature of evaluations of authenticity, and such connections are ubiquitous in foodie talk. We can see just how significant a connection to a place is by contrasting the case of generic, supermarket versions of food that are the same everywhere. Supermarket bagels, like mass-produced Parmesan cheese and fast-food pizza, are difficult to construe to foodies as authentic.

Simplicity

'Simple' food is authentic because of the honesty and effortlessness it conveys, a trait that harkens back to the association between authenticity and individual sincerity, or being "true to oneself." Not only does authenticity connote positive values like sincerity and truthfulness, but it also emphasizes food's distance from the complexities and manufactured quality of modern industrialized life. For this reason, 'simple' food is commonly associated with small-scale producers (often identified in terms of individual producers or family farmers), "fresh" unprocessed foods (which are unadulterated and "true" to themselves), and handmade, artisanal foods (frequently depicted as produced by authentic, sincere craftspeople devoted to their work and not motivated by greed or money). Simplicity is sought not just in the food itself—as in a 'simple' fresh-picked peach—but also in the ways that food is produced, processed and presented—without excess fussiness, preparation, or detail. Food is deemed authentic when it is seen to emerge fresh from a simple way of life, or a simple mode of presentation, and maintains its straightforwardness all the way to the plate.

More concretely, foodie discourse valorizes simplicity in examples like labor-intensive (non-industrial) techniques for harvesting potatoes, 'simple' presentation styles in upscale restaurants, non-manufactured foods like hand-made tortillas or home-made ricotta, and the 'simple' pleasures of a vine-ripened, organic tomato harvested on a family farm. Like authenticity more generally, simplicity must be understood as a dynamic social construction that is highly dependent on social context, rather than a static feature inherent to the food itself. To remind readers that this term is not a straightforward descriptor, we use single quotation marks ('simple'). Clearly it is more time-efficient and less labor-intensive to buy tortillas at the grocery store than to shape them individually by hand after a lengthy process of soaking corn and mixing dough. However, the 'simple' process of hand-made tortilla production is emblematic of the equation of simplicity with authenticity and the positive appraisal of both.

While the terms 'simple' and 'simplicity' are not always explicitly employed or defined, connotations of simplicity are frequently imbued in descriptions of food producers as 'simple' people using 'simple,' small-scale and non-industrial production techniques, or in images of foods that lack pretension, and instead respect the purity of 'simple,' high-quality ingredients. Simplicity can be found in various locations: The food itself, the mode of food production, the way of life of food producers, the method of food preparation, food's presentation and the setting for consumption. Each form of simplicity contributes toward an overall perception of food's authenticity.

Examples of simplicity in food itself include single, whole foods like a "perfect peach" (*Gourmet*, July 2004), or Japanese small plates, which "are often a meditation on a single ingredient flavored simply and respectfully" (*San Francisco Chronicle*, May 5, 2006, p. E10). Gourmet food writers can also appreciate dishes that are a simple combination of basic ingredients: "The guacamole, made of ripe avocados, chopped tomatoes, cilantro, onions and fresh jalapenos, could not have been simpler—or tastier" (*New York Times*, Mar. 5, 2006, p. 14WC.10). That same restaurant review goes on to praise other simple dishes in a way that hints at why simplicity is linked to authenticity: "The appetizer ceviche de camarones—shrimp marinated in lemon juice, chopped onions, corn, cilantro and chili—was another fresh and honest option. The black bean soup was a hearty and tasty rendition of the basic dish, not too thick and with just the right kick." The implied counterpoint to the simple guacamole is the overwrought, complicated guacamole that would represent a dishonest corruption of the original, authentic version. Likewise, the honesty of the shrimp appetizer derives from its simplicity, with the implication being that complexity in this case would be dishonest, a clear violation of the standards of authenticity. This coupling of simplicity and honesty was mentioned by Theresa Callebaut, an interviewee from Boston in response to the question, "Is authentic food important to you?" She said, "Yes, I think it is . . . our

Christmas Eve dinner that I told you about, I'm not going to add a whole bunch of different herbs to that meat, but it's going to be really good-quality beef. I want it to just taste, I guess the word is honest, what it is."

Claims of simplicity are used even when the food itself seems quite complex from the standpoint of the average American diner. For example, Sir Terence Conran, "noted British designer and restaurateur," is lauded in a *Saveur* book review for his love of the simple things in life: "[Sir Terence] wants plain good food: a bowl of crab or lobster bisque, a tomato salad or some oeufs en gelée, a nice poached turbot with beurre blanc or a wood-grilled rabbit with plenty of garlic and fresh herbs" (*Saveur*, March 2004, p. 20). A description of these dishes as simple does not reflect their inherent simplicity, but is an assertion that they are authentic versions of classic dishes, and further indicates that the value of 'simplicity' is highly dependent on social context.

Simplicity can be conceptualized by foodies in ways that extend beyond the food's substance to the way food is produced. Foodie discourse provides a wealth of detail about food production and preparation, allowing us to see what sorts of production conditions are valued and viewed as linked to authentic food. Simple modes of food production (agriculture, livestock, and harvesting) are just as important to evaluations of food's authenticity as is the simplicity of food itself. 'Simple' production is most commonly equated with small-scale, non-industrial, and organic methods. Foodies show a clear preference for non-industrial production processes, and very rarely praise industrially-produced food. 'Simple' methods are argued to produce more delicious food, but they are also upheld as an end in themselves and serve as part of a nostalgic evocation of agrarian ideals and the authentic, honest, pre-modern life they imply.

In addition to providing superior taste, 'simple' production methods are often described as motivated by a devotion to purity and integrity in food production that insulates them from the negative associations of complex chemicals and industrial processes.[35] A restaurant's "house-made" mozzarella is praised, as are the organic eggs from a small poulty operation where not only are the chickens not squeezed into cages, but they "listen to Grateful Dead music while they swing on small trapeze bars" (*Food & Wine*, August 2004, p. 116). Witness the positive evaluation of one restaurateur's usage of pork and vegetables from a small farmer: "His seasonal farmer's plate ($34) is his pride and joy. This past week, it consisted of four different preparations of pork cut from the same side of pig brought in from a farm in [a nearby town], and served with vegetables from the same farmer's garden" (*Gourmet*, Dec. 2, 2006, p. M4). Small scale is clearly equated with simplicity and authenticity, as on a grocery shopping trip in Corsica, when a writer recounted delight upon finding, "that nonchain grocery stores often stocked a few jars of hand-labeled honey, a housewife's jams, or some surplus bottles of a neighbor's olive oil" (*Gourmet*, August 2004, p. 92). Through small-scale production, the authenticity of the lives and values of those carrying out food production is preserved and conveyed to consumers. In an article about farmers who hand-pick their potatoes, the author writes, "[t]hey do so partly because heirloom varieties bruise easily, but mostly because doing things the old-fashioned unmechanized way is what the [farmers profiled] care about" (*Saveur*, November 2004, p. 54).

Intimately connected to 'simple' production methods are the 'simple' ways of life of those individuals who produce authentic food. In a profile of the 'simple' Kalamata olive, we learn that "the annual Kalamata harvest dictates the rhythms of a simple existence" invoking a world where "there is . . . no dearth of ruddy-faced old timers plodding along on donkeys" (*Saveur*, November 2004, pp. 92, 94). Elsewhere the gourmet reader is invited to a family gathering in rural Jordan with the following description: "[i]t's a little agricultural paradise of fruit and olive orchards and fields where Bedouin tend crops and herd sheep, [a family member's] so-called villa is a rustic, simple three-room structure built over a small cave that has been continuously inhabited for centuries" (*Gourmet*, May 2004, pp. 118, 123). The pre-modern, simple way of life is an ideal source for authentic food.

'Simple' ways of life are linked not only with 'simple' production but also with the 'simple' preparation of food. For example, in an article set in rural Louisiana, the authors offer a glowing portrait of a black female cook's 'un-schooled,' intuitive cooking technique: " '[I]t's from my mama's kitchen,' she said. 'I cannot tell you how to do it because she never taught me to measure anything. You just add seasoning and spice until it's right' " (*Gourmet*, April 2004, p. 52). Just as self-taught artists represent authentic self-expression and produce authentic art, unschooled cooks seemingly lacking in commercial motivations produce authentic foods.

'Simple' food preparation can also be invoked without the rural or unschooled connotations of rusticity. Chefs at expensive restaurants can produce food 'simply' by cooking without commercial motivation, and only with single-minded artistic fervor, as we see in a restaurant review: "There's nothing calculated or commercial about Quince: It is simply two exceptional people sharing everything they know about the pleasures of the table. And for those caught up by the couple's passion, it can be transforming" (*Gourmet*, July 2004, p. 30). We see another example in a review of a restaurant where three chefs run a simple operation; they serve "straight-ahead home-cooked food, and the price is right. I wonder if tighter service may better translate the enthusiasm and generous soul these three young men bring to their restaurant" (*New York Times*, Jan. 22, 2006, p. 14CN.8). What could be more authentic than food enthusiastically produced by three generous souls? The valuing of 'simplicity' is also seen in the specific techniques of food preparation. We see this in an article celebrating the tempura made by Japanese masters. We learn that this "[t]empura must have sincerity," and that to produce this authentic artifact, simplicity is essential: "Top-notch tempura all comes down to simple things exquisitely done" (*Saveur*, December 2004, p. 84).

Simplicity in food's preparation is exceptionally ambiguous, since perceptions of what makes something simple to prepare, as opposed to difficult or complicated, vary widely. In the interviews, we asked about "simple" food that the respondents would prepare. This question allowed foodies to describe food that was relatively easy (for them) to prepare, but still qualified in their minds as good food. The answers ranged from basic marinara sauce to grilled salmon to "a really simple vinaigrette with, not even with vinegar necessarily, just with, say, lemon juice and some olive oil." Sometimes foodies would explicitly emphasize the simplicity of their own cooking, although it would seem that many people might disagree with that description. This was the case with Fiona Callworth, an interviewee from Boston, who responded in the following way when asked, "What's an example of a simple dish that you might cook?"

> Oh, I've got this really good, you got to pay attention because this is so easy to make, this is so good. You buy some cod, take a handful (I'm just going to do one serving), a handful of green beans, take two fingerling potatoes. You've got to have heavy cream and lemon juice and you've got to have a whole bunch of frying pans because it all gets cooked at the same time, so you've got to be able to work the pans at the same time. You take the fish, dry it, obviously, salt and pepper it. Melt butter, cut the fingerlings, put them in and start cooking them with some salt and pepper. Then put the fish in, then put the green beans in another pan. So you've got three pans with butters working. As you're browning all of those, go over to the other pan, squeeze half a lemon and pour some heavy cream in. You know, obviously, you don't want to get fat so you got to, you know, three tablespoons or something, four tablespoons, you let that reduce. Be careful with that, watch that because you want it to kind of thicken to give it some intensity but you don't want to burn it. Then go over and work on your other pans, boom, boom, boom. It really happens very quickly. People get all freaked out and they say this is a big deal. It's a very simple thing. Then you put the potatoes down, put the fish on top, put the green beans on top of that, and then you pour the sauce on. This is so good, I'm telling you, I could eat it almost every night, it's really good. That is a very simple dish.

Preparing dishes by hand, especially hand preparation of components of dishes for which mass-produced versions abound, is one of the most important signals of simplicity and authenticity in food preparation. *Bon Appétit*'s editor-at-large reports that "the only Mexican food worth eating is made by hand" (January 2004, p. 43), and we see time and again a preference for hand-made rather than machine-made tortillas (even though hand-made tortillas have become a rarity in the lives of working people in Central American and Mexico). Physical evidence of the 'simple' process of making food by hand, and the unstandardized results, are depicted as aesthetically-pleasing and superior, as with chocolate: "His cocoa-dusted truffles have the misshapen look of miniature spuds—or as Helen says, 'You can tell he's made them with his own very strong hands'" (*Food & Wine*, February 2004, p. 47). 'Simple,' hand-made food is valorized as a "true" version and hence more authentic compared to haute cuisine traditions criticized as overblown, overworked, or fussy. Hand-making foods is also evidence of a distance from the ubiquitous mechanization and industrialization of modern life. This idea came forth in an interview with Chad Tucker, a 47-year-old librarian living in the Midwest. When asked the question, "What is authentic food to you?", he responded that "It's just food that's prepared simply. That would be food that's not prepared from some processed product, where you don't pour your lettuce out of a vacuum sealed bag, food that is prepared by someone who has some sense of interest in how the food is made."

Moving closer to the consumption end of the food chain, 'simplicity' in food's presentation is another valuable signal of its authenticity. Take, for example, the exultation of simple shapes and color: "my favorite [dish] was rice balls, a Japanese-style convenience food. Three elegant and self-contained ovals were formed from milky white grains, each ball with its own deep green strip of dried seaweed as handle. Inside was a simple filling of salmon" (*New York Times*, Mar. 19, 2006, p. 14NJ.12). Although it requires an aesthetic disposition to distinguish between simple elegance and banality, food scores highly when it finds the right balance between a presentation that is too fussy to be honest, and too commonplace to be interesting. We can see this successful display of simplicity without banality in a restaurant's wild boar sausage dish: "The three succulent slices were splayed on a bed of mild choucroute and were topped with an artistic forest of enoki mushrooms and a dollop of whole-grain mustard on the side. It was both delicate and bold, simply but evocatively presented" (*San Francisco Chronicle*, Apr. 23, 2006, p. 23).

The foodies we interviewed occasionally mentioned that they didn't want dishes to look overly "precious" or "fussy" in their presentation on the plate, indicating that such a presentation had a falseness or pretentiousness to it. A good example of a preference for simplicity in presentation and an aversion to fussiness arose in an interview with Nancy Light, a 51-year-old working in marketing. She said, "Authentic food to me is simple and natural food and presentation which supports what is the indigenous quality of that particular food . . . like in the summer maybe a salad that's field greens and fresh peaches and citrus salad dressing and some toasted almonds." Going on to highlight other variants of simplicity we cover in this section, she added, "That would be sort of simple authentic, from the garden, you've just picked it and fresh picked tomato and you're drizzling extra virgin olive oil and throwing a handful of basil. You know, that's wonderfully authentic and rich food."

Finally, simplicity is heralded as an important quality of the setting in which food is consumed. To the extent that food is served and eaten in simple settings, it is more likely to be perceived as authentic. As one might expect in the age of omnivorousness (see Chapter 1), the stuffy and highly formal dining etiquette associated with traditional snobbery appears almost to *disqualify* foods as authentic—consider that Mario Batali's most formal dining venture in New York City, Del Posto, was the food critics' least favorite of Batali's many ventures. Our interview with Fern Osborne, a 30-year-old living in the Pacific Northwest, revealed an aversion to formal restaurant experiences that was fairly typical in our sample:

> I definitely am put off by a stuffy atmosphere. Even if the food is supposed to be phenomenal . . . I just don't like the idea of having, you know, some expectation about what I should look like. I don't have a problem looking nice enough for a restaurant, but if there's an expectation of wearing, you know, a jacket and tie, that kind of puts me off, for my husband or whatever. So generally if it's a sort of stuffy atmosphere, I would say, I don't like the formality.

'Simple' dining at restaurants where formal dining etiquette is absent is often upheld as a pure food experience in gourmet food writing. In an article about Italy's Lipari Islands, we read that "[s]ome people will tell you [the city of Lipari] has the best restaurants in the islands, but Giovanna and I decide that they are just the most formal. Like everything about Lipari, most of the food is overworked and commercial . . . Eventually, we find some small, authentic restaurants on the island . . ." (*Gourmet*, January 2004, p. 90). Simplicity—akin to humbleness—in restaurant décor is cherished by many gourmet food writers, and is taken as evidence of a straightforward and honest food experience. The pretension and complicated etiquette of the past, formerly part of the haute cuisine package, is now evidence of inauthenticity. A review of a Long Island restaurant makes the case for the value of a simple setting:

> Turn off your cellphone. (The signals disturb the fryer for the frites, the menu remarks in an aside that lets you know you're in the kind of place that takes food seriously without taking itself too seriously.) . . . [in this restaurant the] cooking is allowed to shine on its own terms, and shine it does . . . It is a countrified and welcoming space, with its bare-wood floors and furniture, barely adorned yellow walls and a festive box of bright red apples at the front desk.
>
> (*New York Times*, Jan. 15, 2006, p. 14NJ.14)

Simplicity in setting and food together can produce an authentic experience, as in a review of an Oakland restaurant where there is a positive evaluation of "the 60-seat restaurant's edgy, unfussy looks, personal service and straightforward seasonal, natural food that avoids the self-conscious cleverness of much fusion cooking" (*San Francisco Chronicle*, Mar. 5, 2006, p. 49).

The preference for simple, even impoverished settings and non-pretentious surroundings is evident in some discussions of the Slow Food movement[36] which denigrate restaurants with Michelin stars for their formality and opulence, and moralistically praise cooking in rural Italy for its "quality, sincerity, and the emotional values of honest cooking"

(*Gourmet*, January 2004, p. 23). We see the positive appraisal of 'simple' rural life applied again in rural Italy where the author expresses a preference to eat among "a backdrop of rusted farm machinery and walls that aren't perpendicular to the ground" and in "an old manor house where chickens peck at your feet" rather than at "solemn" Michelin-starred restaurants with "stodgy" food (*Gourmet*, January 2004, pp. 46–48).

To the extent that 'simple' settings exist outside of modern life, their simplicity is authentic not only for its straightforwardness but also for its distance from the complexities of life in advanced industrialized societies. And the same can be said of the location of simplicity in food itself, in the mode of food production, the way of life of food producers, the method of food preparation, food's presentation, and the setting for consumption.

Personal Connection

For people who seek authenticity in their lives, the connection between an identifiable producer and a cultural artifact is an essential part of cultural experiences. When we like a painting, we frequently ask, "Who painted it?" Admiration of a building is commonly accompanied with an appreciation of the architectural visionary behind the structure. As with other forms of cultural consumption, we evaluate authenticity in food by connecting the food to the visionary behind the plate—whether that be in the initial stages of food production, or in the cooking process. It is easy to see how identity is linked to authenticity: The uniqueness, originality, and sincerity of an identifiable individual or group finds expression in their cultural production. Food is no different from any other art in this way. Just as mass-produced anonymous art purchased from a big box store is not typically deemed authentic, food is perceived as good and authentic when it is linked to specific creators with honest intentions—intentions that are not limited to making a quick buck. By establishing food as having an idiosyncratic connection to a specified creative talent or family tradition, authentic food is distinguished as "quality" artful food, and distant from industrial foods' faceless, mass-produced lineage, obvious commercial motivations, and unfortunate dearth of authenticity. (This trend, of course, obscures the cultural and economic privilege of eating outside the industrial food system that feeds most Americans—something that we discuss in Chapter 5.) One way that the authenticity of personalized food is established is by conjuring images of individual artistic creativity. The personalities used to signal artistry and authenticity were mainly chefs, most commonly men, cooking in elite restaurant settings. Many of our interviewees had favorite chefs whom they cast in this light. David Teitelbaum, a 34-year-old journalist from New York, praised French chef, Joël Robuchon: "[he] definitely is a genius, and his place L'Atelier in Paris is fantastic." Ted Darby, a retired lobbyist from Washington, DC, provided a clear example of the importance of the individual behind the food:

> There's a restaurant here called Mini Bar. The chef is a guy by the name of Jose Andres, who you will hear more about. He's going to start very soon a new television show in English about the cooking of Spain. He actually lives here and has three or four restaurants here, but he's from Spain. And he's sort of the Julia Child of Spain . . . Jose Andres worked for a while for Ferran Adrià of El Bulli in Rosas, Spain. So he's learned a lot of the techniques there. But he's just an extraordinary, creative guy.

Foodie discourse is replete with references to famous chefs such as Jean-Georges Vongerichten, Alain Ducasse, Alice Waters, and Thomas Keller, as well as countless references to less famous chefs. These chefs are treated as culinary artists who put their personal stamp on food, like a sculptor or an *auteur* director, and create an authentic and original piece of culinary art that can be juxtaposed against the artless world of industrial food and chain restaurants. A review of new chefs in France explicitly connects chefs to the art world: "Each of these chefs has his own distinct personal style, but they are united, like a school of painters, by certain shared traits and convictions" (*Gourmet*, January 2004, p. 55). Perhaps reflecting a general appreciation for Japanese art and culture, Japanese chefs are frequently portrayed as artists: "Michikazu Ueyama, the owner and sushi chef, slices fish with the best of them, and his presentations are sheer artistry" (*New York Times*, Mar. 12, 2006, p. 14WC12).

Other times personalized food was constituted as authentic by establishing a kind of culinary artisanry or folk art, within specific family traditions of food production, such as the Theos, a Greek family who run a ranch in Colorado (*Gourmet*, June 2004, pp. 124–127), or the Romanengo family who have made and sold gourmet candies in the same shop in Genoa for centuries (*Saveur*, December 2004, pp. 68–77). The foods produced or cooked by these named families are upheld as authentic because their origins are traceable to personalities and the individual creativity of family members, which is assumed to have a positive influence on food, rendering it part of a specific authentic artisan lineage and differentiating it from faceless industrial food. In these cases, the folk-art family chefs and artisanal producers are depicted as possessing great taste, and the particular foods they choose to eat, even when they are common dishes, are made special and distinct through the personal and artistic associations they bring to the table. Sometimes naming individuals involved in food creation has neither a high art nor folk art mode, but can still contribute to food's authenticity by connoting uniqueness and attention to detail. In this way we can read of Olivier Baussan, a French multi-millionaire who spends his free time fishing off the coast of Corsica (*Food & Wine*, April 2004, pp. 122–130), and the Van Wyck family, which makes traditional Southern food in their catering business (*Food & Wine*, May 2004, pp. 142–149).

Naming individual personalities in gourmet food writing—in the high art or artisan/folk art mode—is most common in a developed country or an affluent setting.[37] Foodie discourse about food experiences in the developing world, where authors often describe food cooked in huts and roadside stands, tends to resemble old-fashioned anthropology, where the colonial "Other" serves as a fascinating and generalized specimen, but the individual personality of the cook or artisan remains unnamed and under-developed. Similarly in our interviews, discussions of foods consumed in developing countries were frequently lauded, but did not name food producers or chefs specifically. After praising and naming a panoply of famous chefs and restaurateurs connected to famous restaurants (including Mario Batali of Babbo, Wiley Dufresne of WD~50, Danny Meyer of Gramercy Tavern, Joël Robuchon of L'Atelier and Dan Barber of Blue Hill), interviewee David Teitelbaum candidly noted, "But then there's all these other, you know, kind of ethnic places that I couldn't even tell you who the chef is ..." Authenticity in these instances is connoted through other discursive strategies, such as geographic specificity, or through ethnic connections.

History and Tradition

In response to the question, "What is authentic food to you?", Faye Taggart, a 64-year-old landscape designer from Maryland, gave us a succinct answer that represents very well this particular dimension of authenticity: "[Food] made the way it was traditionally made with the ingredients that it was traditionally made with ... That it's cooked in the manner that it's supposed to be cooked." Similarly, Timothy Bauer responded, "Authentic food to me is food that is true to the culture from which it came ... So by authentic I mean, if I went to the Philippines that's how it would traditionally be prepared. Or if I went to Thailand, that's the way it would be prepared. Not modified for American tastes."

More broadly in foodie discourse, we frequently encounter the idea that we know whether we are getting the "real" or authentic version of something by comparing it to a set of established standards, conventions, or traditions. In order to make such a comparison, though, we need a tradition as a reference point. Food is often framed as authentic through connecting it to a specific historical tradition, which is commonly (but not exclusively) linked to an ethno-cultural tradition. This connection demonstrates not only that the authentic food has stood the test of time and been deemed timelessly appropriate rather than an ephemeral food fad, but also that it is true to its origins and has maintained its integrity. Both historicism and references to ethno-cultural traditions are present in this dimension of authenticity, but our emphasis in this section is on the historical dimension of tradition. (Authenticity as it is specifically connected to ethnocultural practices and communities is described below.) For example, mentioning the fact that whole goats have been roasted over hot coals in Monterrey, Mexico since the 1700s (*Saveur*, June/July 2004, p. 44) is a way to identify the food—*Cabrito al pastor*—as historically based and authentic. About Vietnamese rolls, we can read that "[t]he Vietnamese were wrapping meat and seafood in greens before 100 B.C." (*Saveur*, August/September 2004, p. 38) and that a Turinese café serving a drink of espresso and chocolate has been operating since 1783 (*Gourmet*, May 2004, p. 171). Historical traditions support the reader's belief in a food's authentic status because historical continuity can be interpreted as authoritative and undeniable, just as historical traditions are used to validate the legitimacy of universities, artwork, orchestras, and museums.

Although a straight reference to a historical tradition is quite common, foodie discourse also frames foods as authentic when tradition forms the foundation for artistic experimentation, working in conjunction with the previous discursive strategy of personalized artistic innovation. Put differently, foodie discourse identifies food as authentic when its creator makes an artistic innovation on historic traditions. As Peterson (1996b) argues in the case of country music, authenticity is generated through adherence to a tradition, while also departing from that tradition in an original, artistic way. For example, a San Francisco restaurant is lauded when it serves an "imaginative variation on classic themes" (*Saveur*, August/September 2004, p. 85), and a chef is praised because his "genius is knowing when to leave [traditional] recipes intact and when to add a twist of his own" (*Food & Wine*, July 2004, p. 177). An article on Icelandic cuisine notes that "[t]he global kitchen may have delivered new ingredients and tastes to Iceland, but its customs are still very much alive. Old dishes are simply updated" (*Gourmet*, April 2004, p. 112). The following passage reveals that although personal creativity is highly valued—providing uniqueness linked to an individual culinary artist—tradition provides limits for creative license:

'At the beginning of a new century,' says [the chef] Decoret, 'cooking in France is no longer about perfecting a monumental and eternal battery of recipes. It's about incessant creativity.' But there's also a decidedly French respect for basics. 'Unlike the

Spaniards,' [another chef] Tartarin says, 'we never forget that we're cooks first, not chemists or magicians.'

(*Gourmet*, January 2004, p. 55)

Like artists working within the conventions of their genre, it would be senseless for French chefs to cook without regard for the basics of French culinary techniques. Creativity is essential, but it must have limits, and a connection to its "essential" foundations—in this case, the French culinary canon—to be deemed authentic.[38]

The construction of food's authenticity through a dialog of traditionalism and artistic creativity occurs predominantly in first-world elite culinary settings; authenticity is not generally identified as a result of such a dialog when the setting is a developing country or when the setting is a poor and rural first-world location. The foods associated with impoverished settings or developing countries are often obscure and unfamiliar to American palates (e.g., duck tongues), and this obscurity is sufficient to legitimate them as authentically original, so that artistic creativity on "classic" European culinary themes is not required for authentic validation. In contrast, food encountered in upscale restaurants in New York, Paris, San Francisco, or other "world-class" cities is most frequently legitimated as authentic through a dialog between tradition and the personal artistry of an individual chef or food producer, where creativity and experimentation came into play.

Ethnic Connection

Consider the following statement of Florence Nagy, a 51-year-old administrative assistant from Pennsylvania: "When I think of authentic I think of ethnicity."

In this statement we see an example of one dimension of authenticity that turned up in the interviews with foodies, but that never quite came to the surface in our reading of food journalism: An overt signal of the ethnicity of food's producers and consumers as an indicator of authenticity. Although food journalism left the evaluation of food according to the ethnic identity of food's producers and consumers implicit—touching on the issue indirectly through the emphases on geography and historicism—the interviewees were quite clear that authentic food of a particular cuisine needed to be cooked and eaten by members of the corresponding ethnic group. In answering the question, "What is authentic food to you?", David Teitelbaum put it this way: "Well, there's kind of this cliché where, you know, you look in a window of a restaurant, if it's an ethnic restaurant, if you see a lot of that ethnicity in a restaurant, it's probably a good sign." These kinds of sentiments linking ethnicity and authenticity were echoed on food blogs. One Chowhound poster, for example, complained that his city's Japanese food "seems like a wasteland of AYCE [all you can eat] or so-so sushi by Chinese or Korean proprietors," and asked, "Can anyone at Chowhound point me to where I can find sushi that is reasonably priced and not made by someone who doesn't even speak Japanese." This query generated considerable interest, and made clear that for many foodies, ethnicity and authentic foods are inextricably linked (http://chowhound.chow.com/topics/354512).

The placing of ethnicity into the understanding of authenticity in food seems to rely on an understanding that a person's ethnicity influences her or his ability to prepare food in the correct manner, both through using the right techniques and recognizing how the food should "really" taste. Michelle Quinlan, a 37-year-old systems analyst from Chicago, is one of our interviewees who makes the connection between ethnicity and authenticity explicit when she says, "I guess you could say the food I had when I was in Senegal was authentic because it was cooked in that country by native Senagalese." Fiona Callworth, an interviewee from Boston, declared, "I wouldn't set foot in an Asian restaurant in the Midwest." When asked to explain, she distinguished between big cities like Chicago and most of the rest of the Midwest, adding, "Let's say you're in Des Moines, Iowa. Not a lot of Asian people in Des Moines, Iowa . . . I wouldn't go to an ethnic restaurant in an area where they don't have the actual ethnic population."

One way to understand the difference in emphasis between the foodies we interviewed and food writers is that the two groups are actually in substantial agreement about the importance of ethnicity to authentic food. In gourmet food writing, the ethnicity of food's producers and consumers is often illustrated through accompanying photographs or is inferable from the geographic details. In addition, when it is mentioned explicitly, it is downplayed somewhat, likely because of the need to avoid statements that might be misconstrued as essentializing and thereby considered politically incorrect. For our purposes, we find that an ethnic connection is an important part of how authenticity is constructed in foodie discourse, but that it is communicated differently, through interpersonal and online foodie conversations rather than through journalistic gourmet writing.

The Cultural Politics of Authenticity

The contemporary emphasis on authentic food is unmistakable, but how are we to understand the quest for authenticity in food? Our explanation of the concern with authenticity starts with a recognition that food consumption, in addition to being about sustenance and visceral pleasure, is also about status. The link between food or dining and status is centuries old and has been the focus of historical studies (e.g., Elias 2000) and contemporary studies of the relationship between socioeconomic status and food preferences (Warde 1997). People's food preferences, like all their cultural preferences, have implications for the way they are seen in social settings, as well as for their self-conception—their identity. Just as with music or literature, the consumption of food is related to how sophisticated, knowledgeable, refined and adventurous we see ourselves, as well as to how we want others to see us in these ways.

Building on the literature on cultural omnivorousness (outlined in Chapter 1), we contend that foodie consumption patterns have become omnivorous. This does not mean that foodies eat everything, but that they carefully select from a wide array of genres. Authenticity is one of the primary characteristics that foodies use for making culinary choices. We are certainly not the first to identify the importance of culinary "authenticity," but our contribution is to draw from empirical data to specify the ways that authenticity is invoked: as geographically specific, 'simple,' personally connected, connected to history, and linked to ethnic producers or consumers. These qualities can be cited on their own, but they are often used together to convey maximum authenticity—consider the simple delights of hand-made confectionary made in a specific town in Italy based on a recipe passed down for generations. This raises the question of why authenticity has become the basis for evaluating food. What does this quality mean to people? Why does it serve as a contemporary basis for cultural distinction?

We argue that authenticity in food is valued because it helps to settle a tension present in contemporary culture. As explored in Chapter 1, we characterize this tension as democracy versus distinction. By democracy we mean that there is a high value in our culture placed on equality and inclusivity. A democratic culture brings together different people. The American ethos is that all are created equal—anyone can have the American dream. Arbitrary and explicit exclusion of some people—discrimination—is culturally illegitimate. As part of the ascendance of this ethos, old-fashioned snobbery is fading away. By snobbery we mean arbitrary distinctions between good and bad, high and low culture. Snobs won't even discuss the potential for Hollywood films or rock music to be considered art. They also insist that classical music and the great books of the Western canon are examples of the pinnacle of human achievement. This cultural disposition has little currency today, and one important reason why is the obvious Eurocentrism it entails. The dissolving of the traditional high art/low art divide is part of a broader decrease in the legitimacy of arbitrary discrimination in society and a movement toward omnivorous cultural consumption.

An emphasis on authentic culture facilitates this side of the tension. By valuing authentic foods, we are freed from the snobbish constraints of placing French food at the top of the food hierarchy. We can appreciate a more inclusive culinary repertoire, and we can also pursue a set of democratic social goals, including valuing the food cultures of marginalized groups, and helping to sustain small-scale and local food producers. Many authentic foods—like a simple roasted, free-range chicken—can also be valued as more sustainable and conducive to personal health. The desire for authenticity dovetails with critiques of the risks of modern industrial society, making it easy to see the positive outcomes associated with a search for authenticity in food choices.

The other side of the democracy versus distinction tension, however, is that the American foodscape remains a terrain for status-seeking where cultural artifacts are used to achieve distinction, and reinforce class boundaries. Although arbitrary discrimination—snobbery—is no longer a viable means to achieve this distinction, it remains an important goal of social interaction. People achieve many different goals through cultural consumption, and distinction is one of them. A focus on authenticity in cultural consumption provides a standard for distinction that is not overtly snobbish, which is to say that it appears to be a reasonable standard rather than an arbitrarily discriminatory standard. And yet authentic foods can be quite difficult to acquire and appreciate. Not only can they be expensive, but knowledge of foods that count as authentic, and the ability to appreciate what sets them off from inauthentic foods, requires an investment of time and a set of cognitive and aesthetic skills that generally accompany higher education and income levels. Because "real" versions of foods are often found only in particular geographic places, only people who can afford to travel have access to those versions. Hand-making foods is typically a more expensive process than industrial production, particularly in industrialized countries like the United States. When individual producers and esteemed chefs attach their name to food products and dining establishments, the price goes up. Although authenticity can clearly not be reduced to rarity, it is nonetheless true that authentic foods are frequently rare, and it is an economic truism that rarity in valued items creates high prices.

In short, authentic foods, despite possessing many genuine democratic qualities, simultaneously facilitate distinction and the perpetuation of taste hierarchies within foodie discourse. Our point is not that all foodies are obsessive status-seekers, but that the authenticity frame works within foodie discourse to facilitate status distinctions—it enables status-seeking people to derive status and develop their identities as foodies from eating authentic foods. The sociological work on omnivorousness in cultural consumption generally acknowledges that omnivorous cultural consumption—where all genres are eligible for high-status people to consume—is not a disavowal of status-seeking. Quite the contrary, it is an alternative "strategy" for deriving status through cultural consumption, but a strategy that is opposed to snobbery.

In this chapter we have identified and described the authenticity frame as an essential characteristic in foodie discourse that allows foods be evaluated as high-quality or prestigious and worthy of elite consumption. Foods are deemed authentic when they can be framed as geographically specific, 'simple,' have a personal connection, are historically grounded, and have an ethnic connection. An emphasis by foodies on these qualities of food can produce a complicated and paradoxical outcome. There are real, democratic social benefits that result from a focus on authenticity. The democratic element of authenticity involves a reconnection with food knowledge, reclamation of lost culinary skills, and sincere investigation into the troubled origins and implications of industrial food production. Food has incredible meaning for foodies, for whom the tactile and practical values of food are important. Status is not everything, as deliciousness in food is also a clear priority for foodies. We do not want to diminish this difference, or belittle the meaning it has for the foodies we interviewed, or the foodies we know personally. Also, at least from our experience, a grass-fed chicken can indeed taste better than its industrial counterpart, and the research suggests it is also more ecologically-sustainable. At the same time, though, when foodies value authenticity in food, they can inadvertently constitute and reproduce a culinary scene rife with cultural hierarchy and elitism.

Omnivorous cultural consumption, not just in food but in all forms of culture, is a way of negotiating the tension between democracy and distinction in our culture. Snobbery is out of fashion, but hierarchy may never be out of style, and the contemporary method for meeting the demands of both democracy and distinction is omnivorousness, which defines quality in culture not by genre but by a focus on authenticity. The five qualities that allow culture to be framed as authentic in food are also central to evaluations of authenticity in other cultural realms. For example, Grazian's (2003) study of the blues in Chicago identifies geography as a central feature of audiences' evaluations of authenticity. The honesty and distance from economic concerns of the individual personalities is yet another dimension of their evaluation as authentic. The personal identity and race of the artists are so central to evaluations of authenticity that it is unthinkable to evaluate music, or any form of art, without linking it to the individual artist. And we understand music, as we do with all art, as part of a tradition that needs to be engaged with and dialoged with. Authenticity in food, and in our culture more generally, is fundamental for discerning omnivorous consumers' evaluations of culture. But it is not the only quality of food and culture that is important to foodies. The next chapter discusses a second quality that is equally significant: Exoticism.

3

THE CULINARY OTHER
SEEKING EXOTICISM

A proud parenting moment: my youngest son ordered the roast duck for his birthday dinner at his favorite restaurant. As the honoree, he got the duck head and promptly opened the beak and exclaimed, "Someone took the tongue!" I had to get him a serving of duck tongues from a Chinese deli a week later to make up for his disappointment.
—Letter from Gretchen Kohl, Alameda, California (*Gourmet*, June 2007, p. 34)

Like authenticity, exoticism is a key element of foodie discourse. As with the case of authenticity, the term "exotic" is not always directly invoked, yet the desire for an exotic food experience underscores many central elements of the American foodscape—the food television shows that take viewers on a culinary adventure using exotic ingredients, the cooking guides that demonstrate how to impress your guests with dishes like grilled Haloumi cheese and pork chops with North African spice paste, the food magazine travelogs showcasing unusual foods from remote climes, and the restaurant reviews enticing readers to venture off the beaten culinary path. Even cruise ships are starting to offer more exotic fare. The director of strategic marketing for Radisson Seven Seas explains: "Food is playing a larger part in everybody's life these days, and not just on vacation . . . They're becoming more adventurous in what they try. You look back 20 years ago, how many sushi places and Thai restaurants were there? Now, they're everywhere.

People are more interested in exotic cuisine" (*Globe & Mail*, Feb. 4, 2006, p. T12).

Just as authenticity is not inherent to food but is constructed in the way we evaluate food, exoticism is in the eye of the beholder. If food is exotic we must ask, exotic to whom? Food experts frame food to highlight certain qualities that produce an evaluation of exoticism relative to the experiences of American foodies. And like the valuation of authenticity, the valuation of exoticism is not unique to food culture, but is part of a larger cultural esteem for exotic experiences. In this chapter, we will explore why the "exotic" is both a valued quality and a controversial concept. After recounting some of these debates, we then describe exoticism in the context of the gourmet foodscape. Most importantly, we ask a critical question of "food adventuring":[39] is the relentless search for exotic new ingredients, new cuisines, and undiscovered foods a positive development? Put differently, is gourmet globetrotting an extension of culinary colonialism, or does it represent a meaningful attempt to experience cuisines (and people) outside the Western culinary canon?

In this chapter we will argue that the exoticism frame within foodie discourse contains both these impulses: It builds on and reproduces certain neo-colonial inequalities, at the same time it represents a cosmopolitan interest in broadening the culinary canon and forming intercultural connections. Before proceeding with our discussion of ethnicity, it is important to reiterate that the valuation of exoticism and authenticity often occur together, intimately commingling in pages of gourmet cookbooks and magazines. Exotic foods are also often authentic foods, and vice versa. Foodie discourse produces strong messages on the commingling qualities of authenticity and exoticism. Avoid inauthentic Chinese buffets, and instead seek out authentic Salvadorean pupusas eaten in dusty downtown restaurants. Shun Italian chain restaurants (however delicious the fresh hot bread might be), while locally-bottled, hand-labeled aged balsamic vinegar from small Italian villages can be bagged and brought home like big-game trophies. Foodie parents are embarrassed by their children's penchant for chicken nuggets and fries, but proudly mention offspring who order duck tongues at a Chinese restaurant.

While the categories of authentic and exotic commingle and are often conflated in popular food writing and academic prose (e.g., Cohen 1988; Heldke 2005), they are not synonymous. We contend that they are worth discussing separately, since they often represent significantly different, distinctive qualities within foods—qualities that are manifest in different combinations, and often in ways that are mutually exclusive. Figure 3.1 provides a set of idealized examples for understanding how we distinguish between authenticity and exoticism. This figure simplifies how foods are categorized in order to highlight the qualities that contribute to authenticity separately from exoticism. For example, a gourmet magazine might distinguish between two exotic ingredients on the basis of authenticity: a mass-produced fish sauce from a Chinese factory is clearly second-rate, and less authentic when compared to a fish sauce produced in small batches in a specific island in Vietnam (and unavailable in North American stores). Other foods, like heirloom tomatoes, are distinguished on the basis of their authenticity (as simple and linked to a historic tradition), but are not particularly exotic in the sense of being socially-remote or norm-breaking—key elements of exoticism explored below. Fast foods are devalued for being mass-produced, ordinary, and placeless, qualities which render them both inauthentic and unexotic.

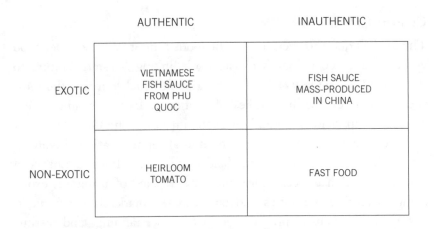

Figure 3.1 Authenticity and exoticism

Our goal here is not to suggest that there are hard and fast categorical distinctions between qualities of authenticity and exoticism, but to argue that they possess different points of emphasis that are worth distinguishing if we wish to understand the complexity of a gourmet foodscape that values certain foods while deprecating others. While the features of exoticism and authenticity certainly co-inhabit the space of the American foodscape, in this chapter we focus on what we mean by exoticism, and flesh out the criteria used to construct food as exotic. This takes us to the heart of debates about what is exotic food in an American foodscape. How are lines of distinction drawn, and how are Euro-American eaters challenged to take up new, exotic dishes outside the culinary mainstream? We argue that although the foodie's desire for new, novel, and exotic flavors *is* indeed part of a colonial legacy, it is not only that, and cannot be reduced to a simple instance of culinary colonialism. The desire to eat the exotic Other also represents the hope for cultural exchange, a cosmopolitan broadening of the culinary canon beyond the narrow valuations of nationally-based Euro-American cuisine. We discuss both of these competing pulls in turn—the drive for social status that is tied to neo-colonial impulses to dominate and possess the cultural resources of the exotic Other, and the democratic drive for inclusion through culinary cosmopolitanism—and then move to discuss the search for exoticism in the American foodscape.

Culinary Colonialism?

The foodie's quest for new and exotic foods cannot be fully understood without reference to Said's classic work linking Western culture to the exotic Other, *Orientalism* (1978), a book which remains the most widely cited text within studies of exoticism. In this seminal piece of scholarship, Said explored how exotic images of the Oriental Other were constructed through Western cultural representations involving art and literature. "The Orient," Said writes, "was almost a European invention, and had been since antiquity a place of romance, exotic beings, haunting memories and landscapes, remarkable experiences" (1978: 1). Orientalism produced a set of understandings and institutions that not only rendered the East "primitive" and inferior, but also secured the West's position as rational, and superior; as such, Orientalist discourse was, and remains, central to Western imperialism. Within this Orientalist dynamic, the appeal of the exotic derives from an adventurous desire to explore and possess the unknown Other. As Said explains, "The Orient at large . . . vacillates between the West's contempt for what is familiar and its shivers of delight in—or fear of—novelty" (59).

Since *Orientalism*, Said's work has informed a great deal of post-colonial scholarship on encounters with the Exotic Other.[40] In this literature, exoticism is understood as "a politically and sexually charged form of othering" (Longley 2000: 23), in which certain cultures and peoples are objectified as "projections of Western fantasies" (Rousseau and Porter 1990: 7). Work on exoticism has explored the construction of the Other within the context of consumer culture, in which cultural difference is increasingly commodified. In an article entitled "Eating the Other," bell hooks remarks that within consumer culture, ethnic diversity becomes "spice, seasoning that can liven up the dull dish that is mainstream white culture" (1992: 21). In *Cannibal Culture: Art, Appropriation, & the Commodification of Difference*, Deborah Root (1996) explores how particular cultures, peoples and objects are coded as 'exotic,' and argues that this pattern relates to a Western colonial attitude that reasserts conquest through commodification. Other scholars illustrate how the popularity of "multicultural products" (Huggan 2000: 91) "ethnotourism" (Roberts 2000), and "culinary tourism" (Molz 2007; Long 2004) derive largely from their exotic appeal. These forms of exoticization extend beyond the aesthetic, as each exercise of 'Othering' draws from and reproduces existing power relations. For instance, Roberts shows how "world cinema" is rooted in an "ideology of conspicuous cosmopolitanism" which "puts the world on display for (largely white) middle-class, First-World audiences" (2000: 109). Indeed, exoticization not only produces the Other, but also "sustains the myth of cultural centrality and superiority of the viewer" (Longley 2000: 23).

More specific to the realm of exotic food, Heldke refers to culinary adventuring as a kind of "cultural colonialism" (2003: xv), a subjective form of colonialism that accompanies and legitimizes economic forms of colonialism, while subordinating and appropriating the food cultures and economies of the Global South. While describing herself as a card-carrying member of the food adventuring club, Heldke describes how she became increasingly uncomfortable as she realized that she was "motivated by a deep desire to have contact with, and to somehow own an experience of, an Exotic Other, as a way of making myself more interesting" (2003: xvi). Heldke recognizes that this attitude is problematic, particularly given its reliance on a neo-colonial notion of the Other as a cultural resource always available to be consumed by more powerful members of the geo-political core.[41] Moreover, culinary exoticism can work to essentialize and stereotype ethnic cultures (e.g., Mexican-Americans) that are expected to present and preserve their cultural heritage for consumption by the dominant culture, often in a context of social and economic inequality where an ethnic community's exotic food is more welcome than members of that ethnic community (Abarca 2004: 8; see also Bentley 1998).

Even though a Western tourist might be uncomfortable attending the funeral rites or birth ceremonies of ethnic Others, the idea of accessing the Other's culinary traditions often goes unquestioned. Might the assumption of universal accessibility support attitudes of cultural colonialism that prop up and reinforce systems of economic colonialism (Heldke 2003: 48)? Do food adventurers "transform the Other into a resource" by projecting a superficial knowledge of the Other's culture (based purely on food, not politics), while assuming that 'we' belong everywhere (Heldke 2003: 48)? These are difficult questions to answer, but the key point is that we need to contextualize the besotted food adventurer's quest for the latest exotic cuisine within a historical pattern of colonial Othering, as well as contemporary neo-colonial realities of economic and cultural inequality. This means realizing that a contemporary food adventurer who wanders around exploring "exotic" cuisines is in some ways like the explorers and conquistadors who preceded colonialization. This does not mean that every cross-cultural meal is an intentional act of colonization or neo-colonial Othering, but it is to say that the exoticism frame within foodie discourse draws from a historical legacy of colonialism as well as contemporary global inequalities. Put differently, the foodie's search for exotic culinary adventures cannot be viewed in a power vacuum, or solely in terms of an individual's intentions, but must be placed in a larger geopolitical context.

Not only can the search for exotic foods be seen as continuous with an Orientalist discourse of Othering, but it also works with the system of status-seeking and distinction described by Bourdieu (explored further in Chapter 5). Finding new exotic cuisines earns foodies a kind of social status—a status that may have been relatively marginal in the past, but which has gained broader currency with the dramatic expansion of gourmet cuisine and food culture (Heldke 2003: xxiii). Narayan (1997: 181) describes how cultural knowledge about ethnic foods "can be used to constitute [a Western eater] as a colonial 'savant,' adding to her worldliness and prestige in much the same manner as 'knowledge' of faraway places she has visited." Status and capital are clearly connected, since seeking distinction through knowledge of exotic foods and cuisines is linked to those with cultural and economic capital. Heldke (2003: xxii) cites a study by the National Restaurant Association on ethnic cuisines, which observes that adventurous "culture-oriented" consumers are the most highly-educated, and have high incomes and the highest percentage of managerial/professional types in their ranks. Economic capital is required for international travel, and is often required to seek out a dining experience beyond food staples, what Bourdieu termed "foods of necessity" as opposed to luxury foods (1984), even though exotic food may be relatively accessible compared to other elite status symbols. As a food adventurer working within the university system, Heldke writes: "sports cars, gigantic houses, and expensive jewelry are not within our budgets; dinner is" (2003: xxiii). Just as Bourdieu (1984) noted how teachers may seek out exotic "peasant" fare to demonstrate their cultural capital, a newspaper food feature describes a group of "bohedonist" bike couriers and pink-collar workers living beyond their means in their pursuit of the best croissants, cheese stores, and single-malt scotch (*Globe & Mail*, May 9, 2007. p. L1).

While foodie status symbols might be relatively affordable compared to a Rolls-Royce or a Rolex, the pursuit of exotic foods is a status strategy employed by those with cultural capital—university professors, students, and the legions of arts workers moonlighting as waiters. Cultural capital is required to appreciate foodie discourse and discern which features of exoticism are worth pursuing. Also, it is important to note that in global geo-political terms, the seekers of exotic food experiences are still relatively affluent. As residents of the United States, foodies reside in the world economic system's geopolitical core—a vantage point that affords them access to commodities from around the world. This vantage point places foodies at the top of commodity chains driven by neo-colonial economic relationships that render marginalized food workers in and from the Global South ineligible to participate in food adventuring in a significant way. In short, while not all food adventurers are economic elites, it is virtually impossible for an impoverished, or marginalized, person to fully participate in foodie culture as a consumer and food adventurer, rather than as a dishwasher in a fashionable restaurant, or a subsistence farmer harvesting cocoa beans for a gourmet chocolate bar.

Culinary Cosmopolitanism?

At the same time as it is essential to recognize the neo-colonial dimensions of the search for the exotic, we question whether culinary adventuring is uniformly malignant and harmful. This question haunted us as we discussed food adventuring with friends, family, and fellow foodies. A recurring narrative emerged in these discussions: Contact with new, "exotic" cuisines was seen to mark a transition from a parochial, Eurocentric lifeworld, to a new kind of cosmopolitan sensibility which affected not just diet, but was part of a critical attitude towards Western culture. In this narrative, learning about and eating exotic new foods represented part of a transition towards cultural cosmopolitanism, understood as a condition of respecting difference, appreciating cultural heterogeneity, and questioning Eurocentrism.

Uma Narayan expresses sympathy for these cosmopolitan culinary narratives; reflecting upon her own caste-based dietary history (defined by vegetarianism and a prohibition on consuming food cooked by non-Brahmins), she expresses a fear of "food parochialism," and suggests that "a willingness to eat the food of Others seems to indicate at least a growing democracy of the palate" (1997: 180). A gustatory appreciation of the foods of groups that are socially distant from ourselves can go hand-in-hand with a broader acceptance of these groups as fellow citizens and neighbors, even if all we know about them is what they eat. Food-court multiculturalism may be the easiest kind of multiculturalism to achieve, and can certainly disguise xenophobic attitudes towards the producers of new exotic foods. While we must remain wary of romanticized ideas about culinary cosmopolitanism (e.g., privileged foodie as "citizen of the world"), we should not throw the foodie baby out with the proverbial bathwater, and overlook the role food can play as a gateway out of cultural parochialism and a prompt challenging Eurocentric prejudices. Narratives of food democracy and cosmopolitan cultural inclusion have some historical resonance in multicultural contexts. Donna Gabaccia's work (1998) on the history of American foodways, for instance, describes how the American foodscape was built not on a Euro-American monoculture, but on the incorporation of ethnic food traditions from around the world—bagels, pizza, pickles—to construct a uniquely heterogeneous sense of American cuisine.

So how do we reconcile these two impulses, the culinary adventuring that smacks of imperialism, on the one hand, with the more admirable aspiration to escape cultural parochialism and experience culinary diversity, on the other? How can we experience the foods of the Other, while not perpetuating colonial relationships and assumptions? Even if foodies reject the valuation of exotic foods and prioritize non-colonial eating, it is not clear that they (we) can achieve greater social justice through an isolated local diet free from outside influences (Born and Purcell 2006). Historically, foods have been fantastic globe-trotters, implanting themselves in remote locations and making their way into regional and national cuisines—like the tomato's role in Italian cuisine (even though its biological origins are in South America), or the role of "curry" in the English diet (even though no dish named "curry" was eaten at the time of Britain's colonization of India). Culinary isolationism is particularly unrealistic in today's age of global travel, transnational commodity chains, and globally integrated food economies.

In conditions of cultural interpenetration and heightened awareness of ecological interdependency, the question of non-colonial eating is not about whether transnational culinary exchanges should take place, and more about how these exchanges can happen through more equitable, less exploitative processes that address political, economic, and cultural privilege.

To re-state the question we posed in the introduction of this chapter: Are culinary adventurers neo-colonial eaters of the Other, or cosmopolitan envoys? We argue that the scholarly debate over how to understand the gourmet's quest for exotic food has been hampered by a search for either/or answers to this question. In keeping with the central argument of this book, foodie culture is not a simple story of snobbery or cultural liberation, but is fundamentally constituted by the tension between a pull of democratic inclusion, and the desire to erect boundaries of exclusivity, distinction, and social status. Drawing from Ulrich Beck's development of the term "cosmopolitan" (2006), we suggest that culinary cosmopolitanism as it is practiced by American foodies today overlaps with a neo-colonial desire to explore and possess the cultural resources of the Other. Culinary cosmopolitanism pushes foodies beyond the world of nationally-bound cuisine, and embraces both the possibility and also the reality that ideas, people, and their cultural artifacts move more fluidly across borders in the globalization era. Beck (2006) usefully distinguishes between philosophical cosmopolitanism (the often unsubstantiated desire to be a "citizen of the world"), and the "really existing" cosmopolitanism taking shape in world risk society. Transnational crises (e.g., avian flu, global warming, global recession) force greater reflexivity about ecological and economic interdependency, and make the development of a cosmopolitan outlook not simply an elite pipe-dream, but a defining feature of the current era (Beck 2006). This is not to deny that "really existing" cosmopolitanism is associated with upper-middle-class and upper-class lifestyles (Hannerz 1996; Lamont 1992: 107), or to obscure the fact that culinary cosmopolitanism occurs in a context of grossly maldistributed power and resources rendering those in the geo-political core of the world system tremendously privileged. However, the point is that globalization processes—globalized risks, global commodity chains, and transnational migration patterns—impact how we think about dinner, and challenge the boundaries of previous dining eras built on nationally-based ideals. Despite all of the limitations of cosmopolitan ideals and "we are the world" imagery, "really existing" culinary cosmopolitanism involves the valuation of exotic foods—a tendency that has challenged hierarchies privileging European cuisine, and particularly French food, above all else. A culinary cosmopolitan perspective resides in a context of tremendous inequality, but it may simultaneously facilitate meaningful cultural exchange, and attempt to link food choices to global risks like climate change.

Of course, the complexity of culinary cosmopolitanism is not always transparent to foodie adventurers, but it is an important part of understanding the Euro-American's contradictory and deeply-rooted desire to seek out and experience the cuisines of the Exotic Other. Narayan writes: "Seemingly simple acts of eating are flavored with complicated, and sometimes contradictory, cultural meanings. Thinking about food can help to reveal the rich and messy textures of our attempts at self-understanding, as well as our interesting and problematic understandings of our relationship to social Other" (1997: 161).

Operationalizing Exoticism

In short, the search for exotic foods is not only complex, but is inherently contradictory given this built-in tension between a neo-colonial search for status and distinction in exotic food choices, and a democratic impulse of cultural inclusion and culinary cosmopolitanism. Understanding something of the complex origins of the valuation of culinary exoticism, we can move from a more philosophical terrain to the social scientific, and operationalize the term "exotic" in order to empirically examine exotic foods in the gourmet foodscape. We suggest a twofold characterization that emphasizes how exotic foods are predicated on (1) social distance; and (2) breaking norms.

Although in popular usage exoticism is often equated with "foreign" or "ethnic" foods, this conception of exotic takes a particular reference point for granted. That reference point typically assumes the perspective of a foodie who is American, cosmopolitan, white, and wealthy. In our analysis, we make this reference point explicit, and identify how exotic foods are socially distant from most of the creators of foodie discourse in the United States. With the central point of production of foodie discourse being food media (i.e., gourmet food magazines and newspaper columns), media primarily produced by and for a white, upper-middle-class audience, foodie discourse generally assumes that eaters have access to considerable economic and cultural capital. The white, upper-middle-class reference point is the basis for demarcating exotic foods as those that are socially distant on the basis of ethnicity, social class, or some combination of these two qualities.[42] Moreover, social distance can have a spatial element, and can either be increased or foreshortened through reference to geography. In this way, the social distance of Australians with European ancestry is much more a function of geographic distance than of ethnicity. A calculus of ethnicity, class, and geographic distance is also used to construe the social distance between working-class Americans and the gourmet food world. For example, working-class African-Americans in New York City and working-class whites in rural Arkansas are socially distant in ways that are different, but which involve the three elements of ethnicity, social class, and geographic distance. So in this first sense of the term, "exotic" refers to foods that are socially distant and considered unusual, novel, and "foreign," assuming that the cultural experience of the affluent Euro-American is the universal reference point.

But is the terrain of "exotic" foods simply about foods that are foreign, or socially distant from the culinary "norm" of relatively affluent, Euro-American food adventurers? A second dimension of exoticism emerged in our reading of foodie discourse, a dimension that we refer to as "norm-breaking" foods. Exotic foods in this sense are not simply foods that are socially distant from the culinary mainstream, but are foods that present difference as radically different, exciting, and desirable. These foods are not simply rare, or unusual, but they violate norms of the culinary and cultural mainstream. This dimension captures how foodie discourse frames exotic foods as foreign to mainstream tastebuds, but also excitingly different, distinct, and even shocking. The need to develop this second category of exoticism is not surprising given the increasing cultural awareness of middle-class American eaters with once-exotic foods like sushi and pad thai. As such, in a globalized multicultural foodscape, exotic foods are not only foods that are different and foreign, but they are also constructed as foods that are norm-breaking. As a socially-constructed category, the precise manifestations of exotic "norm-breaking" are constantly in flux given the dynamic nature of food norms in a globalized foodscape. For example, while it was once considered norm-breaking to eat raw fish, now the mere presence of sashimi on a menu is sometimes enough to warrant the scorn of a food critic. The second dimension of the term "exotic," then, refers to foods that aren't simply socially-distant on the basis of ethnicity or social class, but are those which manage to shock middle-American, non-foodie sensibilities, breaking food norms that allow the eater to stand aside as unique, special, and distinctly adventuresome.

The two dimensions of exoticism are summarized in Figure 3.2 (p. 110). Understanding these two axes can help us understand how food can be framed along a spectrum of exoticism, from strongly-exotic to weakly-exotic, though even weakly-exotic food can be seen as highly-desirable and legitimated as worthy in an omnivorous cultural context. The X axis represents foods that can be socially-distant or socially-proximate—qualities of Otherness that are achieved either through ethnic difference, social class, geographic location, or some combination of these factors. On the Y axis, we indicate how foods can be seen as relatively normal, versus relatively norm-breaking. Examples of weakly-exotic foods are found in the upper-left and lower-right quadrants, where foods are framed as either socially-distant or norm-breaking. Strongly exotic foods are found in the upper-right quandrant and are framed as both socially-distant and norm-breaking. So while the veal cheek ravioli served in an upscale Manhattan restaurant is exotic enough to be suitable for gourmet consumption, the tongue of a duck cooked Peking-style is more exotic yet. Poppadums are familiar as a starchy snack and break no norms about what counts as food, but their association with a socially-distant group makes them exotic enough, and clearly more exotic than a more familiar starchy snack,

French fries.[43] The status system of exoticism we describe suggests that the omnivore will tend to avoid the lower-left quadrant and gravitate toward the other three quadrants.

From Figure 3.2 it is clear that "rarity" is an essential part of the valuation of exoticism, as it is with authenticity. Exotic foods are often rare foods, like a $100 square watermelon grown in a glass container and flown in from Malaysia. Even if exotic foods themselves are readily-available (as is the case with organ meats), they are rare by virtue of the fact that mainstream American eaters infrequently consume them. The argument that aesthetic value depends, at least in part, on rarity has been made by Veblen (1994 [1899]) and is also evident in Bourdieu's (1993) distinction between fields of mass and restricted production. While Veblen wrote about the role of rarity a hundred years ago (1994 [1899]), what is different today is the onset of omnivorous status systems where rarity or price alone cannot operate as an effective symbol of value. In an omnivorous era, valued exotic foods can be non-rare foods from a socially-distant context (e.g., street food in Burma), or can be parts of an animal that are relatively cheap, but distasteful to mainstream eaters. To be clear, what is *complex* about the omnivorous culinary context is that

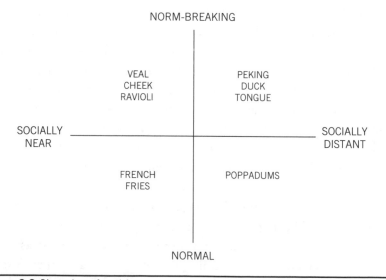

Figure 3.2 Dimensions of exoticism

rarity alone is not a sufficient quality to explain how and why certain kinds of authentic or exotic foods are valued. In short, rarity is a necessary but not sufficient condition to understand the legitimation of high-status foods in an omnivorous era, and requires further elaboration, as we have tried to do in these chapters on authenticity and exoticism.[44]

In the next section we bring this graphical depiction of exoticism to life by looking at how exoticism is articulated in gourmet food discourse. As in the chapter on authenticity, we draw from examples in food journalism and our interviews. We will see how foodies deal with geography, social distance, ethnic differences, and norm-breaking to construct an idea of what "exotic" is, and then use that idea to strike a balance between democracy and distinction.

Exoticism as Distance

Most of the foodies we interviewed placed a high value on foods from different countries and non-European ethnicities. As part of life in an era of globalization, many of our foodie respondents had traveled extensively, and reported that through that travel, they gained an interest in different cuisines. In the words of Timothy Bauer, a 68-year-old from Washington, DC:

> I really got interested in just trying all sorts of different food, particularly ethnic foods. I don't know if that derived out of my experience in the Philippines or not but I was really sort of interested in, you know, Laotian food or food from Ecuador, or food from Indonesia, or Southern Thai food, I mean all these different sorts of foods other than the sort of standard, sort of European-slash-American food.

Foodie respondents also emphasized their access to many different global cuisines within major United States cities. Neil Taverna, a 25-year-old living in Brooklyn, reported that "New York tends to be exotic because you can sort of, you know, can find a group of, you know, immigrants somewhere in the city that have . . . real restaurants they run." The presence of cuisines from multiple cultures was not only noted in major cities, but was universally valued by the foodies in our sample, even though they did not always use the term "exotic" to describe them. While many respondents disliked formal restaurants, or fashionable restaurants, many spoke positively about "little, ethnic restaurants." Melissa Trent, a 58-year-old attorney, insisted that she was "not into trendy restaurants because they are not always good," but said, "I like the ethnic restaurants. The little, ethnic restaurants . . . the ethnic food is usually the stuff I can't make, or I don't know how to make. So you know, it's just different."

In our examination of food journalism we also witnessed how unusual foods from different places around the world were highly valued. We read about delicacies like *mistela negra*, which is new red wine dosed with brandy (though, we also read, it is not available in the United States) (*Saveur*, March 2004, p. 62), ram horn nut, which also goes by the name of water caltrop (*Gourmet*, January 2004, p. 104), and *brocciu*, which is a fluffy sheep's-milk cheese from Corsica (*Gourmet*, August 2004, p. 92). We also learned about unfamiliar dishes such as *O-a-chian*, a Taiwanese dish of oysters with scrambled eggs (*Saveur*, March 2004, p. 37), a Spanish chef's foie gras with cotton candy and avocado-tomato sorbet (*Food & Wine*, May 2004, p. 74), and *snoek*, a hot-smoked fish eaten with doughy bread and jam in South Africa (*Food & Wine*, May 2004, p. 169). We learned that when visiting Japanese restaurants we should not "play it safe by ordering Japanese standards," and instead move towards more exotic dishes like a Kazu sushi cake that is "quickly and dramatically singed with a blowtorch" (*New York Times*, Mar. 19, 2006, p. 14NJ.21), or umeboshi, "the Japanese pickled plums that are brined in red shiso leaves to impart a pinkish tint" and aged over decades (*San Francisco Chronicle*, May 5, 2006, p. E.10).

Foodie discourse contains a fundamental impulse to draw attention to exotic new ingredients and dishes. Most magazine and newspaper writing features some element of identifying new culinary trends and hot new foods, as well as identifying what foods and cuisines are considered passé. Educating readers about the fashion cycles of cuisine—what is the hot new exotic cuisine or ingredient, and what is now pedestrian and passé—can be seen as part of the democratizing function of gastronomy in that it publicizes information about what is included within the contemporary repertoire of "good" food. Likewise, many of our interviewees were enthusiastic to discuss foods that they perceived as new and interesting, such as in the following excerpt from our interview with Ted Darby: "I'm supposed to cook a turken tonight. Do you know what a turken is?" (Interviewer: "No.") "Turken is, another name for it is a naked necked chicken. A turken is a breed of chicken, but it tends to be sort of, apparently they're great egg layers and they have a kind of meat that tends to be somewhat tougher than other chickens. And so you have to, they advise you to cook it wet, in some kind of wet cooking method, or very slow, gentle cooking so you don't toughen it up more than necessary." At the same time as foodies publicize information about exciting new foods—like turken—these fashion cycles work to provide a source of status and distinction by alerting foodies to the possibility of foods and ingredients that they can be the first to read about, or, better yet, consume, and a way to distinguish themselves from less knowledgeable eaters.

Of course, not all "new" foods are equally valued by foodies. Exoticism is a key frame for valorizing certain new foods, while rejecting others. We understand exoticism as existing in both strong and weak forms. The strong forms are attached to foods that are discursively constructed as foods of people who are socially, economically and geographically most distant from the American foodie. At one end of the spectrum of social distancing and Othering are foods associated with poor, rural people of color in developing countries. In these instances, heightened social distance on the level of class, race, and ethnicity works synergistically with geographic space to construct foods as strongly exotic. These are the foods of Vietnamese fishermen, or the Bedouin of Jordan— groups that are both geographically and socially (ethnically, and in terms of class) extremely far from the lives of the foodies who are the dominant creators of American foodie discourse.

Interestingly, strong exoticism, based on prominent forms of social and geographic distance, is less frequent in foodie discourse than the weak form of exoticism associated with food and people who are only somewhat socially and geographically distant from American foodies.

This finding supports Heldke's observation that "we like our exoticism somewhat familiar, recognizable, *controllable*," put into terms that we understand and can relate to (2003: 19). Fairly common in foodie discourse are descriptions or narratives that highlight limited commonalities to shorten the social distance to a foreign setting and present a moderate or weak kind of exoticism or Othering. These exotic foods and cuisines are strange, but can still be understood and enjoyed; they are made familiar and palatable through descriptions that emphasize familiar iconography and recognized food preparation techniques and ingredients. For example, we read about Thai chefs who cook foie gras with sweet potatoes for the upper middle class, inserting a familiar foodie ingredient that closes the class gap though not the ethnicity gap. A review of an upscale restaurant in São Paulo, Brazil moderates the unusualness of the case-study by emphasizing "the area's glamorous surroundings . . . stores like Armani, Versace, Christian Dior, Louis Vuitton," and asserting that "families come to Antiquarius [restaurant] for home-style cooking in an elegant but laid back setting" (*Food & Wine*, June, 2004, p. 46). The food eaten at this restaurant is somewhat unusual, "minced salt cod with julienne potatoes and fried egg sprinkled with pressed hot-pepper oil" (ibid.), but not so foreign that it cannot be comprehended. Similarly an Arab fusion restaurant in San Francisco is described with adjectives like "exotic," "eccentric," "wacky," and "odd," and introduced with the injunction to "walk toward the light—the exotic crimson light emanating from Saha's doorway," but ultimately the exotic food is familiar, described as "comfort food with an air of mystery" (*San Francisco Chronicle*, Nov. 10, 2006, p. E.6).

The valuation of weak exoticism was strongly evident in our interviews with foodies. For example, Fiona Callworth, a 54-year-old Boston woman, spoke positively about an "unusual" meal involving Navajo food served in a hospital cafeteria in Page, Arizona. Kelly Jones, a 41-year-old clergywoman from New York State, articulates a sense of food as weakly exotic in response to a question about how her tastes have changed over time. Her answer contextualizes a breakfast dish in terms of her global travels: "[T]ravels to Italy or going to El Salvador, eating Salvadorian food, that's all expanded my palate. You know, having beans and cream for breakfast is something I love, you know, with a good corn tortilla. It's something that I never would have thought of had I not had the chance to travel in El Salvador." The geographic distance of the food's origins provides some element of exoticism, as does the unique pairing of tortillas, beans, and cream as a breakfast dish, but these are relatively familiar ingredients to most Americans.

Besides geographic distance, another way that exoticism manifests is through an emphasis on social distance. An emphasis on social distance facilitates Othering, and focuses on a lack of knowledge, or through a presentation of pre-modern peoples—even if those people reside in Europe or the United States. In this vein, we read of "pasta made by women who measure weeks in flour and seasons in egg yolks and every fold and crevice of noodle can seem as eloquent as a sigh" (*Gourmet*, January 2004, p. 46). Similarly, we read about food that is produced and consumed in "a medieval Italian town" that "rises from oblivion in the mountains of Abruzzo" (*Gourmet*, September 2004, p. 139). The emphasis on "medieval," and the hyperbole of "oblivion," stresses the remote exoticism of the area to American audiences, even though the contemporary Italian inhabitants (citizens of a G8 country no less) would probably not agree that their home represents "oblivion."

While the geographic distance is small compared to overseas travel articles, the socially distant exotic Other clearly persists within the United States in food journalism. A restaurant review describes a Japanese restaurant with "mysteriously crunchy raw octopus pickle," but the real story of the meal is the charmingly ethnic, but easily confused, hostess and co-owner:

> she answers the telephone, garnishes plates . . . conducts conversations with the employees and works out each table's check. She also delivers those checks in a smiling rapid-fire falsetto: Thank you thank you very much thank you thank you very much, she says, her hands clasped over her tummy, and bowing from the waist. On our second visit, she mistook our table of long-patient and very hungry diners for others who had actually received and

eaten their food, so we heard the tune twice. And then, when we finally did leave our table, we heard more singsong, goodbye, goodbye, thank you very much, goodbye, goodbye, goodbye, thank you thank you thank you.

(*New York Times*, Mar. 19, 2006, p. 14NJ.21)

A surprising number of travel articles in gourmet magazines frame rural America as Other, constructing foods as exotic based on gaps in cultural knowledge or economic capital, rather than ethnicity. These articles are set in rural areas within the United States, often the rural South, Midwest, or Southwest, away from the major urban culinary centers. Social distance is maintained by focusing on the food of people who are portrayed as relatively impoverished and/or uneducated, and possessing unusual food norms or a lack of knowledge. Take, for example, an article that describes Arkansas as "a serious pie lode," where the authors, Jane and Michael Stern, meet the owners and patrons of truck stops and diners (*Gourmet*, August 2004, pp. 32, 127). The authors report that upon explaining that they hail from Connecticut, one stranger they encounter reveals that he thinks that Connecticut is in Canada. They "don't bother making the fine point that Canada and Connecticut are different places" because the especially good Arkansan coconut pie has arrived (*Gourmet*, August 2004, p. 127). Worthy food can be discursively constructed through a similar Othering based on class difference but without the rural setting. Harry Quinn, a 43-year-old communications technology worker in the Bay Area, expresses this kind of exoticism when he says, "I'm a huge fan of the old American cafe, you know, where you want to get a hot turkey sandwich or chicken fried steak. And it could look like a real hole-in-the-wall, you know, but you go in and they've got some world class stuff going on."

As we note above, food's rarity is a central (but not exhaustive) element of the constitution of exoticism in foodie discourse. In this context, rare foods are often sourced from highly specific geographic locations, and are not readily accessible to most United States eaters. A focus on exoticism associated with rarity allows a relatively subtle validation of distinction along with cultural and economic capital. Food that is unknown or obscure because it is in scarce supply, or because it is not available to American audiences, is often highly recommended. One author describes eating a cheese called "Flixer, a nutty number made only from the milk of 12 very talented Swiss ewes" (*Food & Wine*, July 2004, p. 171). We are told that "[t]he Palacios brand of Spanish chorizo, made in the Rioja region, is the only authentic Spanish chorizo imported into the United States" (*Saveur*, May 2004, p. 95). Other ingredients that are explicitly mentioned as difficult or even impossible to acquire in the United States include ang-chim crabs (*Saveur*, March 2004, p. 44), and botifarra negra (Catalonian blood sausage) (*Saveur*, March 2004, p. 66). Some rare ingredients are not foreign at all, but are highly scarce, such as fresh hearts of peach palm flown to New York from Hawaii (*Gourmet*, November 2004, p. 48).

Within food journalism, there is often no need to explicitly state that a certain food is rare and difficult to acquire because it is clear from the context. In travel articles, for instance, food is valorized for being from a very specific place and time, and the readers understand that they must go to the food because the food will not be coming to them through mass distribution channels. The same implicit rarity was evident in restaurant reviews, features on small producers, and articles focusing on family traditions.

The traveling described by our interviewees and within the food journalism we read covered the globe. However, the coverage was uneven insofar as there was far more attention paid to foods from the United States primarily, and secondarily from Europe, with much less attention to foods from other locations.[45] These findings suggest that assumptions about foodies' interest in global cuisine are overstated, even in magazines that consistently carry travel features. The dominant focus for culinary omnivores is overwhelmingly situated in locations in advanced-industrialized countries, with the discourse focused on travel to or within a developed-world setting. Africa, for instance, almost never appears in foodie discourse. This tendency suggests that culinary cosmopolitanism is not a global democracy where any and all cuisines are deemed interesting, and supports the idea that gourmet food culture remains strongly situated in the North-American and European core, with other global food cultures added intermittently in ways that do not fundamentally challenge a Eurocentric culinary canon.

Exciting Food: Food that breaks Norms

The second dimension of exoticism that emerged in our examination of foodie discourse was a focus on food that is exciting, outrageous, inappropriate, daring, and generally not accepted by mainstream American eaters. Gourmet cuisine has traditionally incorporated norm-breaking foods, such as frog legs and raw oysters, which rest outside the realm of what many middle-class and working-class American eaters would consider appetizing or even edible, at least initially. The inclusion of exotically norm-breaking foods is a strong tendency for gourmet food writers who need to continually identify new dishes for their audiences. This analysis of food's legitimation through norm-breaking helps us to understand a gourmet magazine's editorial comment that "[n]othing is more boring than sashimi . . . When I'm eating raw fish in a Japanese restaurant, I practically pass out in mid-bite" (*Bon Appétit*, January 2004, p. 36). In the recent past, raw fish was a norm-breaking food for American omnivores. However, since raw fish is the new normal for this group, it can no longer be legitimated on this basis, and new norm-breaking foods (e.g., beef cheeks) must be found. The search for familiarity is subtly mocked, as with a *New York Times* restaurant review that concludes, "What, no chocolate cake? No crème brûlée? No tiramisu? I didn't miss them, although some diners might. But if you're an adventurous eater longing for new and exciting combinations done well, Mosaic may be just what you're looking for" (Feb. 5, 2006, p. 14LI.12). A similar disdain for the familiar and popular styles of Mexican-American food is expressed in another *New York Times* restaurant review:

> As with many Mexican-themed places, there are combination plates. Most are more of the same, with too much rice and beans alongside too much of the main dishes: burrito and taco, fajitas, taco salad and quesadilla, black-bean burrito and cheese-stuffed tortilla. Then there's the nacho supremo, which builds a tower

of corn tortilla, refried beans, meat or vegetables, Monterey Jack cheese and sauce. We skipped them, in favor of the more specific, more exotic categories.

(*New York Times*, Mar. 5, 2006. p. 14NJ.12)

Like the preference for ingredients from socially-distant sources, norm-breaking food provides a relatively subtle way for food writing to confer distinction and status through the quest for exoticism. Such exciting exotic food may violate norms of purity versus impurity, or food versus non-food, such as "[a Corsican cheese selection which includes] chèvre '*avec habitants*'—a cheese so ripe that little, maggot-type worms had taken up residence inside" (*Gourmet*, August 2004, p. 93). (The maggots are removed before the cheese is eaten.) We see valorization of norm-breaking food in a profile of Monterrey, Mexico, featuring "fritada de cabrito (cabrito [goat] stewed in its blood), machitos (roasted sausages of cabrito heart, liver, and tripe), and cabecita (whole baby goat's head). I had already ordered goat's head once, and that seemed sufficient. But I ate everything else" (*Saveur*, June/July 2004, p. 47).[46]

Norm-breaking exotic food is not only eaten outside the United States. Among groups of people and immigrant communities who are socially- and/or geographically-distant from the culinary core of privileged white urbanites, we find food that pushes the limits, breaking norms to construct the exotic as a source of Other. The social distance of immigrant communities within the United States facilitates the valorization of many norm-breaking, exotic foods as Other. On a ranch in rural Colorado, a Greek-American family makes its own sausages: "There was much smacking of lips and rubbing of bellies as the sweetbreads, lungs, spleen, and hearts, were laid out in ribbons on the fell, spiced with salt, pepper, and oregano, and then wrapped in the small intestine to make the fat, lumpy, three-foot-long sausage" (*Gourmet*, June 2004, p. 126).

When food flagrantly violates social or culinary conventions, it creates a bold spectacle of norm-breaking exoticism that confers distinction, and this is especially evident in the gourmet focus on eating offal found in elite restaurants, an exotic food ingredient made socially distant by its link to consumption by working peoples—even though the trend is most firmly rooted in upscale restaurants.[47] In elite Manhattan restaurants, like Thomas Keller's Per Se, chefs and diners alike seem to gain prestige by participating in this form of culinary exoticism which is simultaneously exclusive, but linked to populist consumption of cheap cuts of meats:

> Keller has said that he loves most of all the challenge of spinning nickel into gold, of transforming cuts of meat many restaurants reserve for forcemeat into the centerpieces of a meal. Though often among the least popular options, these dishes—ox tripe morphed from rubber bands into tender ribbons soft as marrow, pastrami-like slices of confit veal heart served with heated bing cherries and Tokyo turnips—are well worth the detour.
>
> (*Gourmet*, Nov. 2004, p. 48)

It is important to note that while our foodie interviewees showed clear preferences for weakly-exotic food based on social and geographic distance, they tended to avoid norm-breaking exotic food, which they often understood as involving things like shrimp heads, dog, insects, and the offal dishes (brain, marrow) offered in many high-end restaurants. Certainly, all of our interviewees clearly expressed a liking for eating new foods and trying unfamiliar cuisines. By valuing exoticism in food, foodies gave expression to this element of being a foodie. However, foodies in the interviews put less emphasis on norm-breaking evaluating food than was documented in food journalism, although they recognized that a norm-breaking standard exists within foodie discourse. Some of our respondents (all men) described trying norm-breaking foods in ways that express mixed emotions about these experiences: They pride themselves on being adventurous eaters, and recognize that eating unusual foods is part of what generates foodie status, at the same time these experiences are not entirely pleasurable. In the words of Fred Huntington, a 44-year-old software engineer: "I had goat testicles in rice wine. Um, it's not something I would be anxious to repeat but it's something I would, it's kind of weird *and cool* to say I've had goat testicles in rice wine" (emphasis ours). Pedro Maradona, a 22-year-old living in New York City, described a meal that included brain at St John restaurant in London: "I guess those are body parts that you never consider being kind of like edible but people do eat them and they prepare them in very nice ways. So that was good." Similarly, Neil Taverna described a meal at a Japanese restaurant that centered on pig's feet: "I'd never had pig feet before, and I like different, weird things, but it was pretty intense."

Although interviewees displayed awareness that norm-breaking foods generated foodie cachet, most of the foodies we talked to were generally not interested in adhering to the standard, particularly when it involved eating forms of meat or types of animals not normally consumed in North America. When asked about exotic food, Jessica Bowes, a 38-year-old journalist in Los Angeles, replied:

> I have friends who if there's something involving sweetbreads or some challenging meat of some kind, they are all over it. And while I say great to you guys, you know . . . I'm not someone who goes out of their way to eat something extremely challenging on a menu. You know, I'd rather be more sure that I'll, that I won't be grossed out.

In response to the same question, Nathalie Underhill, an administrative assistant from Pennsylvania, made this comment:

> Um, exotic to me would be, I don't know, escargot. Or I know I said I like Vietnamese food but I also watch shows where what people eat on the streets of Vietnam would not be what I would want to eat. Like the coddled, the half raw egg with the little baby duck inside or something. [Laughs.] So exotic to me would mean probably something we're not used to having here or seeing unless you would go to that type of place where, in a neighborhood where that's what they would actually cook. So I think that's what exotic would mean to me.

Melissa Trent, a 58-year-old lawyer in Los Angeles, responded to the question of whether she was interested in exotic food in this way: "[I]t doesn't really do it for me. Like, I mean, I've eaten lardo and I've eaten brains, and I've eaten weird stuff, but it's not . . . I like more mainstream food."

We argue that exoticism is an important strategy for validating foods in an omnivorous culinary discourse. The search for socially- and geographically distant and norm-breaking foods allows foodies to signal distinction without offending democratic sensibilities through overt snobbery. Exoticism suggests a potentially radical democratization of gourmet culture through openness to non-European culinary traditions, yet our reading of foodie discourse suggests that the relationship of the exotic frame to ideologies of democracy and distinction is both complex and contradictory.

On the one hand, democratic ideologies are clearly manifest in the omnivore's increasing openness to new foods and cuisines, particularly from non-European immigrant communities. As Gabaccia suggests, America's multi-ethnic foodways "suggest tolerance and curiosity," along with "a willingness to digest, and to make [multi-ethnic dishes] part of one's individual identity" (1998: 9). In addition, openness to exotic norm-breaking foods, like offal, could be seen as establishing a kind of cosmopolitan culinary solidarity with cooks worldwide who cannot afford to waste the multiple, edible parts of an animal.

On the other hand, valuing foods for their foreignness and unusualness inherently establishes standards for distinction. As with the framing of authenticity, the framing of exoticism presents a dialectical tension between democratic ideology and an ideology of distinction. Omnivorous food culture's concern with exoticism explicitly widens the scope of worthy foods, but exoticism also maintains an implicit focus on foods that can require considerable economic and cultural capital to obtain. The rarity and obscurity of many exotic foods leave them relatively inaccessible to most Americans.

The broadening of the repertoire of worthy foods is concomitant with the demarcation of other food preferences as banal, undistinguished, or unsophisticated. In the case of the exotic frame, this situates foodies firmly at the colonial center where they hold the power to determine what is interesting, unusual, and exciting this season, and create criteria for what is validated as gourmet fashions change.[48] Western colonialism has traditionally rested upon the idea that the ethnic Other "is not a part of human culture in the full sense, but is a resource I may mine, harvest, develop, exploit or otherwise utilize" (Heldke 2003: 46–47), and this ideal is confirmed in the selective mining, and rejection, of certain ethnic foods as interesting and unusual one moment, and over-exposed the next. As *Gourmet* magazine declares in its listing of "What's Now, What's Next," the white rice feeding more than a billion Chinese people is now considered passé, while Black Chinese rice is deemed interesting, unusual, and "stunning" (*Gourmet*, January 2004, p. 26). The same issue declares that the country of Nepal is horribly "Now," while Bhutan is considered the "Next" sexy culinary hotspot (*Gourmet*, January 2004, p. 29).

While the search for exotic foods offers the potential for cosmopolitan understandings of social inequality and political marginalization, it is not always clear that culinary pursuits facilitate these understandings. Looking at gourmet travel writing, which is a common type of gourmet food writing that connects foods to socially distant people and places, we find reasons for skepticism. Travel articles revel in the exotic geographic settings and extreme social distance, providing a wealth of details about foreign people and places. These articles are narratives that tell a story about the role of food in people's lives that deviate significantly from an accounting of the food alone. Although we read about many details of foreign people and places, we almost never learn about the serious social problems that exist in many of these exotic locations. As a result, gourmet food travel writing provides what Heldke (2003: 58) describes as:

> a superficial image of a culture, an image that treats that culture as if it were designed for my use and pleasure. This way of eating is harmful both to colonizer and colonized, for it reifies and reduces colonized people, substitutes for authentic relations to

food the exotic quick fix and normalized colonialism, encouraging us to condone it in its other, more destructive economic and political forms.

Our finding of the different emphasis on norm-breaking exoticism between food journalists and our interviewees allows us to draw some inferences about the dynamics of the American gastronomic field. Bourdieu's (1993) analysis of cultural fields demonstrates that any given cultural field encompasses people (cultural producers and audiences) with varying amounts of both economic capital and symbolic capital (prestige within the field). The most prestige within a field accrues to those who position themselves at the avant-garde of cultural production as well as of cultural consumption. If we assume that gourmet food writers, as the experts in the field with cultural authority and institutional legitimacy, hold the more highly valued symbolic capital, then the comparison with foodies seems to indicate that norm-breaking exoticism is a dominant form of symbolic capital in gourmet food. In other words, shocking or norm-breaking food is avant-garde within the culinary field. Just as symbolist poetry is more esoteric and difficult than romance novels within the literary field, within the gourmet field eating offal is more esoteric and difficult than eating fast food. Preferring strongly exotic food appears to be unnecessary within the gourmet field for foodies. However, for the experts who need to maintain their cultural legitimacy and leading positions in the field, a preference for strongly-exotic foods is highly valued.

To support this idea, we can point to the fact that foods that are at one time strongly-exotic, such as sushi in the United States, can become only weakly-exotic over time, and will thereby not serve as well for distinction. Those who position themselves as the avant-garde, therefore, will have to emphasize the most strongly-exotic foods to maintain their position. These foods (e.g., tartare de cheval—raw horse meat) are typically "difficult" and esoteric in the sense that they present a problem for the average American eater to enjoy because they violate norms concerning the nature of food, particularly as it relates to the consumption of specific animals and specific animal parts.

In sum, our reading of foodie discourse suggests that while the exotic frame can be part of a democratic ideology of cosmopolitan openness and equality to multiple ethnic cuisines, it also draws from post-colonial ideologies of status and distinction that pass exclusionary, and arbitrary, judgments on entire nations and populations; at the same time they perpetuate harmful stereotypes of naïve, unknowledge-able Others. Nonetheless, the possibility for culinary cosmopolitanism cannot be completely discounted within foodie culture. Food adven-turer and writer, Jeffrey Alford, for instance, critiques fellow cookbook author Angela Murrills for her lack of reflexivity and class privilege in a book interweaving food writing with a narrative about the search for the perfect vacation home in the South of France (Alford 2004). In Alford's words:

> In *Hot Sun Cool Shadow*, this house-buying story is like icing on a cake, only in this case I'd prefer my cake without icing. Given the fact that less than 5 per cent of the world's population will in a life-time have a chance to fly in an airplane, the trials and tribulations of purchasing a second house in a country 6,000 miles away . . . is a story that is hardly compelling. Shouldn't publishers have motives other than selling the highest numbers of books to readers with the highest average incomes?
>
> (2004: D7)

Alford's own food writing is heavily guided by a cosmopolitan ideology that pays particular tribute to the culinary traditions of Asian countries (Alford and Duguid 2000, 1998), and provides readers not just with recipes of the socially-distant Other, but with a relatively-nuanced cultural picture of the peoples and cultures behind the foods. Still, Alford appears surprised by a ubiquitous element of culinary discourse—its consistent tendency to present elites as the legitimate arbiters of good taste in an omnivorous era, even when foods are pulled from the cook-books of socially-distant, exotic working people. Our reading of gourmet food writing suggests that gourmet publishers are not simply aspiring to sell cookbooks to high-income elites—although clearly that may be one goal, they would prefer to sell as many cookbooks as possible. Instead, they are using a narrative that is consistent with the culinary discourse we identify: One that relies on social elites in the geo-political core to define the importance of authenticity and exoticism in an omnivorous cultural terrain.

4

FOODIE POLITICS
THIS IS ONE DELICIOUS REVOLUTION!

The notion that "food is political" has become a kind of common sense. This seemingly obvious idea is actually quite complex, and this chapter explores the political world of the foodie. We want to avoid posing a question about food politics in simple yes or no terms—are foodies politicized eaters, or apolitical hedonists? Clearly, the contemporary food scene is replete with political issues, particularly issues of environmental sustainability. Shoppers across the country spend the summer months toting canvas bags with farmers' market produce, and many home-cooks serve only free-range organic meats to dinner guests. A burger joint in New York City's East Village avoids fuel-burning, cross-country deliveries since, as the owner states, "I want this to be an ethical burger" (*New York Times*, Feb. 13, 2008, p.F5). Michael Pollan has become a kind of journalistic folk hero, and his bestselling critique of the industrial food complex, *The Omnivore's Dilemma* (2006), won the 2007 James Beard Award for best food writing, and is widely read by foodies (including the foodies we interviewed).

Although the foodie world appears to have become more politicized— or at least, more conscious of environmental issues—these political commitments are not straightforward. For instance, many foodies remain devoted sensualists and are committed above all to the pursuit of "taste" and pleasure. This might mean eating locally grown produce, but it can also involve a meal of veal chops, foie gras, and live lobsters, all consumed with a focus on authentic and exotic food adventuring. Ethical eating might involve a meal of supremely tender organically-raised lamb chops, but that lamb might be raised in Idaho and consumed 600 miles away in San Francisco.

Food is deeply politicized, by which we mean interlarded with relationships of power and privilege. Most everyday food choices both reflect and reproduce societal power divisions of economic and cultural capital (Belasco 2005: 217; Lefebvre 2002; Smith 1987). As Mintz insists, the meaning human beings give to food cannot be isolated from questions of power, since food's "internal meaning" is intrinsically connected to political-economic structures and large-scale institutions, which Mintz classified as generating "external meaning" (1996: 30). While all food is political, what is not clear is *how* food is politicized in foodie discourse. We therefore start with a simple question: How are food politics framed? Which issues are given prominence, and which issues are neglected? To get at the question of food politics, we eschew simple yes/no answers for a more subtle approach that focuses on how political issues are framed in food discourse and embodied in the lifeworlds and words of foodies themselves. We argue that food politics is best conceptualized as a broad discourse where ideologies of consumerism and citizenship shape different understandings of how food relates to equity, social justice, and sustainability.

This chapter begins with a brief accounting of the rise of political eating, followed by a description of the ideological tensions latent within foodie politics. We then sketch out and analyze how political issues are framed in the popular discursive sources we study, drawing from gourmet food journalism[49] and our interviews with foodies. Following this presentation of key themes and topics in foodie politics, we draw from our interview data in greater depth to demonstrate some of the nuance and tension in the lived experience of foodie politics.

To foreshadow our findings, we find that the discourse of foodie politics is in keeping with contemporary trends of ethical consumption (Johnston 2008; Hilton 2003), and is characterized by a tension between ideologies of consumerism and citizenship. When consumerism prevails, as it so often does, foodies are urged to make a difference through individual consumption acts such as shopping, dining or eating. Consumerism also facilitates the link between political eating and status, a point made in existing critiques of organics and local eating as "bourgeois piggery" (Johnston 2007; Guthman 2003). Consumerism frames a vision of food politics as win-win: These shopping acts benefit the environment, and they are, above all else, pleasing to the palate. A consumer-ethics framing suggests that foodies can have it all—eat delicious foods that are both exotic and local, and have a clear conscience. While this approach to food politics has appealing elements, like accessibility and ease of use (e.g., *Bon Appétit*'s "50 Easy Ways to Eat Green"), its focus on individual commodity consumption may serve to draw attention away from the structural causes and collective solutions required to fix the industrial food system (see Guthman 2007; Szasz 2007), a limitation we explore throughout this chapter. While we argue that an individual consumer-ethics framing is hegemonic, it exists in tension with competing citizenship-based food politics. A citizen-based frame of political eating challenges consumerism's focus on consumption and consumer choice, and puts forward collective, democratic projects that redefine consumer pleasures and assert citizens' authority over food resources. A political frame based on citizenship ideals is broadly inclusive and aims at equalizing benefits across individuals (so not just wealthy individuals can enjoy locally-grown, sustainable, fairly-produced foods). In this way, our analysis of food politics, and of the tension between consumerism and citizenship, demonstrates the political version of the "democracy versus distinction" tension we explore throughout this book.

Political Eating: A Historical Perspective

Both contemporary foodies and traditional gourmets prioritize food as an aesthetic and sensual concern: Food is valued when it is delicious. However, foodie discourse also recognizes the political dimensions of food production and consumption. Good food is frequently constructed to meet both aesthetic and moral criteria, and is commonly understood as both politically palatable and delicious. The bridging of aesthetic with political concerns alters the dynamics of culinary discourse, impacting how food is evaluated. In this section, we explore the origins of the overlap between moral and aesthetic evaluation in the contemporary foodscape. To understand the significance of contemporary food politics, it is useful to go back in time, at least briefly, and see how political food and gourmet food occupied two relatively different and distinct realms in the post-war period, and how these concerns came together in contemporary foodie discourse.[50]

The realm of America's gourmet culture has historically been dominated by a search for delicious food, rather than politically-correct fare. Of course, delicious food was not just any food. While exceptions prevail, the general historical trend involved an equation between high-status food and French haute cuisine, as well as a relatively clear divide between highbrow and lowbrow food (Kuh 2001; Kamp 2006). The search for high-status delicious food meant that political concerns were quite marginal, if not absent altogether from *Gourmet* magazine. In issues of *Gourmet* from the 1950s, 1960s, 1970s, and 1980s, we find articles profiling exclusive restaurants, travel writing featuring exotic foods, and recipes for hosting a fabulous dinner party, with no discernible political awareness. The quintessential exemplar of high-status, French-oriented gourmet culture is the socialite, gastronome, and unapologetic snob, Lucius Beebe. From the 1930s up until the 1960s, Beebe regaled readers with tales of epicurean excess involving exotic game, caviar, and expensive wine. Beebe described New York's high-end French restaurant, Le Pavillon, as "flourishing in a midst of mink and monocles, gilt and mirrors reminiscent of the best Paris restaurants" (as in Kuh 2001: 31). Notions of the "good life" for classical American gourmets drew heavily from French culinary standards, but these French status symbols were gradually popularized to the North American middle class through public personalities like Julia Child. Child's television show and bestselling book, *Mastering the Art of French Cooking* (1961), explicitly aimed to take French food off its cultural pedestal and teach French cooking techniques to servantless American housewives.

While gourmets spent the 1960s learning how to cook French classics like *boeuf bourguignon* and *sole à la normande*, the food politicos that emerged in the late 1960s and 1970s were famous for their brown rice and healthy (if heavy) breads.[51] Belasco (1989) documented the emerging food politicos of the 1960s and 1970s, dubbing them the "countercuisine"—a group that was heavily invested in exploring the political implications of food choices. The countercuisine was not a unified, monolithic movement, but operated from multiple vantage points such as food co-ops, the peace movement, and 'back to the land' lifestyles. A common thread that united diverse culinary interests was a focus on unearthing the political implications of food choices. White bread was decried as a symbol for an industrial era of soulless convenience foods, while "brown rice became the icon of antimodernity," and a mechanism for standing (and eating) in solidarity with the world's oppressed peoples (Belasco 1989: 27, 49). A thoughtful process of food preparation was highly valued. For example, a column on "Bread Bakin'" by columnist "mother bird" advised readers to "not be discouraged by a few bricks, or even a lot of bricks—they're all building blocks" (Belasco 1989: 46). Another central tenet of the countercuisine's political food was vegetarianism. The wastefulness of a meat-based lifestyle was widely publicized through Lappé's bestselling treatise, *Diet for a Small Planet* (1971). Countercultural hippies prioritized "moral" food choices, like vegetarianism, over gourmet decadence. Exemplifying this trait, Lappé's book included recipes such as "scrambled tofu," a "thinking person's cheesecake" made with cottage cheese and egg whites, "Betty the Peacenik gingerbread," "soybean pie," and "Hearty Tomato Soup (like Campbell's never dreamed of)" (1971).

While the realms of gourmets and the countercuisine were relatively distinct in the 1960s, 1970s, and 1980s, this divide gradually diminished as ideals of the countercuisine were incorporated into the mainstream food system (Belasco 1989), and gourmet culture itself came to take on new concerns and adopt new, more diverse ways of eating. For example, the widely-read *New York Times* food columnist, Craig Claiborne, expanded his writing beyond the world of upscale French-related cuisine and wrote profiles of cheap ethnic eateries. Perhaps most emblematic of this blurring was the emergence of Alice Waters and her Berkeley restaurant, Chez Panisse, as a culinary icon. While much can be written about Alice Waters, and Chez Panisse itself had many different chefs with different styles of cooking, what is key to our argument here is how Waters's spectacular success reflects the convergence of the concerns of gourmets and the countercuisine. More specifically, Chez Panisse incorporated an appreciation of French gastronomy (the classical concern of American gourmets) with the countercuisine's emphasis on food prepared with care and political awareness. The influence of French cuisine on Chez Panisse was strongly evident—both in Waters's acknowledgment of the important influence of time she spent in France, and also in the food itself. Chez Panisse's opening night menu was classically French, and included *pâté en croûte* and a classically-prepared *canard aux olives*, made with a bevy of French sauce essentials like *fond brun* and demi-glace (McNamee 2007: 2–3). Of course, Chez Panisse was (and is) no simple French restaurant. As the restaurant moved from a local hot-spot to a national culinary icon, Waters worked to pioneer a style of New American cooking focused on fresh, local, seasonal ingredients sourced through close relationships with local farmers. In the words of Waters's biographer, Thomas McNamee: "[Waters's] conception of a moral community based on good food and goodwill has helped to spawn a new generation of artisans and farmers. Like her, they are committed to stewardship of the land and waters" (2007: 6–7).

While some might find this depiction of Waters's culinary leadership exaggerated, the quotation and its invocation of "moral community" neatly encapsulates the ethos expressed through the contemporary foodie era—an era where the political credentials of one's dinner can matter just as much as classical gourmet concerns like taste and authenticity. Put simply, many foodies are gourmets with a political bent. Tellingly, in 2008 an introduction to *Best Food Writing* began with the following words: "Food ought to be the simplest thing in the world. Since when did it become so politicized?" (Hughes 2008: ix). The same collection leads off with six essays on food politics under the heading, "Food Fights," but the book also includes pieces discussing classic gourmet concerns like culinary techniques and specialized ingredients. Today, many foodies not only understand what an authentic ceviche is, but they also worry about whether the seafood that made up their ceviche is from a sustainable source. Taking over Julia Child's role as a populist gourmet educator, *New York Times* columnist Mark Bittman is known for his role popularizing no-knead home-made breads and accessible gourmet meals, but his voice also weighs in on political food issues like the virtues of local versus organic foods (Bittman 2007: 2). On the Gourmet.com website, foodies can learn how to cook delicious dishes with celery root, at the same time they read about the paucity of agricultural initiatives in President Obama's financial stimulus package, or how they can enjoy yogurt without the guilt of plastic packaging.

In short, foodie discourse combines political issues with a continued interest in classical gourmet concerns. This means that relative to earlier eras, the contemporary evaluative schema for food is even more complex, and the criteria that are upheld as important frequently involve an intricate intermingling of aesthetic and political concerns. Two caveats are in order. First, this is not a simple additive process— foodie discourse does not simply "add" the politics of the countercuisine to gourmet concerns. Foodies take up political and gourmet concerns in ways that are new, thereby creating a new culinary discourse and adjudication standards. For instance, foodies frequently distinguish themselves from the countercuisine, which is commonly depicted as moralistic, druggy, and tasteless. A feature on brown rice in *Saveur* makes clear that the rice they profile is not the bland, virtuous brown rice that emerged from the "torpor of hippie-era cooking" (*Saveur*, May 2008, p. 75). In an article about the First Family's White House chef, culinary journalist Christy Harrison lauds Alice Waters and the sustainable food movement (led by "outspoken, committed chefs") for making clear that delicious, sustainable food "doesn't just mean granola and tofu" (Harrison 2009).

A second caveat: foodie discourse has a critical political component, but it is not *necessarily* political. As with any discourse, elements of foodie discourse are selectively taken up and modified by foodies, and food politics is no exception. This means that not all foodies are interested in the politics of their plates, and some self-consciously reject any suggestion that they should ponder the living conditions of industrial chicken, or feel shameful about the food miles of imported raspberries. Our point here is not that all foodies are food politicos, but that foodie *discourse* has taken up issues of food politics alongside traditional epicurean concerns like taste. While much of foodie discourse is avowedly apolitical, focusing exclusively on aesthetic concerns, politics is a relatively new and significant stream. Chefs, authors, and other culinary personalities can position themselves not simply as experts on aesthetic matters (e.g., the proper way of cooking venison), but as public intellectuals speaking out on topics like sustainability and public health. The Obamas' decision to hire Chicago chef Sam Kass[52] to work in the White House was newsworthy not because of his cooking techniques (which are probably decent), but because Kass has a stated political commitment to sourcing healthy, local food (Burros 2009).

The merging of the aesthetic and political concerns evident in the contemporary foodscape is of particular interest to us because of the consequent tensions it produces. Although aesthetic and political concerns are sometimes harmonious, they are also frequently in conflict. New Zealand lamb may be delicious and tender, yet it racks up copious food miles. Local produce can be environmentally responsible and promote economic development, but few foodies want an exclusive relationship with local foods in the long winter months. Harmony can be found in the example of the wild-caught salmon; it has a texture and flavor that many foodies find aesthetically superior to conventionally farmed Atlantic salmon, and it achieves the political goal of avoiding the environmental risks associated with salmon farming. At the same time that wild salmon is considered an ethically and aesthetically superior product, its price is frequently three times that of farmed salmon, raising questions about which socio-economic classes can afford to eat ethical food. Wild salmon's eco-credentials are also open to discussion, since its high price reflects the dwindling fish stocks and uncertain sustainability of wild salmon fisheries. All of these examples speak to the difficulty of balancing aesthetic and political concerns in foodie discourse. Given the complexity and contradictions within foodie discourse, we believe it is important to investigate which concerns are highlighted in the contemporary foodscape, and how boundaries are drawn around "good" or "worthy" food. Which political goals are prioritized when these distinctions are made, and which tend to recede into the political background?

Competing Ideologies in Foodie Politics

To address this question and shed light on foodie politics, we examine the competing ideologies at play in foodie discourse. As with all discourse, foodie politics is not monochromatic. Different ideologies compete to encourage particular understandings of complex food issues like sustainability and food access. To be clear, our focus in this chapter is on the food discourse presented in popular sources that constitute the dominant foodie public sphere, rather than the many food subcultures (or subaltern counterpublics) which range from freegan dumpster diving to community food security activism, and present very different visions of food and social change.

When food politics are discussed in the popular gourmet food media and in our interviews with foodies, two ideologies—consumerism and citizenship—guide and shape understanding of these issues. Whereas consumerism enables a view of foodie politics that exacerbates status distinctions, the realm of citizenship entails a collective politics targeting social and ecological problems in the food system. Of course, in the real world of food consumption, citizenship and consumerism intermingle. A bunch of organic arugula can mean multiple things depending on who buys it, where it is grown, the conditions of its production, and how it is transported and sold. Rather than see consumerism and citizenship as discrete entities, it is useful to conceptualize them as ideal-typical end points on a spectrum of food politics. While consumerism exerts a hegemonic presence on the foodscape, shaping everyday elements of foodie common sense, critical dimensions of citizenship can also be observed in foodie culture, as we shall see below.

The terms consumerism and citizenship are conceptually baggy in everyday parlance. This has led to the commonplace observation that consumers now practice citizenship through their shopping decisions, and the emergence of a hybrid concept of the citizen-consumer (e.g., Johnston 2008; Arnould 2007; Schudson 2007; Shaw, Newholm and Dickinson 2006; Slocum 2004). It is not that consumers never behave as citizens at the grocery store, but it is important to unpack the meaning behind these terms, since thoughtlessly collapsing "citizens" into "consumers" can obfuscate some significant differences and contradictions.[53] While "consumption" refers fairly straightforwardly to "using up" goods and services, consumerism refers to an ideology suggesting a way of life dedicated to the possession and use of consumer goods (Kellner 1983: 74), rooted in the capitalist necessity of selling an ever-expanding roster of commodities in a globalized economy (Gottdiener 2000: 281; Sklair 2001). Consumerism presents a world where individual consumer choice is the optimal social condition. In terms of food consumption, consumerism involves asking questions like, "What foods should I choose to maximize my pleasure?", or "How should I eat to be healthy and protect my family?" In terms more specific to food politics, the ideology of consumerism encourages a frame of understanding, what we call a consumer-ethics frame, suggesting that individual consumer strategies are optimal strategies for addressing system-wide problems in the food system like environmental deterioration. In this context, ethical eating is presented as a win-win situation where individual lifestyle choices are thought to simultaneously address eco-social issues, like carbon emissions, while producing individual benefits, like delicious-tasting food.

While consumerism is the dominant ideology guiding understanding of food politics, a second ideology—citizenship—is also present within foodie discourse.[54] Citizenship involves collective struggles to reclaim and preserve democratic control—not just over the state, but over social life, culture, and ecological resources. While consumers maximize individual self-interest through commodity choice, citizens prioritize the collective good, which means that individual self-interest and pleasure can be trumped in the interest of improving sustainability or equity. In short, citizenship struggles are distinguished by a collective, needs-oriented responsibility to ensure the survival and well-being of other beings, both human and non-human. Put in terms more specific to food politics, the ideology of citizenship generates a frame, what we term a political-eating frame, that prioritizes structural solutions over individual consumer choice, challenges the dominance of individual pleasures over larger political-environmental principles, and uses public sphere discussions to reflexively engage with food system contradictions. A political-eating frame moves beyond convenience and taste to address questions like, "What collective and structural changes are required to produce a just and sustainable food system?"

One of the key findings in our study of foodie discourse is the dominance of ideologies of consumerism, and the concomitant prominence of a consumer-ethics frame heavily focused on individual "eco"[55] commodity choices used to construct a green lifestyle. This is not altogether surprising, particularly since neo-liberal ideologies, with their pro-market, anti-state agendas, have globally dominated political and economic life since the 1980s. A frame of individual consumer ethics fits neatly with the neo-liberal emphasis on market choice as the ultimate arbiter of the collective good, often at the expense of state action, regulation, and institution-building. It is within this context that a larger trend of ethical consumption emerged in the 1980s, originating in concern that collective consumption patterns were producing a range of negative outcomes like pollution, chemical contamination, and global warming.[56] These consumer projects have resuscitated a classical ethics concern—What is the good life?—but with a more specific consumer twist: What should I buy? Asking, "What should I buy?" turns out to be very closely related to the question, "What should I eat?", as food commodities have been central in numerous ethical consumption projects like fair-trade coffee and humanely-raised meat.

The political agency of consumers is up for debate (Micheletti et al. 2004; Zukin and Maguire 2004; Soper 2004; Slater 1997; Gabriel and Lang 2006; Scammell 2000),[57] and what remains unclear is how effective consumer-focused strategies are at redressing the food system's numerous failings. Szasz (2007) critiques a focus on individualized consumer solutions for addressing environmental problems on both ecological and political-economic grounds.[58] Szasz emphasizes that individualized, commodified consumer solutions are not only frequently ineffectual, but inevitably have a class dimension, since consumer-based solutions require a substantial outlay of capital that only a small section of society can afford to do consistently. Besides the class implications, the availability of consumer commodities reduces the urgency the public feels about environmental issues and thus reduces government action. Szasz argues that "political anesthesia is *the* important unintended consequence" of individual commodity approaches (2007: 195), and this political process is even more troublesome when you factor in the class implications: why would states act to regulate and protect the food supply if their most affluent and influential members have the disposable income to purchase commodities that allow them to opt out?

Having laid out the key ideological contest at play in consumer politics, we return to our earlier question: How are food politics conceptualized in foodie discourse? The primary objective in the next section is to describe key themes of food politics, while also providing an analysis of how the ideologies of consumerism and citizenship manifest within this discourse.

The Discourse of Foodie Politics

While we have argued that foodie concerns about sustainable agriculture and free-range eggs are part and parcel of a larger ethical consumption trend, the emergence of foodie politics is a relatively recent phenomenon. Flipping through the pages of *Gourmet* magazine from the 1950s, or even the 1980s, a reader fails to find interviews with agricultural theorists or exposés of industrial chicken operations.[59] In these historic issues, food is discussed in apolitical terms—as separate and apart from citizenship issues of social justice or sustainability. In the years when we systematically investigated food journalism (2004–2008), the place of politics in foodie discourse evolved significantly. Although explicit political concerns had been raised for many years, if not decades, it was during this period that these concerns gained tremendous visibility. When we first conducted a systematic reading of *Bon Appétit, Gourmet, Food & Wine*, and *Saveur* in 2004, we found virtually no in-depth reporting on environmental, political or social food issues, although there were numerous passing references to local, organic, or seasonal food. By 2007 and 2008, we noticed that certain food issues, particularly local eating, sustainability, and animal welfare, were featured in greater depth and with greater frequency. The "politics of the plate" were in the public eye, well symbolized by the continued media attention and sustained sales of Michael Pollan's tome, *The Omnivore's Dilemma* (2006). In January 2008 *Gourmet* magazine launched a new website featuring a prominent section on "food politics" inaugurated by an interview with Pollan.[60] When we conducted our interviews in 2008, all our interviewees showed an awareness of explicit political dimensions of food practices, even if not all of them expressed a willingness to prioritize these political concerns in their eating habits (a topic discussed below).

While passing references to local, organic, and seasonal foods are now ubiquitous in foodie discourse, it is important to distinguish these references from in-depth coverage of food issues like sustainability and farmer livelihood. Although in-depth coverage in 2008 is more frequent today than when we started this research in 2004, many magazine issues and newspaper dining sections still focus exclusively on classical gourmet concerns like recipes, restaurant reviews, and travel pieces.[61] The prevailing way of understanding gourmet eating is still relatively apolitical, and continues to promote an understanding of affluent Western lifestyles as unconnected to the inequitable and unsustainable global flows of resources, people, and capital.

This brings us back to our starting question of how food politics are being framed in foodie discourse, when these issues are raised. Three topics are regularly observed in foodie discourse: (1) local eating; (2) organic/sustainable food; and (3) animal welfare. These topical themes are organizational heuristics, rather than discrete, self-contained categories with monochromatic messages. Like ethical consumption trends more broadly, these topics contain elements of internal contradictions and ambiguity. A desire to protect the environment is overlaid with personal motivations like pursuing good taste and protecting one's health. Overall, foodie discourse relies heavily on an individual consumer-ethics frame focused on how individuals can shop, dine out and cook in order to protect the environment and feel better about their place in consumer society. These contradictions will be drawn out below in our discussion of local food, organic/sustainable eating, and animal welfare. Following this discussion, we examine conspicuous absences of certain political issues, particularly issues of labor rights and social justice that animate a great deal of food activism nationally and globally (e.g., CFSC 2008; Nyeleni Declaration 2007), but which are virtually absent from our examination of foodie discourse.

"Fresh, Local, Seasonal. Everybody's Doing It"

The virtues of locally-grown food are so prominent within contemporary foodie culture that the "buy local" mantra has reached near common-sense status. The focus on local and seasonal food has created buzzwords out of these terms, and there is probably no more important determinant of food's quality than the use of local and seasonal ingredients. Recipes featuring local ingredients encourage readers to "celebrate what's great now . . . with a dinner that puts local, seasonal food front and center" (*Bon Appétit*, Feb. 2008, p. 98). An ice-cream shop and bakery is lauded for preparing its goods using "local fruit" (*New York Times*, 18 June 2008, F1), and readers are guided on a mental tour through the colorful aisles of an "indoor public market selling pristine local food" (*New York Times*, 2 Jan. 2008, F1). Several of our interviewees described themselves as "locavores," and many of them valued local food purchased in farmers' markets.

Although foodie discourse identifies great aesthetic benefits associated with local and seasonal ingredients—i.e., they tend to be the most fresh and flavorful—the focus on local and seasonal foods is also justified in political terms. The most commonly cited justification for eating locally is to reduce greenhouse gas emissions and to support local farmers. One article proclaims, "Fresh, local, seasonal. Everybody's doing it, most of us by shopping at farmers' markets, which is definitely a carbon footstep in the right direction" (*Bon Appétit*, Apr. 2008, p. 113). The specific environmental benefit of local eating relates to the concept of food miles. Food that is local and seasonal requires shorter transportation than food that is imported from out of the region. Less transportation results in fewer greenhouse gas emissions. Although there is debate about the environmental and political implications of prioritizing (and fetishizing) local market solutions

(Desrochers and Shimzu 2008; DuPuis and Goodman 2005; Eaton 2008; Andrée 2006), foodie discourse has generally adopted this idea as conventional wisdom.

And so, among political comments in foodie discourse, we see a great advocacy of local eating. For example, from an article on vegetables: "We all know that eating in-season, locally grown produce is best—it's beneficial for the environment, for our health, and for the flavor of the dishes we prepare" (*Bon Appétit*, Feb. 2008, p. 105). Another example comes from a review of an Oregon restaurant named Tilth: "Maria Hines, Tilth's owner and chef, pays more than lip service to the adjectives local and seasonal, and she has created a restaurant that's very much of its moment, not only in its attention to food miles but also in its menu structure" (*New York Times*, 27 Feb., 2008, p. F4).

A concern for "food miles" was echoed in our interviews, where concern for the environment was frequently cited as a criterion for valuing local food. Gillian Edelman, a 48-year-old journalist living in the Bay Area, stated: "I mean there's been a whole renewed emphasis on buying locally as a way to not only support smaller, more local farmers, but to also reduce your carbon imprint by, you know, buying food that hasn't been imported from Chile or Mexico. So that shapes my shopping habits." Another interviewee, Michelle Quinlan, a 37-year-old analyst living in Chicago, re-defined "organic" to include concerns about food miles, stating, "Part of the definition of organic to me is local, you know. So what difference does it make that they didn't use any pesticides growing it on the other side of the world. I've since made up for that ten-fold with all the petroleum it took to get it to this side of the world!" To be sure, in addition to a concern for minimizing food miles, local and seasonal foods were preferred for a range of reasons (e.g., taste) that had nothing to do with the environment. In this sense, the political dimensions of food do not have discrete boundaries and are blurred with other dimensions, such as health consequences and aesthetic criteria.

While appeals to the "local" abound, celebratory statements are not always accompanied by a discussion of the political concerns associated with the locavore trend. For example, a special feature on "Cooking Vacations" exalts the regional cuisine of Shanagarry, Ireland by stating, "With the sea just half a mile away, even the fish is local here" (*Gourmet*, May 2008, p. 80). Yet how are readers to reconcile an appeal for "local" Irish fish with the fact that they must travel across an ocean to savor these "local" ingredients? Our analysis of gourmet food discourse suggests that the goodness of the local is framed in a variety of ways that do not always connect the issue of local eating to substantive political and environmental concerns—like supporting local economies or significantly reducing fossil fuel consumption. In fact, local food is frequently framed as a fashionable practice demanded by the latest trends. A *San Francisco Chronicle* food critic remarks, "There is nothing groundbreaking about cooking with local and seasonal ingredients these days—it's practically required for any new, trendy restaurant in Northern California" (23 Jan. 2008, p. F5). An article entitled, "Spoonbread gets a seasonal makeover," offers tips on how to update classic comfort foods to "mirror today's culinary trends . . . with the addition of the Bay Area's seasonal and local ingredients" (*San Francisco Chronicle*, 2 Apr. 2008, p. F1). In other cases, the current emphasis on buying local is embedded within a narrative of established gourmet tradition. As one editorial comments, " 'Going green' may be the latest trend, but for us, local, sustainable, and organic ingredients have always been in style" (*Bon Appétit*, Feb. 2008, p. 4). Even within this appeal to culinary tradition, the desire for local foods is framed as fashionable, with less of an emphasis on the serious political and environmental issues underlying the movement for local eating. We do not dispute the fact that the local has achieved trendy status, nor do we wish to suggest that all food writing must provide substantive analysis of the reasons to eat local. However, it is worth examining the discursive significance of framing local eating so consistently and commonly as an issue of fashion. Rather than substantially engaging with the political issues of local eating, the framing of local as a culinary fashion fits within a frame of individualized consumer ethics where discerning foodies can have it all—delicious local food, a clear conscience, and participation within the latest consumer trends.

While discussions of local eating vary in the amount of attention given to political objectives, what is remarkably consistent, and a key element of a consumer-ethics frame present in the great majority of sources we examined, was the presentation of local eating as win-win: Political objectives are presented as being in complete harmony with gourmet objectives of finding delicious food. When eating locally is politicized within foodie discourse, it is frequently presented in a way that upholds, and even optimizes, consumer choices by providing access to the most delicious foods available. Even when local eating is framed as a way to address collective goals, like the environment and farmer welfare, taste is the ultimate value, as seen in this excerpt from the *Bon Appétit* "Green Issue":

> Line-caught, grass-fed, cage-free; buy local, choose sustainable, go for organic when you can—these words and phrases have become a mantra for many of us by now. The reasoning is simple: It's good for you (research shows that organic produce really does have more nutrients), it's good for the local economy (who would you rather support, a farmer you know or a nameless conglomerate?), and it's good for the environment (generally, the less distance food has to travel to get to your plate, the better). But *perhaps the most important reason? Food produced this way and cooked with care simply tastes better.*
>
> (*Bon Appétit*, Feb. 2008, p. 88; emphasis ours)

By suggesting that "the reasoning is simple," the mutual benefits of political and gourmet objectives are again constructed as common sense. Yet even as readers are applauded for their knowledge of political issues, they are assured that these need not compromise a foodie's "most important" concern: Taste. The editorial of the same issue sums up the ethos of the consumer-ethics frame as follows: "since better for the world means better tasting, this is one delicious revolution" (*Bon Appétit*, Feb. 2008, p. 4). In our interviews, foodies also frequently presented local eating as both progressive and delicious, as in the following quotation from Chad Tucker, a 47-year-old living in the Midwest: "I'd much prefer to buy carrots that were grown within the state rather than California, say. And often because it is a good idea to support local farmers, but also I find that the flavor is much better. They tend to be grown on smaller scale farms and they tend to taste like something rather than hydroponic water."

In some instances, the underlying tensions and potential contradictions involved with local eating are unearthed, but reconciled in the interest of maintaining gourmet choice. One such conflict arises between the ethics of eating locally and the continued embrace of consumer choice, particularly in regards to long-distance, exotic foods. A *Saveur* article entitled "Praising Far-Flung Fruit," explicitly describes the tension between eating locally and enjoying exotic foods:

> Sure, we at *Saveur* are ardent supporters of the locavore movement; after all, do any foods taste quite as nice as those raised a stone's throw from home? Well, yes, as a matter of fact, at least when it comes to the exotic ASIAN FRUITS now showing up with increasing frequency on our shores. We're crazy for sweet rambutans, native to Malaysia; tangy longans, from southern China; dragon fruits, popular in Vietnam; and delightfully funky-smelling durians, originally from Indonesia. With their otherworldly looks and wonderfully complex flavors, these are foods from afar that we're happy to sink our teeth into.
>
> (*Saveur*, Jan./Feb. 2008, p. 53)

The tension between local desires and global choices is also seen in a survey of Community Supported Agriculture (CSA) customers who rate "local" as the most important quality in their food shopping, but list bananas as their favorite fruit or vegetable (*San Francisco Chronicle*, Jun. 25 2008, p. F1). Similarly in our interviews, most of the foodies we spoke with valued local eating and many praised farmers' markets, and at the same time they valued foods that came from distant regions and countries. Sometimes, this involved a different kind of ethical criteria, as in the case of Harry Quinn, a 43-year-old in California: "While I don't necessarily know where my local El Salvadorian market gets his meat, you know, I'd rather give my money to them. So between being ethical in knowing where your food comes from, I want to give my money to someone who cares."

On the subject of consumer choice, it is worth noting that while local eating is consistently praised throughout the foodie discourse we studied, mainstream journalistic sources never suggest that foodies prioritize their political commitments over taste and restrict long-distance foods—a move that would inevitably push environmental commitments and gourmet objectives into tension. The closest we come to this is a *Bon Appétit* interview, entitled "Expert Advice from the Locavores," with Alison Smith and J. B. MacKinnon, a Vancouver couple who kick-started the 100-mile diet and who wrote a book describing their experiences of eating exclusively food produced and grown in their local area (defined as within 100 miles [160 km] of their home town) for one year. According to the article, Smith and MacKinnon's primary goal was to "reduce the use of fossil fuels in the production and transportation of food," but they soon learned of several additional benefits, including "a sense of community in the practice of meeting our local farmers and knowing them by name," as well as the "unexpected pleasure . . . [of] having a story attached to the things you are eating" (*Bon Appétit*, Feb. 2008, p. 27). Even though Smith and MacKinnon's book (2007) is honest about the limitations and hard-ships of an exclusively local diet (which eliminates foods like sugar, coffee, chocolate, olive oil, and wheat), it is significant that *Bon Appétit*'s emphasis is on the consumer-ethics frame, and the win-win benefits experienced from eating locally.

This is not to diminish the significance of a secondary, but important, political eating frame that rejects consumer choice maximization, partic-ularly the choice to consume long-distance foods, in the interest of maximizing the social and ecological benefits of local eating. This came across most strongly in a small sub-sample of our interviews, rather than in the food journalism we exampled. For example, in comparing her decision to buy through a community-supported agriculture project versus Whole Foods, Michelle Quinlan commented on the importance of local eating versus long-distance organics:

it takes less petroleum, to get [the food] here, and it's a community thing, you know, you're making an investment, you know where your food is from, you know? I get regular invitations to go up there and meet [the farmers], they have open houses, you can choose your level of involvement. But if I go to Whole Foods and I buy an organic, quote unquote, apple from Australia, you know, that's very abstract.

Another interviewee, Sarah Driscoll, stated her decision to reduce her consumption of long-distance fruits and vegetables:

I don't buy bananas and mangos and papayas, and pineapple almost ever, even though I really like them. Because I just try and enjoy what I can get here. So, I don't know, I think that's, again it's about being connected. I like there to be roots underneath my plate that I can trace.

Kevin D'Angelo, who lives in the Seattle area, described how on his last trip for groceries, he "looked through the vegetable section and passed most of them because they were from California or Mexico and I am avoiding buying foods that are from that distance." Nathaniel Snider, a 38-year-old engineer, not only reduces his consumption of long-distance produce, but has a regular food blog that helps people increase their consumption of local food. This kind of commitment to eating locally, and eschewing some of the choices of consumer culture, is connected to less mainstream elements of foodie discourse that we didn't systematically investigate, but certainly took note of. For example, a group food blog, called "Eat Local Challenge" (eatlocalchallenge.com), states that they are "committed to challenging themselves to eat mainly local food," and provides tips, recipes, and motivation for those striving to eat mainly local food across the country. These kinds of foodie projects are noteworthy because they highlight a vision of local eating by pleasure-seeking citizens (rather than pleasure-prioritizing consumers) who are willing to make significant personal sacrifices to reduce the carbon emissions of their daily diet.

"Organic Food: Better for You, Better for the Environment, and still Great-tasting"

Just as with eating locally and seasonally, eating foods that are certified organic, or are thought to be natural and "sustainable," is now mainstream. In foodie discourse, the sometimes interchangeable use of "organic" and "sustainable" refers to an often-nebulous set of practices regarding food production (reflecting the debate over when farming and fishing can legitimately be called organic or sustainable). Predominantly, these terms arise in food journalism and in our interviews to refer to food production that avoids harm to the environment from the use of toxic or otherwise poisonous chemicals (e.g., pesticides and fertilizers) or through farming practices that degrade the integrity and quality of soil and water. These terms also refer to food production that supports the enduring survival of natural (not genetically-modified) plant and animal species.

Within the dominant foodie discourse, the win-win logic of the consumer-ethics frame presents organic and sustainably grown foods as good for the environment, but above all else, delicious. In the words of Joe Bastianich, restaurateur and business partner with Mario Batali, "[h]aving a sustainable business is the way of the future ... But our fundamental principle is better product. We're doing what we're doing to elevate the dining experience" (*Bon Appétit*, Feb. 2008, p. 39). Similarly, an article on progressive aquaculture tells of a salmon farm in northwest Scotland that has "won several awards in the UK, not only for its sustainable aquaculture practices, but also for the quality of the fish itself, which has a buttery texture and sweetly meaty flavour" (*Saveur*, June 2008, p. 86). The framing of sustainable and gourmet as coterminous works to legitimize consumer pleasures, even when they involve long-distance travel and an extremely privileged point of orientation. The concept of Community Supported Fisheries, for instance, becomes a means to hire one's "own personal lobsterman" and enjoy "the entire catch from an individual lobster trap for $2,995 a season"; the catch is conveniently shipped anywhere in the country overnight (*Gourmet*, June 2008, p. 24). Those who shell out for this service will be gratified to know that "10 percent of the profits will go to the Gulf of Maine Research Institute."

The goodness of organic and sustainably grown foods is also framed as positively related to gourmet objectives by coupling environmental issues with consumer health concerns. In this way, the consumer ethics frame is win-win-win: foodies choose organic foods to benefit the planet, and the palate, as well as their personal health. A story about the rising popularity of sardines, for example, emphasizes their "status as a sustainable seafood choice and heart-healthy protein packed with omega-3 fatty acids," as well as "the sweet, rich flesh and flavorful skin of the sardines" (*Bon Appétit*, Feb. 2008, p. 22). Google executive chef, Charlie Ayers, explains the motivation behind "Google's food revolution" as follows: "They wanted power foods that would leave their minions stimulated and energetic after lunch, not slumped over their keyboards . . . And they wanted it done with the highest quality organic, sustainable-sourced ingredients" (*San Francisco Chronicle*, May 7, 2008, p. F6). In our food interviews, a preference for organic food was also based on dual concerns of health and environmental sustainability. When asked to explain her preference for organic food, Karen Weiss, a 49-year-old homeopath in California, replied: "Because I feel very strongly both for the health and well-being of the earth as well as my family, that I don't want to be putting pesticides into the ground, and the run-off into the water table, and the toxicity in our bodies." In some instances, health and energy benefits are framed as the primary motivation for organic food choices, while the environmental issues are left implicit and unexplored. For example, Melissa Trent stated that she looked for naturally-raised, antibiotic-free meat, but was clear that this was for health reasons, not environmental concerns. When asked about ethical food choice, Norman Arbus, a 56-year-old New Yorker, replied: "I would buy organic food provided that it's not horrifically more expensive," and stated his motivation clearly: "I think it's healthier." Florence Nagy, a 51-year-old administrative assistant in Pennsylvania, also clearly stated that "[h]ealth is very important. That's the number one priority."

As with locavorism, food discourse on organics and sustainability acknowledges some ambiguities and contradictions.[62] For example, several interviewees acknowledged that tension between eating locally and eating long-distance organic. Nathaniel Snider clearly described his rationale for buying local over organic, but noted that he also buys organic because:

> I like how it has a lower impact on nature and on the workers. And I think it's a better way to grow because it requires a bit more diversification in the agricultural system than just giant monocultures. That's not always the case, as many people have explored. But at least most of the farms I buy from, they grow twenty or thirty different crops, and they, you know, they have to rotate them to keep the productivity up and also to help prevent pests from getting established.

These contradictions are not thoroughly explored within food journalism, but they are present. For example, a *Gourmet* article lists a series of questions that plague consumers when shopping for seafood: "How to weigh the health benefits of consuming fish against the risk of eating those from contaminated waters? What about overfishing and sustainability?" (*Gourmet*, June 2008). Drawing attention to further consumer tensions, another article highlights the degree of mystery surrounding the terms "organic, natural, and free-range," and asks: "We see these labels every time we shop for chicken, but what do they really mean?" (*Bon Appétit*, Feb. 2008, p. 131).

Clearly, foodies face a complicated foodscape as they attempt to make ethical decisions about what labels to trust, what foods are truly "green," and whether organic foods can always be considered sustainable choices. These contradictions speak to the limits of individually focused consumer strategies in achieving food system sustainability, and the need for regulatory oversight and state intervention.[63] In addition, when one considers how elite consumers consume a grossly disproportionate share of global food resources, the strategy of substituting organic foods for conventionally produced products seems woefully inadequate. Rather than highlight the complexity of these issues, the consumer-ethics framing commonly works to resolve such tensions by offering simple, clear prescriptions to ease a conflicted foodie conscience, while still allowing for the maximization of delicious eating. For example, a book review praises Rick Moonen's *Fish Without a Doubt* for drafting "a blueprint for minimizing hand-wringing in the store and kitchen and maximizing pleasure at the table" (*Gourmet*, June 2008).

As per the ideology of consumerism, consumption is commonly presented as a means to address environmental issues, and gourmet food writing works to direct foodies toward appropriate sites and products. For instance, a listing of "the best eco-friendly restaurants" offers "ten spots where you can dine with a clear conscience" (*Bon Appétit*, Feb. 2008, p. 24). These include a "modern American restaurant . . . with a two-acre organic farm, fruit orchard, composting system, and biodiesel-fueled heating system," as well as "a seafood spot in Georgetown" where the chef not only "knows the geographic origins of the fish he serves . . . but he also knows when it was caught, how it was caught, and even the name of the fisherman who caught it" (ibid.). Food writing features an array of "green" products, such as "good for the planet" vinyl place mats, where "easy care equals green (and guilt-free) when no washing or dry cleaning is required" (*Bon Appétit*, Apr. 2008, p. 56). A special feature on "the country tote" describes a carryall made from recycled coffee-bean bags: "Burlap bags that previously held fair-trade coffee beans give the bag a conscience—and a cool artsy air" (*Bon Appétit*, Feb. 2008, p. 35).

Within gourmet food writing, a consumer-ethics frame enforces the win-win logic by creating distance from culinary counterculture movements of the past that privileged politics over taste. Instead, readers are repeatedly assured that being "green" does not require one to relinquish the pursuit of fine food and good living. In the introduction to a feature on organic brown rice, the author admits her surprise to find that the rice "was good, uncommonly good, and completely unlike the comparatively tough, bland-tasting brown rice I remember eating during San Francisco's counterculture heyday, when consuming the nutrient-packed food was an act more of virtue than of pleasure" (*Saveur*, May 2008, p. 68). She reiterates this distinction in the article's conclusion, stating that "the most tangible evidence of the benefits of the kind of attentive, adaptive farming . . . is the rice itself. Having emerged from the torpor of hippie-era cooking, brown rice is no longer merely a substitute for white rice. It is a food that stands on its own" (ibid.,

p. 75). The contrast between today's eco-delicious meals and the "hippie" politics of the past is also seen in an article on whole-grains: "now that everyone is going green, it's become stylish to combine eco-friendly with glam," and although whole-grains were at "one time relegated to the land of lentil loaf," they have since shed the grunginess of their 1960s hippy status (*San Francisco Chronicle*, 7 May 2008, p. F1). By distancing foodie pleasures from countercultural practices of past—the tough brown rice and flavorless lentil loaves of yesteryear—a consumer-ethics framing affirms that foodies can have their cake and eat it too, enjoying ethical foods while still prioritizing good taste.

We should note that the ethical-consumption frame emerged as a dominant pattern within the data, but we again emphasize that foodie discourse is not monochromatic. As with the topic of local eating, we found limited, but significant, evidence of in-depth discussions around issues of organic food and sustainability, and instances where citizenship objectives and structural concerns were featured (as opposed to green-shopping guides). A significant minority of our interviewees articulated a political-eating frame where environmental concerns about food appeared more significant than their own personal concern over health and taste. For example, Chad Tucker described the expansion of his concern from personal health to the broader environment: "I think primarily my initial reason to buy organic food was concerns about various pesticides and so forth, and that sort of grew into a broader understanding of the effects of conventional agriculture on the land and so forth, and whether it's sustainable." Some of the articles in our sample of gourmet magazines featured a political-eating frame, including one on farmer and long-time sustainable agriculture advocate Wendell Berry, whose food philosophy "marries agrarian and environmental ideologies," but situates these concerns within a broader commitment to "the political and social well-being of the nation" (*Gourmet*, Feb. 2008, p. 72). Two of the magazines included discussions of the United States farm bill that presented a complex picture of related political, social, economic and ecological issues in the food system (e.g., *Gourmet*, April 2008, p. 90). The politics of food in America was listed as the final item in the *Saveur* 100, an annual list of prominent issues in the world of food. The entry, written by Michael Pollan and entitled "The Year the Farm Bill Became Sexy," states that "for the past few years, a political movement centred around food has been bubbling in America, and 2007 was the year it spilled over onto the national stage" (*Saveur*, Jan./Feb. 2008, p. 76).

While we do not dispute Pollan's observation that political issues, particularly environmental issues associated with the industrial food system, are now on the table for foodies, we do believe that it is important and significant to examine *how* food politics are predominantly presented. Even though important exceptions exist, our analysis of foodie discourse finds that food politics are primarily framed through a lens of consumerist ideology that encourages a particular understanding of the complex issues around food. A consumer-ethics frame focuses less on mobilizing collective citizen-based politics to alter the food system, and more on individual food choices that acknowledge concerns about the food system, while affirming classic consumer considerations like price, taste, and convenience.

These considerations continue to play a substantial role determining food choice, as demonstrated by the majority of foodies in our sample. For instance, one foodie, Trish Lincoln, describes her personal approach as "a good balance of pragmatism, but accommodating ethics," and admits that ethical concerns would not prevent her from buying the ingredients she needs for a particular recipe. Pedro Maradona, a 22-year-old New Yorker working in the music industry, stated that while he was concerned about excessive food packaging when making food choices, "in the end I think that . . . I'll end up picking something mostly based on, well first of all my budget, and then also just my interest." Timothy Bauer, a retired lawyer, describes himself as "a big fan of organic food and food that is sort of grown the old-fashioned way," but in the same passage describes why he shops for red meat at Costco: "it's much less expensive than, as you might guess, than going to a really high-end butcher shop." When asked why he prefers organic food, Timothy Bauer explains, "Most of the time it tastes better [laughs]," and goes on to emphasize the importance of taste, along with the win-win mantra of the consumer-ethics frame:

as a person who [cooks] . . . I want my food to really taste like something. That's what eating is all about, so you taste something and you think, "Wow. That really tastes like a tomato," or whatever. Or, "Wow. That really tastes like watercress." So, taste I'd say is paramount . . . the fact of the matter is, I don't have to sacrifice. It's not as if I'm buying something healthy but sacrificing taste. In most cases it tastes a lot better.

Another participant, Ted Darby, explains that he tries to buy sustainable food whenever "given a reasonable choice," but that ethics does not usually trump other consumer considerations like convenience or expense: "By reasonable I mean at some point you can pursue buying the most ethical food possible, at either a considerable expense or a considerable inconvenience. And I wouldn't say that we go to great inconvenience or great expense . . . ethics is a factor, but not the determining factor in what we buy." While individual consumer ethics permit the entry of other considerations beyond cost, taste, and convenience—like sustainability concerns—they do not trump consumer concerns for the majority of the foodies we interviewed. Within foodie writing, these issues are most often presented as readily harmonious with dominant gourmet objectives—as a win-win situation where individual consumer strategies can deliver foodie pleasures, while also addressing the pressing environmental issues in the food system.

To be clear, the environmental issues that are engaged by gourmet food discourse are profoundly important, and it is both significant and important that they are even mentioned—particularly given the virtual absence of these issues in earlier decades. This suggests that the apolitical eating of past gourmets has diminished legitimacy, and that political and environmental issues must increasingly be taken into account within foodie discourse. However, the framing of these issues predominantly as a matter of individual consumer ethics and shopping choice—like the more general framing of environmental issues as individual shopping choices (Szasz 2007)—works to lessen collective understanding of the severity of environmental problems in the food system, and mitigate the need for collective action above and beyond individual commodity consumption.

Animal Welfare: "Love the Environment as much as you love Meat?"

The third major political aspect of foodie discourse concerns the rights of animals. As with the environmentalism animating local and organic food purchases, the animal rights movement has a long history and a broad base that obviously extends beyond contemporary foodie discourse. At the same time, the conflict between animal rights and farming animals for food and dairy products is particularly acute, for the obvious reason that people eat animals and animal products.

For foodies, the particular issues that arise around animal welfare are not the classic concerns of the countercuisine's vegetarianism—to not eat meat. Instead, vegetarian meals are advocated to avoid the excessive meat consumption associated with energy-intensive lifestyles, and concern is expressed for the conditions under which farm animals are raised before they are slaughtered for human consumption. The ethical-consumer frame is the dominant mode of understanding these issues, and promotes a win-win logic suggesting that vegetarian meals and humanely-raised meat were not only ethical but also delicious. Within this focus, and in a pattern mirroring the consumer ethics framing described in previous sections, the politics of vegetarianism and concern for animal welfare are constructed in harmony with individual gourmet objectives, and as part of a green eco-lifestyle package that is kind to the earth, guilt-free, and delicious. An article in the *New York Times* reports that "[m]any chefs believe absolutely that meat from happy, healthy animals tastes better" (*New York Times*, 16 Jan. 2008, p. F1). An article entitled "Mollycoddling Lamb for Tender Eating" describes a farmer who has worked with the likes of chef Thomas Keller (and is said to "pamper" his lambs) and who shares the philosophy that "raising animals naturally and humanely will result in better meat. Sold under the Pure Bred label, it is excellently tender and flavorful" (*New York Times*, 12 Mar. 2008, p. F2).

Besides promoting humane meat as tastier than its industrial counterpart, gourmet food writing frequently describes meat-free meals as defensibly delicious. We are invited to celebrate the 25th anniversary of the *Moosewood Cookbook* as a "Meatless Milestone" in gourmet food history when Deborah Madison "bridged the divide between a principled commitment to eating compassionately and a decidedly sensuous approach to food" (*Saveur*, Jan./Feb. 2008, p. 51). Providing evidence that meat-free can in fact be tasty, we read of bulgar burgers that "don't try to hide their meatless nature and instead celebrate their graincentric origins with wonderful texture and a hint of Middle Eastern spice" (*Gourmet*, June 2008, p. 70). And in a more forthright statement of this same fact, a reviewer deems the menu at one vegetarian restaurant "proof that you can do away with all flesh and hold onto hedonism, at least if you keep enough butter, cream, cheese and wine at hand" (*New York Times*, 19 Mar. 2008, p. F1). The bottom line is that "going vegetarian is more appealing than ever" (*Saveur*, Apr. 2008, p. 22).

Even though vegetarian food is framed as aesthetically appealing, the foodie discourse as a whole does not promote wholesale vegetarianism, and instead works to re-define meat-eating as ethical. Vegetarianism is practiced for many different reasons, but one main reason is the belief that humans should not kill animals for food. This idea appeared only a handful of times within our interviews, and has virtually no traction within the larger foodie discourse. Foodie flexitarians—meaning "vegetarians who aren't that strict and meat-eaters who are striving for a more health-conscious, planet-friendly diet" (Bittman 2007: ix)—have displaced the vegetarians of the 1960s countercuisine. Flexitarianism allows foodies to eat meat and still have the moral high ground by avoiding industrially-raised livestock. Vegetarian meals are presented as delicious foodie choices, much like making a particular dish with "ethnic" spicing, but a meatless lifestyle is not significantly discussed, and never advocated. Conceptualizing meat-eating as just one food choice among many is in keeping with the consumer-ethics frame's emphasis on maximizing consumer choice. Exemplifying this flexitarian philosophy, one of our respondents, Norman Arbus, self-identified as a vegetarian, also noted that he eats fish and frequently cooks elaborate meat dishes for friends when entertaining.

Alongside the narrative about the contemporary deliciousness of vegetarian cuisine, the carnal delights of meat-eating are reconciled with ethical objectives, suggesting that gourmands need not forge a meatless diet in order to practice responsible food politics. One way this framing strategy works is by revealing some of the realities of animal slaughter, thereby making meat-eaters more accountable for their carnivorous diet. Visceral accounts of butchering—singeing "the hair from a pig's head with a blowtorch", cutting "the legs just so for prosciutto"—demonstrate how the meat-eating author keeps her eyes open to the realities of animal consumption, and thereby gains a "new respect for the meat on [the] plate" that eases the conscience, and even creates pleasure in the process (*Bon Appétit*, Feb. 2008, p. 112). The article continues: "I had seen these pigs in every manifestation: roaming around, dismembered, hanging in salt, and now on my plate. Although the *Lion King* song 'Circle of Life' floated through my mind, I had to admit that witnessing this cycle was satisfying and even—dare I say?— exciting" (*Bon Appétit*, Feb. 2008, p. 112). Another example is found in an article on the perspective of some leading chefs on animal slaughter:

> How far will chefs go to display their empathy and respect for the animals they cook? All the way, it seems, to the barnyard and the slaughterhouse. Leading chefs like Mr. [Jamie] Oliver, Dan Barber and David Burke seem to be wallowing in—and advertising—a new intimacy with the animals they cook. Not long ago, chefs got credit simply for knowing the breed of the pigs or chickens they served . . . Now, it seems, intimacy with the animals during their life—and preferably, their death—is required.
>
> (*New York Times*, 16 Jan. 2008, p. F1)

As further testimony that carnivorousness can be reconciled with ethical eating, meat-eating is almost exclusively framed as delicious in foodie discourse we studied. This reflects the dominance of an individual consumer-ethics frame that emphasizes consumerism's offering of choice and food pleasures. Harry Quinn described an interest in grass-fed meat, but this is overshadowed by his absolute devotion to the taste of meat, as witnessed by his food blog devoted entirely to meat. His interview includes loving tributes to dishes like pork roast braised in milk, bacon, a barbecue sauce that uses duck jelly, whole braised rabbit, and a roast chicken rubbed with salt and roasted on a high heat that "just comes out like chicken candy, and the skin, you know, pops when you cut it because the salt has dried the skin a bit and made it crispy, but the breast meat is still juicy, when you cut into it, it just runs with juice. It's amazing."

Food writing displays a similar devotion to the aesthetics of meat-eating. In an article titled "Why I'm Not a Vegetarian," one food writer describes her own conversion "from devoted vegetarian to meat-loving omnivore" (*Bon Appétit*, Feb. 2008, p. 6)—a shift that she admits was motivated entirely by hedonistic pursuits: "My reunion with meat had nothing to do with anemia or anything so easily explained away. It had to do with flavor and the hunger for it. It had to do with heat and muscle and fat, and the sparks that fly when they meet" (*Bon Appétit*, Feb. 2008, p. 77). This revelation is then tempered by the code of ethics she brings to each meal, described in the article's closing paragraph:

> For me, eating meat will never be a slapdash decision. I'm still picky about what crosses my fork: how it was raised, how it lived, how it died, and, of course, how it tastes. I do my best to buy meat raised humanely and by local producers . . . But every day I thank heaven for sausage, and for the dream it snuck in on.
>
> (*Bon Appétit*, Feb. 2008, p. 77)

Thus, while the personal struggle at the centre of the article could be perceived as evidence of a contradiction between ethical and gourmet objectives, the conclusion works to resolve this tension through a commitment to ethical meat production. Combine this information with facts regarding the nutritional benefits of these products—"meat from free-range chickens . . . has 21 percent less fat, 30 percent less saturated fat, 28 percent fewer calories, 50 percent more vitamin A, and 100 percent more omega-3s than regular chicken meat" (*Bon Appétit*, Feb. 2008, p. 44)—and humanely raised animal products provide a near seamless resolution between the demands of ethical responsibility and gourmet desire.

Within gourmet food discourse, humanely-raised meat is also cele-brated as a way to ease the foodie conscience. One headline exclaims:

"Love the environment as much as you love meat? Eat guilt-free with these eco-conscious recipes for pan-seared steaks, crispy cutlets, and bison meatballs" (*Bon Appétit*, Feb. 2008, p. 4). A restaurant review describes how "even the conscience is stroked, by the kitchen's exclusive use of cage-free eggs, organic flour, wild fish and grass-fed beef." The reviewer playfully hints at the presence of self-interest by remarking that "when two people plow through a whole roast chicken . . . it's nice to know that it was once free-roaming" (*New York Times*, Jan. 30 2008, p. F6). Such comments seem to indicate a degree of self-reflexivity within a form of food ethics that often presents the desire to ease the consumer conscience as a primary objective, if not *the* primary objective. There were other flickers of contradiction, and moments when citizenship concerns are evident, particularly when political and environmental principles take precedence over individual self-interest. While most of our foodie respondents stated that they altered their meat consumption for health reasons (Florence Nagy remarked, "I don't think that I don't eat meat for any ethical reason, I just don't think it digests well"), a handful of respondents demonstrated a sophisticated understanding of the complex ecological politics of meat-eating. Sarah Driscoll noted that "I mean I eat meat, but I pretty much only eat meat that I feel is raised ethically. And unfortunately I can't even include certified organic meat in that because a lot of certified organic meat is still factory feedlot. Um, so that's always a consideration of mine when I'm consuming animal protein and eggs or milk or cheese." Gillian Edelman described an engagement with meat-politics that involved a high degree of honesty, reflexivity, and willingness to forgo consumer choice:

> you know, meat is the big conundrum for me because I do buy grassfed beef but I don't always buy it. And I just in fact read last week that big article in the *New York Times* by Mark Bittman about the factory farm movement and stuff. And certainly I knew about that but it made me think once again, I've got to cut down on our meat consumption because that's good for global warming, and you know, I should stay away from this mass produced beef.

And so in fact this week, I cooked, it was harder, I cooked less meat in my . . . in what I cooked for my family, as a result of that article.

This quotation demonstrates how foodies engage with public sphere discussions around food politics, and suggests that the private realm of eating and food preparation is deeply integrated with public sphere spaces of food blogs and newspaper forums. Foodies may prepare food within their kitchens, but their ideas are situated within larger public sphere discussions of food's political implications.

In terms of food writing, the tension between environmental concerns and a desire for meat becomes visible in a *Saveur* book review of three cookbooks promoting vegetarian meals as an appealing addition to the average foodie's diet. After providing a generally favorable review of each of these texts, the author admits that she is skeptical of a depiction of vegetarian cooking as simply an opportunity to expand one's culinary repertoire, for she has gone through periods of committed vegetarianism that involved an element of sacrifice and restricted choice. She states:

> I'll confess that the purist in me—the one who endured the nut loaves and worse in the name of avoiding meat—finds something wishy-washy in all this big-tent vegetarianism. After all, long before the flexitarians decided to think twice about where their food came from, the unglamorous duty of raising consciousness about the environmental and ethical depredations of heedless carnivores fell upon a hard core of committed vegetarians and vegans . . . Maybe that's why I felt more than a little glee on reading *Veganomicon* . . . an exuberant and unapologetic vegan cookbook by Isa Chandra Moskowitz and Terry Hope Romero.
>
> (*Saveur*, Apr. 2008, p. 24)

In her critique of what she sees as "wishy-washy" vegetarianism, this reviewer challenges the consumer-ethics frame, and its postulation of a win-win world where no sacrifices are required to eat ethically. Nevertheless, this article was one of a handful of outliers within a gourmet food discourse that consistently promotes occasional vegetarian meals and humanely-raised meat consumption as ethical practices that unequivocally enhance the gourmet experience, as per the win-win message of a consumer-ethics frame. Thus, the popular foodie discourse we study generally presents gourmet food culture as entirely congruent with ethical meat-eating and optional vegetarian meals. While there is minimal space for critical engagement with the complexities of meat-eating, some of our respondents took up a political-eating frame in their approach to meat-eating, and saw their personal meat consumption not just as a source of pleasure, but as a link to environmental degradation, and an arena to challenge the prioritization of consumer choice.

Thematic Absences

The above sections document that important environmental issues are raised in foodie discourse—issues like local eating, sustainable food production, and humane animal husbandry. These issues signify the emergence of citizenship concerns into the gourmet foodscape, even though these concerns are predominantly framed through an indi-vidualized consumer-ethics frame advocating a win-win, eco-lifestyle approach to food politics where consumerism remains central. While the presence of these issues in the gourmet foodscape is significant, and suggests that the apolitical eating of an earlier gourmet era has lost legitimacy, other food politics issues are almost entirely occluded from the gourmet foodscape. The major discursive omission concerns issues of social justice, food security, national food sovereignty, and labor exploitation. These issues were virtually absent in our study of foodie discourse, aside from a few passing endorsements of "fair-trade," and some acknowledgment of labor issues in our interviews. This omission is significant, since the food system has been critiqued by social movement actors and organizations on multiple scales, from the local community food security projects to globally-scaled resistance to the WTO agricultural trade negotiations (see, for example, Raynolds, Murray and Wilkinson 2007; Wright and Middendorf 2008). While issues of social justice and inequality in the food system can only be briefly explored here, it is important to indicate the significance of their virtual absence in our sample of foodie discourse. Most significantly for our argument, the non-appearance of labor and inequality issues suggests the dominance of consumerism and an individualized consumer-ethics framing of food politics. Perhaps this is because "red" concerns like labor rights and global inequality are more difficult to frame as part of a win-win logic that makes these foods taste more delicious. The relative absence of labor issues also speaks to the marginality of a citizen approach to food politics where eaters tackle issues outside their own palates, like global equity and justice.

Activists and academics have critiqued the food system not only for its environmental failings, but also for its role in creating and reproducing class inequality at a national and global scale (Fold and Pritchard 2005). The global food system is tremendously inequitable, and contains at least three tiers—a top tier focused on post-Fordist niche markets (e.g., organic, quality, 'authentic' specialty foods), a second tier of 'mass' market foods, and a lower tier of 'surplus' food aid for those unable to access food through market mechanisms. Recent decades have seen the consolidation of a neo-liberal agro-economic model where countries in the Global South specialize in cash crop commodity production (e.g., avocados, strawberries) to generate export revenue, and where food security is defined through niche market specialization in global markets (McMichael 2000). The neo-liberal reorganization of agriculture is associated with a significant decline in peasant access to non-market subsistence land, which is in turn linked to problems of hunger, rural out-migration, poverty, and urban unemployment impacting the lives of millions in the Global South (Araghi 2000). While the availability of new exotic fruits and vegetables in northern food stores is routinely lauded in foodie discourse, accompanying social justice issues are not significantly discussed—even though this economic pattern is linked to global disparities of nutrition and health. In response to these global trade inequities, food sovereignty has emerged as an important demand of farmers organizations in the Global South, who argue that farmers should have the right to produce foods for subsistence purposes before focusing on exports for wealthy consumers. Global farmers' organizations, like Via Campesina, critique the neo-liberal paradigm of export orientation for its reliance on an unfair set of WTO trade rules that protects agriculture in the Global North, while leaving farmers in the Global South vulnerable to price fluctuations (Rosset 2006). A reliance on the global market for subsistence food needs was particularly troublesome with the 2007/8 global financial instability, and the associated global food crisis that saw both food prices and hunger levels increase dramatically (Bello 2008).

While issues of inequality in the global agricultural system were absent in our analysis of foodie discourse, there was some patchy evidence of global and national labor issues within foodie discourse that signify the presence of a secondary, but still significant, political-eating frame. While none of the magazines we studied included profiles of labor issues or the inequality embedded in global commodity chains, the March 2009 issue of *Gourmet* did feature an exposé of the appalling conditions of tomato workers in Florida, suggesting that journalistic coverage of labor issues may increase in future years as food politics becomes a more established element in the gourmet foodscape. Also, a few of our interviewees, like Kelly Jones, a clergywoman from upstate New York, mentioned that they looked for fair-trade products, like coffee and sugar. Nathaniel Snider reported that just that morning he had gone out of his way to buy fair-trade, certified organic sugar because "the sugar industry has some pretty dark sides to it." Kevin D'Angelo mentioned that although he primarily buys local products, he has given a great deal of thought to the political impact of his coffee habit, and noted that "the philosopher Peter Singer has made a case that people should still buy foods that are fair-trade that come from distances because it's providing an economic benefit to those other areas." On the subject of domestic labor issues, one respondent, Sarah Driscoll, stated her preference for produce from a particular company because "it's one of the only farms in the country that have benefits to their farm workers, and so ethically speaking, ya, you're paying more but there's a decision there to take care of the people who are growing your food."

In addition to the minimal discussion of the human implications of global supply chains, the issue of a stratified food system is occluded within foodie discussions of exotic food adventuring. As explored in Chapter 3, exotic foods are highly valued in foodie discourse, but never significantly questioned, even though this style of eating frequently involves a process of ethnic Othering that normalizes the affluence and geopolitical privilege of affluent and globally mobile elites. While eating locally is presented as a common-sense norm for foodies to aspire to, the world is simultaneously presented as a tasting menu that is ripe for the taking. Many of our foodie interviewees speak glowingly about the foods they consumed in different countries, and how foreign travel has changed their diet for the better. This speaks to the popular, but problematic, phenomenon of "foodie travel." In terms of food journalism, foodie travel is highly prominent, and never problematized. For example, *Gourmet*'s special issue on "Cooking Vacations" entices readers with "a collection of truly amazing places to visit," that include a range of experiences from "a luxurious week in a country villa with a teacher all your own," or the opportunity to "camp in the jungle and learn exotic tropical dishes" (*Gourmet*, May 2008, p. 8). While enticing, the extravagant journeys described throughout this issue are divorced from global relations of power, and areas with limited economic and social infrastructure are presented to the intrepid foodie as a form of adventure: "Little did we realize just how far off the tourist track we would go, to villages where gringos are an anomaly, banks don't exist, and hotels are bare-bones basic" (*Gourmet*, May 2008, p. 170). Lest we give the impression that such examples were confined to this special issue of *Gourmet*, it is worth noting that we found similar examples in the "Travel Issue" of *Bon Appétit*, in which food writers "globe-trot far and wide to find the best places to eat, drink, and cook, from Parisian bistros to Malaysian street vendors" (May 2008, p. 8). Similarly, the "Special Road Trip Issue" of *Saveur* pronounces: "We live in a day and age when gastro-tourism is one of the fastest growing segments of the travel industry and where cooking shows are abandoning kitchen studios in favor of formats that take viewers on the road in search of great food" (June 2008, p. 28). Given that the need to reduce carbon emissions is frequently cited within calls for more localized food consumption, it is notable that environmental issues are entirely absent from this celebration of "culinary-themed travel tales" (ibid.).

Foodies Speak: Balancing Pleasure and Politics

In this section we draw from our interviews with foodies to build on our description of foodie discourse, and describe some of the nuances of food politics on the ground. In our interviews, we found that foodie perspectives could be characterized as predominantly fitting into each of the three frames: the individual consumer-ethics frame, the political-eating frame, and an apolitical-eating frame. While we categorize our respondents' responses as fitting mainly within one of the three frames, in many instances we observe that a single person can articulate multiple frames. This makes sense, since frames offer competing explanations that shape understanding of specific issues, and are not comprehensive idea packages that orient all elements of social life. One particular frame might guide a foodie's understanding in one area of the lifeworld (e.g., deciding whether or not to purchase organic produce for one's children), but not another (e.g., deciding where to make a dinner reservation for a special occasion). While the different food political frames can coexist, by and large, we find that the individual consumer-ethics frame is the frame most consistently espoused by our foodie respondents. An overall disposition of apolitical eating was next most common, and a political-eating frame was least common. Our sampling method and sample size do not allow us to generalize about the relative frequencies of these frames to other foodies. In addition, we specifically asked questions about ethics and politics, and so we are not surprised to see these frames more prominently in our interviews than was the case in food journalism. In general, each framing of food politics displays a high degree of nuance in the interview data, which we describe below.

To begin, it is important to note that even though most respondents drew on the win-win frame of consumer ethics, few foodies presented ethical concerns as *fully* compatible with their gourmet preferences. That is, many of those respondents whose overall orientation was predominantly situated within a consumer-ethics frame described their own ethical orientation with a degree of nuance and complexity often lacking in the magazines and newspapers we surveyed. For some, this complexity arose from an awareness of privileging certain ethical concerns over others, and the persistence of classic consumer concerns like price, convenience, and taste. Fern Osborne, a 30-year-old living in Portland, admitted that she's "pretty conscious about the ethical issues in terms of the way that animals are being treated, but I'm not always so, I mean I'm aware of, but I don't think I'm always making my buying decisions based on environmental impact." It is also noteworthy that the respondents who are most dedicated to buying locally-produced foods acknowledge that this practice is made possible in large part due to their geographical location, where, as Trish Lincoln puts it, they are "lucky to have a lot of options for local ingredients." Therefore, even though most foodies articulate their sense of ethics in terms of green commodity consumption, some participants supplement the win-win consumer-ethics framing with a degree of reflexivity that is not nearly as prevalent in the magazine and newspaper data.

Related to the consumer-ethics frame, another important nuance that arose in our conversations with foodies was the importance of retailers in foodie politics, dispelling the atomistic notion that food politics primarily involves consumers. Commodity choices were seen as an important means to make social and ecological change in the food system, but great weight was given to market retailers to enable and influence these decisions, further suggesting that private-sector actors are key players in the constitution of food politics discourse (Johnston 2008). Several participants suggested that ethical food decisions can be effectively dealt with by entrusting ethical responsibility to market retailers. Consumer choice of shopping venues—whether they be farmers' markets, food co-ops or natural food supermarkets like Whole Foods Market—was thought to ease the ethical burden, and lessen the need for consumer reflexivity about individual products. Fred Huntington, a 44-year-old living in California, asserted that "most of the places we shop don't offer anything that I can think of that would violate any sort of ethics." While a few respondents criticized Whole Foods Market for a predatory growth strategy that drives small companies out of business, it was simultaneously praised as providing more local and organic options. Theresa Callebaut spoke about how "shopping at Whole Foods takes some of that worry away about whether it's ethical or not ethical." In the following excerpt, Dennis Nolan elaborates on this idea in the context of his local food co-op, and articulates the win-win logic of the ethical consumer frame:

> One of the reasons that I do go to the co-op that I go to is, is that they are quite stringent about what they sell. So as a result I end up paying between, probably about a twenty percent premium across the board. And in return for that, basically I get several things back. One of them is that most of my ethical concerns I don't have to worry too hard about because they're very strongly interested in promoting local and organic produce, both of which are important to me . . . but the other aspect of that is that . . . the food does tend to taste better.

While the consumer-ethics frame dominated our interview data, there were other instances in our data, and certain individuals who talked about food politics in much greater depth, acknowledged contradictions in great detail, spoke about collective struggles/issues around food, and were willing to significantly redefine and even sacrifice consumer pleasures for the sake of collective betterment. These respondents, like Karen Weiss, insisted that "food is very political," and expressed a deep engagement with food politics that extended well beyond the eco-lifestyle politics focused on consumer benefits. Instead, the environmental issues around food were framed as much broader than the scale of individual bodies and taste preferences. Kevin D'Angelo criticized industrial food on precisely these grounds:

> Industrial food is processed using a lot of fertilizer, a lot of pesticides, a lot of herbicides, and there are side effects to those chemicals not only to the farmlands where they're applied, but also to the run offs to the streams and rivers and ocean, and also to their production. I look at organic agriculture as being less destructive to the environment than industrial agriculture. So where possible I buy organic products.

Respondents who draw heavily on the political-eating frame tend to view their own relationship to food as defined in large part by their political commitments to environmental and social concerns, and a handful of participants even identify as "ethicureans."[64] Foodies articulating a political-eating frame tend to gather information from a variety of sources beyond mainstream media including blogs (many of them are bloggers themselves), academic discussions, and conversations with other politically-motivated foodies at their local food co-op. Foodies oriented towards the political-eating frame embrace the contradictions of food politics, and discuss complex issues such as the tension between the goals of local and organic, the contradictions of "big organic," and the exploitative practices of large corporations who are tapping into "eco" lifestyles as a superficial marketing niche. Sarah Driscoll expressed a desire to "strengthen what the term 'organic' means" because it is "increasingly becoming a vehicle for higher profit." In another interview, Michelle Quinlan provided an extensive history of the organic movement in California, explaining that the 1990 California Organic Food Act was quite different in its original form than when it emerged from the House and Senate. In her view, the outcome of this process is that "a lot is lost on the general public about what organic means." Strategies for dealing with food politics contradictions are often described in highly-reflexive terms, which suggest that this style of political eating is not about a codified set of rules for consumption, but a process of thinking and engaging with the food system. For instance, Nathaniel Snider explained that he is

> prioritizing local over organic because I think it's important, especially in California where we have this rampant urbanization and the pressure on the land, I think it's important to support the local food system, and the farmers who live within a hundred or two hundred miles . . . But then I will also buy organic generally when given the choice because I like how it has a lower impact on nature and on the workers.

While the political-eating frame was a significant presence within our interviews, there was even more evidence of apolitical eating—instances where eating well is the dominant motivation, and where political and environmental commitments are completely absent from the discussion. These respondents expressed no concern about the ethical or political dimensions of their food choices, and offered responses such as Fiona Callworth's: "Am I ethical? No, probably not. I'd have to say that I'm not ethical. [Laughs.] You know, a chicken's a chicken. [Laughs.]" When asked if buying organic is important, Faye Taggart replied that the cost factor is a turn-off:

> I think for the most part [organics] is a rip-off. However, I know that the generation below me worships it, and you know, I respect their choices and they may turn out to be correct. But non-organic milk hasn't killed me yet and it probably isn't likely to do so. So, to me, there's no, it's extra price for something that is not of value to me.

Foodies who displayed an apolitical approach to eating saw the sensual experience and collective sharing of food as preeminent factors, even when these goals led them to purchase organic foods. For instance, when asked if ethical concerns influenced her food shopping, Faye Taggart responded: "I'm not very good about that . . . But I have been thinking about switching over to Bell and Evan's chicken because I've decided that the reason I don't like chicken very much is because it doesn't taste like anything. So any time I buy an actually organic, properly grown chicken, it tastes like chicken." A less common construction of apolitical eating involved acknowledging ethical issues, but then rejecting them as untenable. Catherine Quilter described her own thought process as follows: "I mean here's the thing, the ethical concerns are there. I have them, and they live in me as a kind of guilty conscience thing . . . but I'm not, I'm too interested in my pleasure to actually impose them on myself." She continued:

> [I]n a perfect world we would be eating seasonally and we wouldn't be shipping food and we would go to the green market and we would only eat organic. I mean, I feel guilty that I don't worry

more about organic versus inorganic. And I think that the guilt . . .
that in the perfect—but it's very difficult to resist raspberries in the
middle of the winter! It's very difficult to, you know, the stuff is
there and I just am too, you know, I'm not going to put the values
ahead of my own pleasure, I'm afraid.

While this foodie's guilt is trumped by her desire for pleasure, this excerpt
illuminates awareness of the underlying tensions that are obscured by the
more popular frame of consumer ethics. Rejecting the win-win assumption of the ethical-consumption frame, this foodie suggests that truly
embracing the ethical ideals of local, seasonal and organic foods would
demand a level of sacrifice she is not willing to make.

Conclusion

Food's political content certainly has made an entry into foodie
discourse—just as Michael Pollan's writing makes an appearance on
bookstore shelves once devoted exclusively to cookbooks and travel
writing. What and how we eat clearly has political implications, particularly since food not only embodies natural resources, but is the by-
product of numerous labor processes that transform seeds and dirt into
elegant creations like duck confit and butternut squash risotto. However,
in our reading of food discourse and our conversations with foodies, for
the most part food is not obviously framed, discussed, or understood in
an explicitly political way. In most instances, food is appealing because
it is delicious, interesting, and worthy of eating. While foodie politics is
an important recent development that integrates issues of the 1960s and
1970s countercuisine with traditional gourmet concerns, it is equally
important to remember that this is not the dominant way food is understood or discussed in foodie discourse.

When food's political implications *are* discussed, the ideology of
consumerism is a dominant influence, along with its emphasis on the
win-win nature of food shopping and eating. When food politics is
conceptualized this way, we can eat delicious local seasonal fresh food
and save the environment at the same time, leaving social justice issues
like poverty and food security relatively marginalized or altogether

absent from the foodscape. This vision of food politics promises easy, market-based solutions where consumers "vote" with their dollar, and where the industrial food system can be readily reorganized to achieve greater sustainability. This framing builds on a neo-liberal vision of environmental change that relies on market mechanisms, and suggests ultimate faith in enlightened, educated consumers' self-interest as the primary motor of social change. Consumer choice is prescribed as an easy and efficient solution to address market failures like sustainability, leaving public sector solutions or regulation of market actors unmentioned and underemphasized. In essence, the market—in the form of educated and enlightened consumer choices—is presented as a solution for market failures, and the suggested focus is on how individuals can ultimately make the "right" choice at the restaurant or grocery store. When faced with the plethora of political concerns that surround our food—and the feelings of guilt that accompany them—the proposed "solution" is to become "an informed consumer" (*San Francisco Chronicle*, 28 May 2008, p. F6).

The ideology of consumerism can be contrasted with a citizen-based approach where food issues like sustainability are debated through collective processes of reflexivity. When a citizenship ideology prevails, food is discussed in a way that involves actors beyond individual consumers and their culinary pursuits. Citizen-based food politics are not dominant actors in the gourmet foodscape, but they do exist. They include social movements that lobby for institutional change in the food system, food bloggers who encourage people to restrict their long-distance food consumption, and food writers who challenge the inequities embedded within global commodity chains for tomatoes. Citizen-based food politics may appreciate and comment on the deliciousness of food, but they also address issues like how the state must act to promote food security, or how to develop legislation that protects food workers.

The difficult systemic challenge of reorganizing the globalized industrial food system raises the question of the role of the individual foodie—somebody who might be understandably overwhelmed by the complexities of contemporary food politics, and more worried about getting dinner on the table. While the occasional purchase at the farmers' market can certainly produce delicious food and likely offers some reduction in greenhouse gas emissions, we think it is important to point out that a wholesale commitment to food politics will likely involve some taste compromises—as with some of the monotonous and unappealing meals described by Smith and MacKinnon in their narrative of eating within a 100-mile (160-km) radius for one year (2007). This is not to say that a citizen framing of foodie-ism eliminates all pleasure. In the *100 Mile Diet*, many of Smith and MacKinnon's meals are described as wonderfully delicious, and would likely appeal to many foodies. Instead, our point here is that citizenship demands that consumer pleasures be reevaluated, redefined, and even restricted to keep them congruent with larger political objectives. This culinary tendency is evident in the foodie world and was seen in our conversations with foodies, but it can be a hard sell when a cornucopia of delicious food is front and center, appealing less to the conscience and more to the stomach.

5

CLASS AND ITS ABSENCE

In this chapter we examine how issues of status distinctions and inequality play out in the gourmet foodscape. Like the broader American discourse surrounding wealth and inequality, the foodie discourse around wealth and class is fraught with contradictions—particularly the contradiction between an overt democratic populism that seeks solidarity with others, and a more covert but perpetual drive to achieve social distance and distinction. In the foodie world, a conversation about cooking with truffles may coexist with an earnest discussion on street food in Juárez, Mexico, which in turn can be accompanied with an in-depth knowledge of food in Spain's most celebrated fine dining restaurant, El Bulli. The term, "foodie" itself contains these contradictions, and is both rejected and embraced for similar reasons—not wanting to appear snobbish.[65]

Not only do foodies attempt to distance themselves from snobbery, but the discourse continually reaffirms an interest in non-elite foods. In our reading of foodie sources like magazines and websites, we are continually surprised by how a fascination with wealth and privilege coexists along with interest in the authentic and exotic foods of the poor—both the American poor and the global poor. Foodies may enjoy elite foods like caviar, truffles, and champagne, but they also passionately seek out roadside huts and "hole-in-the-wall" ethnic restaurants. While class inequality is in the fore of the gourmet foodscape, it is typically not discussed explicitly. To address its ambiguous status, in the first part of this chapter we look at food writing to investigate how inequality is framed for a foodie audience. Understanding the framing of inequality in foodie discourse can help us better understand how foodies balance goals of democracy (being in solidarity with other food lovers) and distinction (holding oneself separate and apart from other eaters). This is a particularly relevant point since a long history of media research shows that media framing of issues both reflects and influences how audiences think about these issues.

In the second half of the chapter, we draw from our interview data to address how foodies balance democracy and distinction, and how they explain their food preferences relative to other types of food and other social classes. These explanations can help us understand how foodie preferences and consumption habits operate as part of a high-status cultural consumption strategy—even while many foodies reject snobbery and decry snooty dining experiences. As discussed in Chapter 1, the sociology of culture has developed a body of research on the topic of "omnivorousness," a term that refers to the contemporary tastes of people with generally high levels of education and also often income. Omnivorousness stands in contrast to the traditional pairing of high socio-economic status with tastes for exclusively highbrow culture, and the pairing of low socio-economic status with tastes for exclusively lowbrow culture. Over the last several decades, sociologists have used survey research to document how people with high levels of education and income tend to have cultural tastes that sample selectively from both traditionally highbrow and traditionally lowbrow genres. For example, the classical music snob of the past century has been replaced by a cultural world where high-status people prefer particular pieces of music and artists from an array of genres, including rock, jazz, rap, and classical music. Based on our interviews, we find that foodies are clearly omnivores: they prefer traditionally highbrow food—i.e. French or haute cuisine—as well as foods from cuisines that traditionally were not consumed by high-status Americans, such as Mexican, Thai, and Indian. In fact, foodies report that they are open to selecting good foods from every tradition. Our interview data include foodies' explanations for their preferences, and these justifications provide a clear window on the question of what the omnivorous consumption pattern means to foodies, and how it can be used to generate a high-status identity.

The overall aim of this chapter is to paint a picture of how food plays a role creating and maintaining status distinctions in the contemporary United States. Of course we acknowledge that foodies' tastes are multifaceted and influenced by many factors other than status, such as geographic location, age, and ethnic background. While foodies are clearly motivated by concerns other than status, at the same time, class and status are inextricably woven into the gourmet foodscape. Class inequality is a relatively invisible phenomenon in the foodie world, yet all of this eating (and talk of eating) takes place in a world marked by tremendous socio-economic disparity—both globally, and within the boundaries of the United States. Our goal here is to describe how food-ies' tastes reflect a concern with class and status that is both shaped and constrained by broader cultural values and beliefs about snobbery, status, and solidarity.

Frames in Gourmet Food Writing: Obscuring Inequality

While gourmet food writing is interested in the foods eaten by poor people, the issues of social inequality and poverty are portrayed as rela-tively unproblematic. To understand this phenomenon, we draw from the scholarly literature that examines how social problems, and the problems of social inequality and poverty in particular, are framed in the media. Framing studies look at messages in the media in order to address questions such as what counts as a problem, what is the nature of a problem, who is responsible for a problem, and how to solve a problem. In this section we employ content analysis to investigate how poverty and inequality are framed in food writing. Our goal is to compare our findings with the findings of prior research on the framing of poverty and inequality in the news.[66]

Although gourmet food writing does not aim to analyze poverty and wealth, food writers can still encourage a particular understanding of these issues without treating them directly. There is ample opportunity for frames of poverty and wealth to emerge because gourmet food magazines contain many lengthy articles in which the production and consumption of food are discussed, including details about who is eating and making food and in which social locations. Moreover, framing can emerge through assumptions and omissions that are involved in the presentation of wealthy or impoverished food scenes and food producers and consumers. Finally, we might expect that because food writing is just as much a cultural product as the food it covers, and so has aesthetic aims of its own, it would not be fruitful to investigate social problems in this discourse. We would argue, however, that it is precisely in cultural and aestheticized texts such as these that sociologists can gain valuable insight about issues of fundamental sociological concern, such as inequality. Indeed a great vein of sociological literature rests on this (neo-Marxist) insight, informing scores of studies in the sociology of culture and cultural studies.

Although there are many elements of a frame that can be analyzed (Altheide 1997: 651–652; Benford and Snow 2000), two of the most important factors involved are the causes of a social condition (i.e., why are people poor and why are people wealthy) and who is involved in the social condition (i.e., who is poor or wealthy) (Entman 1993). When a cause is attributed to a condition, we can also make inferences about whether an issue is being presented as a serious social problem and the nature of that problem. In the case of poverty, when poor people or impoverished locations are the subject of an article, the following questions arise. What kinds of claims are made for why this poverty exists? Are the causes personal or societal? Are people responsible for their own poverty, or does poverty result from structural conditions in the social environment, such as the shifting of factory work out of the United States to developing countries or recessionary periods of the domestic economy? Similarly, trends in presenting certain groups as poor can indicate that poverty is being framed as truly an issue for, say, particular ethnic groups or age groups.

Prior research on the framing of poverty has focused on the news media, and has found that poverty is framed predominantly as a problem for African-Americans and the working-age unemployed (Gilens 1999). Additionally, poverty is framed as caused by the actions of individuals who do not do what is necessary to ensure they have good jobs. By focusing on poor people's roles in creating their own poverty, rather than the role of broader economic factors, news stories tend to imply that the solution to poverty is in the hands of individuals who need to pull themselves out of poverty (Iyengar 1990). Additionally, poverty in the news media is framed disproportionately as a problem for particular groups in particular social settings. The overall impression from news media is that poverty is disproportionately a problem for "undeserving" African-Americans (Gilens 1999).[67]

The depiction of poverty in food writing strikes a different tone, and raises questions that cannot be fully answered by previous studies on the news media. Unlike in research on news media, the vast majority of instances of poverty in gourmet food writing are presented without *any* explicit or implicit suggestions for causes of that poverty; both structural (at the level of the city, region, or nation) and personal explanations are lacking, suggesting that poverty is naturalized and normalized in gourmet writing. In those very few instances when a cause is suggested, it is most often structural, as suggested by the following example: "By the time of the Industrial Revolution . . . inexpensive wool from Britain had all but wiped out [the village's] reason for being. Left without a livelihood, the villagers set off for Belgium, Argentina, Australia, and, especially, Canada" (*Gourmet*, Sept. 2004, p. 139).

Because explanations for poverty (individual or structural) are relatively rare, poverty in gourmet food writing is most often presented as a characteristic of an environment or a location, rather than attached to identifiable individuals. Poverty is simply part of a place. For example, descriptions of run-down buildings or "destitute" rural regions where food is produced or consumed indicate that poverty is present without labeling groups or individuals as "poor," leaving the identities of the poor mostly unspecified. A good example comes from an article that says of its setting, the "region cannot afford good schools and healthcare" (*Saveur*, Nov. 2004, p. 97); a state of poverty is indicated, but it is not linked to individuals identified in the article, nor is it further explored since the focus of the article is on the delicious foods of rural Greece.

The lack of an explanation for poverty goes hand in hand with a vague description of who is poor. In this way we read in various articles of food that is available in "a Depression-era, ramshackle area," in "a backdrop of rusted farm machinery and walls that aren't perpendicular to the ground," in a "beat-up" tavern where the manager lives next door in "a trailer," in towns that are "dinky and depressed, with failing bakeries," or in "a cinder-block garage hidden from easy view."

Also in contrast to findings from the news, poverty in food journalism is not disproportionately associated with African-Americans or Africans. Similarly, no mention is made of unemployment; instead, when poverty is linked to identifiable people, they are usually employed—as the cooks and servers featured in the article. There is no replication in these data of the findings from news media that poverty is framed as a problem of the "undeserving," to use the term of prior research (Gilens 1996). Clearly, the frames that can describe how poverty is portrayed in the news cannot describe how poverty is portrayed in gourmet food writing. Instead, poverty is framed as a vague and almost abstract condition that requires no serious analysis, but is instead a backdrop for delicious food.

How does an analysis of the framing of wealth compare to the framing of poverty? Are the causes of wealth and the identities of the wealthy described in food writing? Prior research does not indicate what to expect about the framing of wealth. It could be the case that, like poverty, wealth is framed as having personal causes. Or wealth could be framed as an outcome with structural origins. Likewise, wealth could be linked to people who are "deserving" (employed) or could be linked to the "undeserving" (unemployed). A close reading of gourmet food writing shows that, as with poverty, wealth is also most often depicted as without a cause. However, in those few cases where a cause is given, the most common cause is inheritance. When there is any explanation given, wealthy people who appear in gourmet food writing are most frequently explained to be members of families of long-standing wealth. Similar to the case for poverty, though, wealth is more frequently a characteristic of the environment than of people, though not quite as frequently detached from identifiable groups and individuals as is poverty. As with poverty, the rarity of causal explanations for wealth goes hand-in-hand with vague descriptions of who is wealthy. And so we read of restaurants in "high-end residential" areas, that serve "the most expensive meals in New York City," and where patrons are "bourgeois" and "wear fur." We also read of food that appeals to "moneyed" urbanites, that is produced in a "paradisiacal enclave of billionaires' thatched cottages," or on a "luxurious" cruise with "suites bigger than many apartments." In general, we do not read details about who the moneyed urbanites, billionaires, and luxury cruise tourists are, nor about the sources of their wealth.[68]

It is interesting to note that race is identifiable or inferable in only a minority of cases, but when it is identifiable, wealth is a characteristic mostly of Europeans or white Americans. There is a contrast with the framing of poverty insofar as race is signaled more frequently with instances of wealth. However, for both poverty and wealth, race is predominantly left unmentioned, largely because wealth is not associated with identifiable individuals in these articles. In addition, the employment status of the wealthy was indicated in only a minority of cases, and it is difficult to draw conclusions about differences with poverty in terms of the "deservingness" of the wealthy. In sum, we find that poverty and wealth are omnipresent, but their causes are largely left unspecified as is a detailed understanding of the individuals or groups in these socio-economic categories. This raises questions about how poverty and wealth are framed in food writing and the implications of the framing, a topic to which we will now turn.

Three Frames for Maintaining Classlessness

Given that the frames found in prior research on journalism appear infrequently in gourmet food writing, we need to identify new frames to better understand how poverty and wealth are framed. To do so, we provide a qualitative reading of the presentation of wealth and poverty, and particularly of *inequality*, in gourmet food writing. We identify these frames interpretively to draw out an understanding of the implications for the portrayal of wealth and poverty. Gourmet food writing does send some messages about wealth, and our method worked to make these covert messages more explicit.

We find that when issues of wealth, poverty, and inequality arise in food writing, three frames are used to obfuscate social inequality. Of the three frames, one romanticizes poverty, another presents poverty as no worse a situation than wealth, and a final frame makes extreme forms of wealth and privilege seem absolutely ordinary. Together, these three frames encourage an understanding of the foodscape as a classless terrain—a place where inequality is insignificant, unimportant, and even irrelevant. This finding sheds light on the conundrum of the United States being a highly inequitable yet relatively 'classless' society,[69] and also speaks to our overall thesis that foodie culture represents a tension between competing ideologies of democratic solidarity on the one hand, and social distinction and exclusion on the other hand. Our analysis of food writing suggests that at least one element of foodie culture is relatively blind to inequality, which makes it easier to support a worldview that overtly proclaims democratic solidarity with the world's rich and poor eaters, while covertly continuing to make and sustain distinctions based on wealth and status. These issues are explored below through a description of the three frames: (1) romanticization of poverty; (2) equality of inequality; (3) ordinariness of privilege.

Romanticization of Poverty

Food writers travel to United States metropolitan centers, to rural America, and to a great number of foreign locations in both the developed and developing world. There are many occasions when articles are set within impoverished environments and involve impoverished people, both domestically and abroad.

Rather than discussing poverty as a social problem, however, there are many occasions when food writers idealize and romanticize poverty.[70] They take readers into environments of squalor and despair and write enthusiastically about them in a way that consistently ignores any negative or harmful aspects of poverty. The enthusiasm concerns the seeming advantages of impoverished environments, creating an idea of the deliciousness of poverty without acknowledging socio-economic hardship. Take, for instance, the following description:

The best food in Arkansas is served in the worst-looking restaurants. If you have a sense of adventure and an appetite for down-home meals, you will eat majestically in derelict shacks by the side of the road and tumbledown buildings on the wrong side of town . . . Craig's Barb-B-Que [is] a shack so unrepentantly dumpy that you've got to love it.

(*Gourmet*, Aug. 2004, p. 32)

The subtext of this description is that food should be valorized *because of* rather than *in spite of* the impoverished conditions in which it is produced and consumed. Other times that message is delivered more explicitly, such as in an article about a restaurant called "Chez Shack" in Vieques, Puerto Rico, that is "an unlikely setting for some sensational food." Why unlikely? Because the food "all had been cooked by a bandana-clad guy in an open-air space the size of a phone booth. Could this get any better?" (*Food & Wine*, November 2004, p. 40). Through a romanticization frame, the difficulties of working in a tiny space, which would entail taking the perspective of the worker, are not selected for salience, but the ambiance of the authentic experience is. In another case, readers are invited to delight in "a scenario that titillates critics and cuisine hounds: a dumpy restaurant off the radar that serves mind-blowing meals." Here, the delicious news is that "the best Chinese food in town" can be found in a "dining room [that] has all the appeal of a homeless shelter" (*San Francisco Chronicle*, 6 Feb. 2008, p. F7). The restaurant review reads much like a dare, suggesting that only the intrepid foodie who is brave enough to venture into such dismal dining quarters is worthy of the delicious food that awaits.

Time and time again, travel articles describe impoverished people and locales as producing food that is all the more delicious for its connection to poverty. A common theme in these romanticized portrayals is their rural or foreign settings—in the remote countryside or in the developing world, it appears easier to imagine poverty as a happy state than in a depressed metropolitan setting, where the food of the poor is most often ignored. A particularly salient example can be found in an article describing the author's quest to find the hottest pepper in the world—the raja pepper grown in northeastern India. The article includes a picture of a farmer's family sitting on the dirt floor of their home and paints a glowing portrayal of rural life: "[M]eats and chilies cure in smoke-blackened huts" in a place "where life has changed little since ancestral times" (*Gourmet*, August 2008, p. 56). The impoverished conditions of the region are brought to the fore in this travel writing—it is mentioned that the pepper harvest will provide the farmer with $400–$750 for the entire year—but the people are straightforwardly presented as content and proud of the pepper they grow and cook with. There is no effort to provide the reader with the farmers' perspective on their income, nor to provide a description of how the pepper harvest may contribute to, or relate to, rural impoverishment. Instead, we learn only that this most amazing pepper is to be found amongst extreme poverty.

The uncritical embrace of poverty as the source of good food can result in the fetishization of the poor. A well-known Turkish chef expounds on this philosophy with an unusual candour:

> I am interested in the food of real people . . . I get very excited when I discover new poor people's dishes, because I believe only poor people can create good food. If a man has money, he can buy anything, but a person who has nothing must create beauty from within.
>
> (*Food & Wine*, July 2004, p. 177)

Clearly, it is just as simplistic to categorically state that only poor people can create good food as it is to say that only rich people can create good food. Yet by romanticizing poverty as producing *better* food than wealth, gourmet food writers are able to create a sense of solidarity with the poor that obscures their own—and the reader's—economic and cultural capital and its relationship to gourmet food culture. By declaring poor food to be better than the food of elites, privileged commentators appear democratic, at the same time they remain safely distant in a privileged cultural position as the arbitrators of good taste. By providing little or no details on the less delicious components of the lives of the poor, both within the United States and throughout the developing world, gourmet food writing frames poverty as removed from harsh political, economic, or social realities. Romanticizing poverty elides its unpleasant problematic nature in favor of an unproblematic sense of classlessness.

Without the quantification of frames, the reader might wonder about the prevalence of a competing frame that presents poverty as a social problem. It is worth noting that throughout our entire sample of gourmet food writing, a competing frame where poverty was presented in the opposite manner, as distinctly unpleasant or undesirable, was almost entirely absent.[71]

The Equality of Inequality

While romanticizing poverty turns a negative into a positive, this second frame asserts that poverty and wealth are cultural equals, close together rather than far apart. To accomplish this, gourmet food writing frequently employs legitimizing contrasts that situate social and cultural elites alongside marginalized sub-cultures/ethnicities and/or working-class people. While this strategy undoubtedly reflects a social distaste for overt social snobbery and acceptance of certain democratic principles, it is not clear that this is simply a case of culinary democratization where *all* food cultures are rendered equal (see Johnston and Baumann 2007). Instead, we contend that legitimizing contrasts work to render references to wealth and poverty more palatable by pairing them semiotically, creating a kind of faux populism that suggests a democratic connection across classes, while minimizing the existence of socio-economic inequality. The "equality of inequality" frame implies that diverse class constituencies are essentially similar, and deliberately underplays the vast economic distances that separate the food realms of the wealthy and the poor. In a profile of street food in India, one of the characters jokes that the sweet milk foam produced by the nameless "*daulat ki chaat* man" is "the inspiration for Ferran Adrià," the renowned molecular gastronomy chef behind El Bulli in Spain (a renowned pilgrimage place for foodies across borders) (*Food & Wine*, July 2006, p. 122). Sometimes the rich and poor are said to share an affinity for one prized ingredient, such as White Lily All Purpose Flour, which is a staple in "biscuit dives and high-end Southern restaurants like

Watershed in Atlanta and Blackberry Farm outside Knoxville" (*New York Times*, 18 June 2008, p. F1). Another example can be found in an article about a family-run catering company that began with the following question:

> What do Bill Clinton, George W. Bush, rap mogul Sean "P. Diddy" Combs, and socialite Martina Rust Connor all have in common with a tractor repairman from the Mississippi Delta? The answer is Van Wyck and Van Wyck; a mother-son event-planning team with big name clients and surprisingly deep country roots.
> (*Food & Wine*, May 2004, p. 144)

In this article, the genteel, Southern family is portrayed as awash in cultural and economic capital through references to Ivy League schooling and multiple celebrity connections. The wedding of the mother and father, we are told, was noted in *Town & Country* magazine as one of the best of the 20th century. In this context, their elite status is clearly referenced, but rendered safely apolitical since the reader is reassured that the family associates with a tractor repairman from the Mississippi Delta. Only later in the article is it revealed that the tractor repairman does not hire the caterers for his gatherings, as is implied in the opening. Rather, the caterers hire *him* to repair their equipment.

Other examples of legitimizing contrasts are frequently found in the description of expensive restaurants. To effectively distance themselves from the stereotype of the snob who is stuck in the antiquated separation of highbrow from lowbrow culture, gourmet food writers are eager to explain expensive restaurants as freed from the arbitrarily rule-bound norms of a snobbish culinary past. To do this they juxtapose the elite status of the restaurant with the casual behavior expected of staff and diners:

> Meals at [The French Laundry and Per Se] are just playful enough to take the edge off the fine dining experience. With a fairly relaxed dress code and a staff that treats all diners like VIPs, the chef and his front-of-the-house team have forged two *truly populist* four-star

restaurants, just as likely to attract middle-manager gourmands on an annual splurge as regulars from neighboring Ducasse.

(*Gourmet*, Nov. 2004, p. 48; emphasis ours)

Although there is little plausibility to the claim that a "populist" restaurant is one where a middle-class patron must carefully save for an annual visit, by characterizing these restaurants as relaxed about status hierarchies, the elite associations presented in this high-end culinary field are underplayed, and legitimized as suitable for a democratic age. These faux-populist themes are also evident in an article on an expensive resort ranch in Colorado which is described as "one of the most luxurious and low-key destinations in the West," a description that is tempered by the fact that the guests "indulge in a flannel-pajamas-and-jeans kind of luxury" (*Food & Wine*, August 2004, p. 112). In a profile of a historic "old-boys" restaurant in Manhattan, the author unintentionally summarizes the contradictions of this frame:

> There's something *wildly incongruous* about the Bar Room at '21,' surely the least formal place in the city to require dinner guests to show up in jacket and tie. The red-checked tablecloths and rec-room décor put you more in mind of a glorified pub than of a luxe venue for seared foie gras with shaved truffles and English peas. In fact it's just this playful collision of highbrow and low, along with the air of Ivy League mischief that clings to the walls, that lends '21' so much of its enduring allure. In this rich man's playground, under a ceiling festooned with tycoon-bequeathed toys, it seems only fitting to order a monstrous burger and accompany it with a decanted grand cru.
>
> (*Gourmet*, September 2004, p. 43; emphasis ours)

The "casualization" of restaurants, especially many expensive restaurants, in the United States is a phenomenon that surely has various long-term causes and is related to the marketing of these businesses, as well as to a broader shift in society away from formality in many social arenas. Notably, reviewers are often quick to point out that the shift to

a more relaxed atmosphere need not signal diminished culinary expertise. For example, one article describes a "relaxed but chic" New York
restaurant that "opened the door for what became a 'downtown' style,
with no neckties, jackets or formality," yet, importantly, "did not take a
casual approach to its food, wine or service" (*New York Times*, 4 June
2008, p. F5). The following example represents a quite different
phenomenon regarding the wildly diverse forms of self-presentation
characteristic of modern urban life. However, the description of this
phenomenon serves equally well as a legitimizing contrast of highbrow
and lowbrow, in this case a listing of the types of people who patronize
a San Francisco restaurant:

> The crowds that surge through Zuni day and night are a living
> exhibit of what San Francisco is all about: investment bankers
> and transvestites, bestudded bike messengers and bespectacled
> intellectuals, models and mooks, tourists gawking at the openly
> necking gays and soigné social swans.
>
> (*Saveur*, Aug./Sept. 2004, p. 77)

A time-honored New York hangout is described in a similar light:
"Nestled among meatpacking plants and hard-core gay bars, Florent
was an anomalously egalitarian enclave beloved in equal measure by
celebrities on the A list and hedonists on the edge." The article is
peppered with celebrity references, including Calvin Klein recalling
some favorite memories of dining alongside "real downtown character
types," as well as the owner's humorous anecdotes about serving the
likes of Johnny Depp and Keanu Reeves. Despite the immense star
status of its patrons, Florent is applauded for its "proudly grungy looks"
and a menu of "Continental-ized diner food with just enough French
bistro chic thrown in" (*New York Times*, 21 May 2008, p. F1).

Another example of a legitimizing contrast between patrons is found
in an article on eating in Malaysia: "Squatting side-by-side next to their
favorite hawker or elbow-to-elbow at small tables in a stall, everyone
from street cleaners to well-to-do businessmen makes time to roll up
their sleeves and makan nasi (eat rice), enjoying the full-flavored noodle

and rice dishes, curries and clay-pot stews that epitomize Malaysian cuisine" (*Food & Wine*, July 2007, p. 244). The juxtaposition of high- and low-status individuals suggests that both wealth and poverty are unproblematic issues in a classless landscape. We see this in another restaurant in the American South whose patrons' "attire ranges from the still-wet camouflage waders to pressed pinstripe suits" (*Gourmet*, Aug. 2004, p. 32).

Within this frame of supposed equality in the face of class inequality, we observed a variant of the "equality of inequality" frame—the use of kitsch, which is employed to add a tone of ironic detachment allowing cultural elites to appreciate lowbrow cultural forms, while legitimizing the economic and cultural distance between social classes. While definitions of kitsch abound, Seabrook (2001: 20) usefully summarizes the kitsch ethic as being "hierarchically nonhierarchical—of bringing highbrow connoisseurship to lowbrow pleasures, and thereby preserving the old High-Low structure of culture as status, though it was necessary to wittily invert it."[72] Inherent in the notion of kitsch is a blurring of boundaries between highbrow and lowbrow. Significantly, the blurring is temporary and fully controlled by those in the more privileged cultural and economic position. In fact, kitsch serves as a method for displaying mastery over the rules of the game of cultural hierarchy. Through kitsch, the obvious tension between highbrow and lowbrow is resolved, and socio-economic and cultural inequality is both legitimized and obscured.

Through kitsch, foods typically associated with people of low cultural and/or economic capital are presented as playful and suitably enjoyed by gourmets, as in *Gourmet*'s mini hot dogs with home-made ketchup served with carrots and home-made "ranch" dip (*Gourmet*, Jan. 2004, p. 75). The distinctly unfunny aspects of eating processed foods by economic necessity rather than by choice are never addressed within our close reading of these magazines. Applying the kitsch ethic, mass-produced lowbrow culinary forms are consistently framed as enjoyable foods, but with a sense of ironic play that simultaneously appropriates and mocks the culinary form being eaten. Such playful mocking is evident, for instance, in the praise of a "deep-fried rabbit appetizer that owes less to the grand commanders of haute cuisine than to Colonel Sanders" (*New York Times*, 2 Apr. 2008, p. F7).

The use of kitsch foods allows gourmet magazines to juxtapose foods with low-status associations alongside actual gourmet foods, thereby presenting culturally-unequal foods as ostensibly equal, and constructing an image of foodies as democratic. The kitsch sub-frame is typically used when discussing foods associated with the American working class—whether white working class or racial minority, or stereotypically lowbrow food. 'Kitsch' items take two major forms. The first form is that of a humble, protean dish like tuna-noodle casserole (e.g., *Gourmet*, May 2004, p. 95) or a hot dog (*Gourmet*, Jan. 2004, p. 75) reworked using high-quality and often expensive ingredients. For example, readers of *Gourmet* are advised to "forget cutting-edge cuisine" and enjoy the down-home pleasure of fried chicken and white gravy (Apr. 2004, p. 26), but with an eye to the quality of the ingredients that is uncharacteristic of the traditional preparation of the dish. This first manifestation is exceedingly common—so much so that *Bon Appétit* named the hamburger its dish of the year in 2004 (for a discussion and content analysis of this phenomenon, see Johnston and Baumann 2007).

Compared to the first form, the second form of kitsch is heavier on the irony. In this second form of kitsch, mass-produced, lowbrow items are appreciated *as is*, without any upscaling of ingredients. The second form is less commonly presented in food magazines. However, from time to time we find jarringly inauthentic or unexotic foods described alongside their authentic or exotic counterparts. For example, *Saveur* has a regular feature entitled [Savoir] "Fare," which lists the hottest food events and anniversaries for the discerning foodie. A consistent feature in this column is the interjection of one or two kitsch elements—like the anniversary of the Tootsie Roll (*Saveur*, Jan./Feb. 2004, p. 22). Also ironically lauded is the birthday of James Kraft, and his "*grand vision*: by 1916 he's patented a nonperishable processed cheese (the precursor to Velveeta), and by 1952 he'd developed Cheez Whiz and his version of macaroni and cheese" (*Saveur*, Dec. 2004, p. 16; emphasis ours). What is significant is not simply the inclusion of these items, but their juxtaposition against events like the anniversary of the birthday of Anton Chekhov, or a sausage festival in the remote Swiss village that serves only 250 people (January 2004, p. 18)—events that require a significant amount of cultural and economic capital to appreciate, let alone attend. In the magazine *Gourmet*, a similar legitimizing contrast and appreciation of 'kitsch' is achieved through Michael and Jane Stern's column entitled, "Road Food." While the magazine in general promotes appreciation of upscale food items and gourmet restaurants, this column serves as a playful reminder of the deliciousness of roadside diners and backwoods America. In the January 2004 issue of *Gourmet*, devoted to projecting "what's next in food," the magazine's editors laud items like "black rice" and South Beach (p. 26) while the voice of the Sterns is interjected to promote hot "next" food items like sweet tea by the pitcher (considered a marker of lower-class taste preferences in the South), doughnuts, gravy, chili dogs, and coffee mugs (p. 43). Similarly, *New York Times* readers are informed of the "$175 Kobe, foie gras and truffle concoction" available at the Burger Shoppe on Wall Street, but advised to choose the "$4 four-ounce burger" in place of its high-end counterpart (*New York Times*, 4 June 2008, p. F8).

As with the romanticization of poverty, a competing frame of wealth as obviously superior to poverty never explicitly appeared in our sample. One could argue that because snobbery is socially unacceptable, such a frame is unlikely to appear. However, we would respond that an acknowledgment of the privileges of wealth does not constitute snobbery, but represents a realistic description of the benefits of possessing ample amounts of economic capital in capitalist societies.

Ordinariness of Privilege

The third frame we found in gourmet food writing served to downplay wealth and elitism as common and ordinary. Privilege was frequently presented in terms that suggested that it was interesting, yet ultimately inconsequential. In contrast, we never encountered a competing frame presenting economic privilege as remarkable for its relative rarity—both within the United States, and globally. Instead we found privilege was acknowledged through "off-hand" and indirect references, creating the impression that although economic privilege exists, it is of minor importance and is commonplace.

Such an impression was frequently created through brief allusions to the high social status of food producers and consumers. Food is regularly linked to individuals who are described as "socialites," to families who are explained to have fortunes earned by a prior or current generation of industrialists, to royalty or descendants of former royalty, to Hollywood celebrities, or to people presented as, among other professions, prominent surgeons, politicians, or financiers. A good example of elite status as ostensibly incidental comes in a story in which a food company executive's dedication to organics is described without any overt reference to economic capital: He "has all his shirts tailored" with organic linens (since as he says, "When you buy from a chain . . . there's always a compromise") (*Gourmet*, Aug. 2008, p. 61). These stories are ostensibly about the food produced and consumed by these people, and their elite status is framed as trifling—relatively unimportant when compared to the individual commitment to food.

In addition to the elite status of individuals, the extreme wealth possessed by these same individuals is also framed as insignificant through "off-hand" comments like the following:

> We browsed artisan showrooms filled with the flamboyant oxcarts for which Sarchí [Costa Rica] is famous. A salesman told us we could personalize one by having our portraits painted on its sides. Françoise told me that while she and her husband did not have an oxcart, personalized or plain, they did have a boat and had spent many summers sailing with their daughters along the coasts of Italy and Corsica.
>
> (*Food & Wine*, July 2004, p. 173)

This contextualization of good food as the concern of wealthy and sophisticated people is a common theme within gourmet food writing, but their wealth is framed as incidental rather than integral to their taste culture (Gans 1999). Another way that wealth was frequently framed as ordinary was through off-handed references to locations where wealthy people live or summer such as Aspen, Nantucket, the Hamptons, the Côte d'Azur, or the island of Capri (e.g., *Food & Wine*,

July 2006, p. 58). One article describes a life that spanned the "estate in Provence and his apartment in Paris," where "meals were gorgeous, profligate rituals that ate up most of the day" (*New York Times*, Feb. 20, 2008, p. F1). Yet another way of normalizing wealth was through casual references to high-cost culinary items that only affluent people can afford, such as Galician beef grilled on an $18,000 custom-made grill (*Gourmet*, June 2004, p. 50), or a "$2,499.95 Delonghi Gran Dama Espresso Maker" (*San Francisco Chronicle*, May 21, 2008, p. F4). In another article, the price of $400 for a meal for two at a Swiss restaurant was explained to be "almost a bargain" because of the high quality of the food in comparison with what $400 would buy in the United States, and also because "an à la carte dinner for two with wine at Alain Ducasse in Paris would probably run you $900" (*Saveur*, June/July 2006, p. 61). In those cases where financial limitations are briefly acknowledged, they are often dismissed in lieu of a dedication to good taste. Responding to questions about the impact of the economic recession on his business, one restaurateur replies: "I'm certainly not the kind who would look at the Dow . . . Does a writer write or not write a book based on the economic climate? Does a songwriter write songs that way?" (*New York Times*, Feb. 20, 2008, p. F1). These questions imply that good food is in the realm of artistry, and such things must not be tainted by the pressures of one's pocketbook.

Quite often the wealthy people featured in the articles are the authors themselves. In one article an author is denied a table at a busy Italian roadside eatery, and he responds by purchasing a large quantity of the proprietor's home-made, extra-virgin balsamic vinegar:

> I cursed him under my breath—Italian is a most satisfying language in which to mutter imprecations, as anybody who has ever watched the third act of any Verdi opera knows—and slunk next door to buy some of his vinegar . . . Pedroni strolled into his store, greeted me as an old friend he hadn't seen in years, and sold me 500 euros' worth of the *extravecchio*. There turned out to be a table for us after all.
>
> (*Gourmet*, Jan. 2004, p. 46)

The fact that the author has a working knowledge of Italian, a familiarity with Verdi, and 500 euros (approximately $615 United States dollars in 2004, when the article was published) to spend on vinegar are minor details in this story of roadside eating. In another article, the author discusses her family's Thanksgiving traditions, which include a meal made by a long-serving, hired "family cook" that is eaten in the family home, which "sleeps only 16" but "looks bigger on the outside" (*Saveur*, November 2006, p. 67).

In gourmet food writing, great wealth and elite status appear frequently, yet they are consistently downplayed, so that the overall message is that they are ordinary and trivial. This third frame works in concert with the others to present not just wealth but class inequality in the same way—entirely unproblematic.[73]

While the food of the poor and the wealthy appear prominently in gourmet food writing, the idea of class inequality as a social problem is virtually absent, as are articles exploring causes of poverty or the identities and perspectives of the poor. Instead, poverty is romanticized and placed on a par with great wealth, while economic privilege is normalized. In general, gourmet food writing in the three magazines and two newspapers we studied in depth entertains at the expense of meaningful critique or analysis of poverty and inequality. To be fair, gourmet food writing does not pretend to offer a critique beyond food. However, our point is that poverty and inequality still make their presence known in this writing, and that the frames employed to present this inequality to audiences both reflect and reproduce notions of the unimportance of class inequality, regardless of intentions.

It seems clear to us that our findings are at least partially driven by the fact that we studied media written for a relatively privileged audience. These frames might not be found in media targeting poor or working-class audiences (although it is worth noting that there are no food magazines written for this demographic). The frames we found would likely resonate with and soothe the social conscience of the wealthy, suggesting that poverty is not a horrible condition but a relatively equal status where great food is still enjoyed. Given the target audience, it is fairly clear that food writers are less likely to write articles that highlight class inequality as a social problem, or explore the food deprivation of the poor. While it is not altogether surprising that media for a privileged audience downplay the significance of inequality, a contribution of this research is to use frame analysis to identify the particular ways in which social inequality—one of the most difficult and pressing issues in the contemporary United States—is accomplished. Another contribution is to document that the gourmet foodscape, as presented in food writing, is characterized by a strong tension between democratic norms of inclusivity and classlessness on the surface, and norms of status-seeking and acceptance of significant inequality just beneath the surface of the discourse. In the rest of this chapter we move from an analysis of class and status in gourmet food writing to an analysis of these issues as they are discussed by foodies themselves.

The Foodie as Omnivore: Rejecting Snobbery and Negotiating Status

Topics of class and status emerged in virtually every interview conducted, allowing us to make some important inferences about how foodies' involvement with food overlaps with their own concerns about status, as well as how their preferences reflect larger cultural trends. To better understand foodies' discussions of status and taste, we turn again to the literature on omnivorousness. We have argued that the symbolic boundaries drawn by foodies between worthy and unworthy food are an instance of omnivorous cultural consumption, and so the logic of evaluation that we find here can be taken as an example of the logic of omnivorousness. In addition to the demographic similarities—education, income, and occupation—between our sample and the demographics of omnivores as reported in other sociological research, we find ample evidence in the responses of our interviewees that their preferences in food qualify as omnivorousness.

Recent research generally characterizes omnivores as high-volume consumers of cultural products from lowbrow and highbrow genres. Translating these studies to understanding food preferences requires some work. Prior research on omnivorousness focuses mostly on artistic consumption such as music appreciation. To take the case of music, one important difference is that music appreciation is entirely optional while everyone must eat. Therefore, in order to establish that an omnivore is a high-volume consumer of food we must specify that omnivores are high-volume consumers in a specific *mode*—a gourmet mode that we characterize as "foodie."[74] What this means is that they understand their food consumption to be particularly cultural and symbolically important, rather than a matter of sustenance alone. We find that, indeed, the interviewees see themselves as frequently, or always, concerned about whether the food they are eating is worthy or good food. This stands in contrast to those who might only occasionally consume in a gourmet mode; for instance, on a special occasion such as a birthday or anniversary meal in a restaurant. The foodies we interviewed described themselves as "obsessed" with food, as working hard to search out different ingredients at different stores, as vigilant in their searching out of new recipes and reading of restaurant reviews. Many of them said they cooked every day, and two of them claimed to have cooked a different meal for every dinner party they had ever thrown. Several of them explained that mediocre restaurant meals or poor-quality ingredients were quite upsetting to them, and that successfully authentic and delicious meals made their day. What is clear is that virtually all of our interviewees consumed food in a gourmet mode daily, which by any metric is a high volume of consumption within the field.

Regarding the second component to omnivorousness, many of our interviewees were explicit about their preference to span brows in food. Within the field of food, brow can be understood as related to several features of food. Because of the particular history of French food in the United States, this cuisine is virtually always highbrow. However, brow can also be strongly determined by expense, so that highbrow food is expensive food in terms of restaurant prices or in terms of pricey ingredients. We found that virtually all of our respondents reported liking expensive food as well as cherishing authentic or exotic inexpensive food, with the standard example being regional or ethnic restaurants that are described as "seedy" or a "hole-in-the-wall." The following excerpt, taken from our interview with Catherine Quilter in New York, is worth quoting at length given how well it depicts brow-spanning in particular and omnivorousness in general:

> I just had a fabulous meal. I went with a friend of mine who knew this neighborhood in New York . . . It was Dominican. And we ate one of the best chickens that I've ever eaten in my life. It's a rotis-serie chicken that they cook and the restaurant is just a very, very inexpensive kind of dive . . . I mean that's authentic . . . in the past I used to get dressed up and go to, you know, I've eaten several meals at a restaurant in New York called Le Bernadin which is a French restaurant which is extraordinary. And my friend who's a professional foodie took me there one time when the chef was basically making a meal for him because he had written a nice article about the place . . . and it was just extraordinary. I mean it was really, really, really something. And then I ate once at Taillevent in Paris . . . And there's another place in Paris called L'Ami Louis, which is a really, really, really simple place, but it has fabulous food . . . but then also, the last time I was in Paris I went . . . to a little place, a wine bar with food run by two, a family that have a farm . . . I get as much pleasure out of that, a sort of cheap student place run by a family who has a farm, as I do about going to Taillevent, I mean I really do. I think I might get more pleasure out of the simpler place in this instance.

Just like Catherine, some other respondents only obliquely describe a preference for both expensive and inexpensive food, focusing on other dimensions of their brow-spanning in food, such as ambiance and culinary traditions. In the case of David Teitelbaum, he described the diversity of the restaurants he likes with a slightly stronger emphasis on expense: "[A] slightly pricier, more ambitious meal, or not more ambi-tious, but pricier. Um, something like The Red Cat, which is in Chelsea in Manhattan . . . for a splurge [I] may go to Blue Village Stone bar, which is in Westchester. But I should say, I'm more than happy to go to, you know, the local Irish pub and order a burger." Fiona Callworth from Boston also emphasized liking both very expensive and inexpensive food when eating out, saying:

> We don't go out very much, but when we go out, we'll spend four hundred dollars on a meal. I mean, we'll spend a massive amount of money, but there are very few restaurants I will go to in Boston . . . Although, you know, I can take great joy in having a hot dog at this really cool hot dog place. I don't eat hot dogs but once a year, but to have a really good hot dog with lots of home-made fixings, pickles and relishes.

Clearly, these respondents are not the "snobs" identified in the sociology of cultural consumption as preferring only highbrow genres within their fields. What these examples demonstrate is that the foodies we interviewed are best understood as omnivores, and that their emphases on authenticity and exoticism should be taken as representative of the underlying logic of omnivorousness.[75] This finding about brow-spanning leads us to a further question: The meaning of this preference for foodies. How do they explain their preference for both lowbrow and highbrow cultural consumption, and what do their explanations suggest about how omnivorousness produces distinction?

We find that foodies explain brow-spanning food preferences as a clear indicator that their cultural consumption is driven by unbiased perceptions of food's quality and by a pure obsession with excellence. This focus on quality and excellence was sharply revealed in the almost universal insistence that good food or good restaurants are not necessarily expensive, or formal. Many of the foodies volunteered the terms "formal" or "stuffy" in describing restaurants they do not like, and most of them reported disliking "fussy" or "pretentious" food. Even foodies who reported having first-hand experience of eating at some of the most expensive restaurants in New York and Paris were clear about their aversion to eating in a traditional highbrow mode. Their opposition to formality and traditional etiquette requirements was perhaps the most strongly and frequently voiced opinion in our interviews. It is clear that the *mode of consumption* was a key consideration in their evaluation of the food. Melissa Trent, a 58-year-old attorney in Los Angeles, is clear about the mode in which she prefers to consume food:

> I don't like snooty restaurants . . . I just don't like really formal, um, stuffy, expensive dining. I think food is so wonderful, and that there's so many great ways to make it, that you, you know, I don't like the, what do you call them, nouvelle restaurants with these little small portions and I don't like stuff like that. I like very traditional, good, healthy food. I love ethnic food. I love to see what people do with foods. But I just don't like the real snooty white tablecloth, fancy restaurants. I think food is supposed to be enjoyed, and I find that inhibits your enjoyment of food.

In a similar vein, interviewees reported being uncomfortable with the elitist connotations they perceived in the term foodie. Dennis Nolan, a software engineer in Chapel Hill, explained his reticence to apply the term "foodie" to himself: "[T]he problem is that the term is used very broadly, and it's used to include people who simply feel an extraordinarily strong desire to spend, you know, tens of thousands of dollars on equipment for their kitchen and then don't cook. [Laughs.] So I don't particularly want to be bundled together with those people if I could avoid it." Traditional snobbery is clearly disliked by foodies. Strikingly, however, foodies are simultaneously able to maintain a symbolic boundary between worthy and unworthy food even in the absence of traditional snobbery. This is precisely what the focus on authenticity and exoticism achieves. By upholding these qualities as central to evaluating food, foodies maintain the symbolic boundary in an overtly meritocratic way. The food is better not because it belongs to the consecrated French canon or because it is consumed in a highbrow mode, but because authenticity and exoticism speak to the purity, integrity, and overall excellence of the food. Foodies understand their preferences as legitimate because these choices demonstrate knowledge and a concern for quality, defined as objectively as possible.

What goes mostly unsaid by foodies, however, is that their choices are, in fact, discriminatory in the sense that they are highly selective, as has been noted by Warde et al. (2008). In describing worthy foods, they are also, by omission, defining categories of unworthy foods. Foodies also routinely make choices that require high levels of cultural capital, and often also high levels of economic capital, and so the foods that they prefer tend to be foods that are not enjoyed by non-foodies, or by most of society. This creates a curious contrast in the case of restaurants that foodies dislike. On the one hand, foodies avoid stuffiness and formality. Yet on the other hand, almost all foodies reported a strong aversion to chain restaurants and fast food. They give various reasons for disliking chain restaurants, which is reasonable given that fast food is neither exotic nor authentic according to the standards of gourmet discourse (see Figure 3.1 in Chapter 3). But what restaurant could be less formal or less stuffy than a chain restaurant? While chain restaurants solve the problem of the need to avoid snobbery, they introduce a new problem of being inauthentic and non-exotic, and, not incidentally, too common to serve as a basis for drawing symbolic boundaries. Consequently, they are often disavowed, or even provoke disgust.[76]

It is clear that omnivorous food choices have an important meaning for foodies in that they consider their choices to be anti-elitist, knowledgeable, and to provide themselves with enjoyment. However, the distinction that their choices facilitate is unmistakable all the same. We interpret this tension between inclusivity and exclusivity to be the guiding principle behind omnivorous consumption. Because overt snobbery is no longer acceptable,[77] the contemporary cultural consumption strategy must move away from the traditional highbrow model. But because cultural consumption is still related to distinction processes and to individuals' social locations, symbolic boundaries must be maintained. Omnivorousness is the solution to this problem.

Conclusions on Class and Status: Minimized but Still Relevant

Through an analysis of class and status in gourmet food writing and in foodies' descriptions of their taste preferences, we find that at the same time the gourmet foodscape is imbued with concerns about quality, politics, ethics, and meaningfulness, it is also permeated with hierarchy and distinction. As generations of scholars, from Thorstein Veblen to

Max Weber to Georg Simmel to Pierre Bourdieu have demonstrated, cultural consumption of all sorts is inevitably wrapped up with class and status. Food is no exception. What we see from our media analysis and our interviews is that the particular engagement with class and status in the gourmet foodscape is shaped and constrained by contemporary cultural values and norms concerning class and status. Namely, class and status are minimized in the foodscape (since nobody wants to be an outright snob), but they are also clearly still relevant as distinctions about quality food are continually made.

We argue that there are important implications of this tendency to obscure status distinctions through tastes and cultural consumption. When this happens in the media, important issues of class inequality and poverty are framed as unimportant or unproblematic. Past research has shown that news media frames often suggest particular causes of and treatments for poverty that blame victims and focus on individual factors over societal factors. We find this research convincing and an important contribution for understanding how the American public views poverty, yet these frames are not found to be applicable to the cultural genre of food writing. Our identification of frames that maintain classlessness by romanticizing poverty and normalizing wealth pushes thinking on the nature of framing past consideration of particular causes and treatments of inequality. Instead, we must consider the ability of frames to dissolve a social problem altogether, so that there is nothing being caused and nothing needing treatment.

Despite disagreements about how to best describe and explain class relations in the United States (Chan and Goldthorpe 2007; Weeden and Grusky 2005), sociologists generally remain convinced that class differences are a central feature of American society and that the degree of social inequality in the United States and globally constitutes an important social problem and a pressing issue of social justice. The same cannot be said, however, for much of the general population. Although prior research finds that class awareness or identification tends to be salient for most individuals (Centers 1949; Guest 1974; Haer 1957; Hodge and Treiman 1968; Jackman and Jackman 1983), and especially so for the working class, the research also finds that

Americans in general are not especially troubled by class inequality. Instead, most Americans find high levels of class inequality acceptable (Bobo 1991; Hochschild 1981; Kluegel and Smith 1986).

One robust finding in the literature is that class location powerfully shapes class consciousness (Wright 1997), and a related finding is that upper-middle-class individuals typically dismiss or trivialize class inequality (Brantlinger 1993; Stuber 2006). Such findings are supported and clarified by our work. The upper-middle-class discourse present in gourmet food writing both reflects and shapes the audience's understanding of class inequality as trivial. As Stuber (2006) notes, although structural accounts of class inequality remain in favor, in recent decades scholars of class inequality have also increasingly taken up cultural approaches to explain stratification outcomes. Such approaches emphasize that the meanings and understandings people have of their social world can play a role in the creation and reproduction of class inequality. Although this idea is not new, having been developed by both Gramsci and Weber among others, studies that adopt this perspective have gained considerable attention as of late (e.g., Bourdieu 1984; Lamont 1992, 2000). Our findings suggest the particular frames through which class inequality is understood as unproblematic and is therefore allowed to remain at high levels in the contemporary United States without generating a great deal of public concern.

Our interview data with foodies suggest that omnivorousness, as a cultural consumption pattern for high-status individuals, meshes well with the classless nature of gourmet food writing. Through their focus on authenticity and exoticism, they can be highly selective in their food preferences, but in a way that takes the emphasis off the exclusivity inherent in their preferences. The result is that, although foodies are interested in much more than status when it comes to food, foodies' tastes contribute to a status system in just the way that contemporary cultural values prescribe—through omnivorous patterns that span lowbrow and highbrow food choices. Traditional snobbism is disavowed and the range of acceptable genres is wide open and more inclusive than ever before; however, it takes a great deal of knowledge and often a lot of money to fully participate as a foodie in the American foodscape.

Our identification of the ways in which class inequality is effectively obfuscated in foodie discourse seems to us a prime example of hegemony (Gramsci 1971). Carroll defines hegemony as "a historically specific organization of consent that rests upon—but cannot be read off—a practical material base" (1992: 8). The concept of hegemony emphasizes that elites cannot rule by force alone—cultural leadership is required to achieve cultural consent, which reinforces class inequality and often works to "short-circuit attempts at critical thinking" by working its way into common sense (Smith 2001: 39). For hegemony's cultural leadership to be effective it must change along with social and historical circumstances; cultural consent is never permanent, and is always in the process of being contested (Hall 2001: 97; Roseberry 1996: 360–361). We interpret the rise of omnivorousness as part of hegemony's continuing evolution. Foodie discourse participates in a broader American discursive field where class inequality is predominantly trivialized. In its obfuscation of class inequality as a social problem, foodie discourse and the logic of omnivorousness it employs help to perpetuate the very inequalities they conceal.

CONCLUSION

MORAL AMBIGUITIES IN THE GOURMET FOODSCAPE

In this book we have sought to answer several key questions about food and culture in the United States. What does the gourmet foodscape look like, and what is a foodie? How do culinary experts and foodies alike draw symbolic boundaries between worthy and unworthy food? What can we learn about cultural boundaries and status distinctions more generally by studying how food is evaluated, and how food's quality is discursively constituted? What political and ethical issues are intertwined with the evaluation and consumption of food?

While there is no easy way to précis our answers to these questions, a few summary statements about foodies are worth reiterating. Foodies have emerged as the descendants of yesteryear's gourmets. Rather than primarily orient themselves to high-status French food, they take interest in a great variety of foods from many global culinary traditions, especially *exotic* foods from distant groups or cultures. They frequently feel just as comfortable in an expensive, but casual, restaurant with a celebrated chef, as they do shopping for wild ramps in a farmers' market, or eating home-made donuts in a Texas truck stop. Foodies treasure food that is delicious, but they also want food that is *authentic*—foods that are simple, made from the heart, and with history and tradition to back them up. Many foodies also value 'eco' food choices—they want foods that are sustainably-produced, organic, and local, and they frequently deem these foods more delicious than their long-distance, industrial counterparts. Finally, foodies are interested in foods consumed by poor people as well as foods found in elite settings, but they typically make very little of the material divides that separate eaters in the American foodscape.

While we hope that this book sheds light on the phenomenon of the "foodie," to be clear, this book is principally an examination of foodie discourse—the ways that foodies talk about, think about, and write about food. Our intention has not been to systematically study food trends or foodies themselves (in their myriad manifestations), but to analyze how food is "framed" in order to shed light on the connections between gourmet food, environmental politics, exotic Othering, and social inequality. With the method of discourse analysis, the study of frames is able to tease out the justifications and ideologies underlying the preferences and identities that people express. Foodie discourse is no exception, and the frames we have studied speak to two central, competing priorities: Democracy and distinction. Based on our analysis of the way that "worthy" food is framed in foodie discourse, we argue that the gourmet foodscape embodies a tension between embracing ideals of meritocracy, equality, and inclusiveness on the one hand, and offering a venue for marking status and for divisive class and identity politics on the other.

The way that foodies draw the boundaries between worthy and unworthy food also centers on an identification of qualities of authenticity and exoticism. When foods are framed in these ways, they are seen as "worthy" and foodies enjoy them in a mode that is not only ostensibly democratic, but undoubtedly more achievable for people with high economic and cultural capital. Authentic and exotic foods are not only frequently expensive, but they are often easier to appreciate by someone who is culturally-sophisticated and educated. We wish to be clear that foodie discourse is characterized by an ideological *tension* between competing ideologies of democracy and distinction, rather than an absolute manifestation of these ideals. In many instances, the impulse for democratic ideals is simply ideological window-dressing on elite cultural practices, and in these instances, the term "faux populist" is more appropriate than democratic, especially when seeing democracy in the sense of political and economic equality. At the same time as foodie discourse possesses many instances of faux-democracy, we cannot deny the democratic impulse within foodie discourse to broaden the cultural canon to include different kinds of foods outside elite repertoires—the foods of working-class people, and ethnic minorities from around the world. While this democratic impulse is real, it is also important to recognize that this cultural broadening occurs in a larger political and material context of tremendous economic inequality, making it difficult for many people to fully partake in the pleasures of foodie culture. Our interpretation of the ways that wealth and poverty are framed in foodie discourse is that this aspect of the gourmet food-scape is severely minimized, and we critique foodie discourse's faux populism for facilitating cultural and social exclusion.

Besides the tension between ideologies of democracy and distinction, another key analytic theme is omnivorousness. Foodies represent a kind of cultural consumer—the omnivore—that sociologists of culture have identified in other realms such as music and the arts. The "rules" for discerning worthy culture under the omnivorousness paradigm are more complicated than the prior highbrow/lowbrow divide (Erickson 2007). For this reason, foodie culture stands to contribute further to the reproduction of social inequality because food knowledge is one way that privileged and high-status people relate to one another. A lack of food knowledge can contribute to a sense of being a cultural outsider from privileged circles.

We also note that the implications of how we eat, and foodie culture more specifically, go beyond class politics to touch on important issues such as the social, ecological, and animal exploitation associated with the industrial food system. The food system is closely intertwined with myriad social and environmental issues—from the labor exploitation of farm workers to the carbon emissions associated with industrial agriculture production and transportation—and these issues have recently come to the fore of the foodie consciousness.

Our investigation of the mainstream gourmet foodscape reveals a food discourse that has in recent times taken up issues of environmental sustainability and animal welfare, but which is largely disconnected from issues of social welfare and social justice on a national and global scale. Within foodie discourse, an ethical consumption frame dominated by an ideology of consumerism is hegemonic. This frame approaches food through a lens of individual commodity choices, employs a win-win logic suggesting that food choices can be both ethical and delicious, and suggests that commodity choices are the paramount way to affect social and environmental change. Employing this frame, foodies display some awareness of environmental issues, and a general (but certainly not exclusive) preference for "eco" friendly choices, like organic foods or foods that are locally grown and produced. While "eco-eating" is certainly a staple of foodie culture, the ultimate valuation for most foodie culture remains *taste*. This tendency was heard both in our foodie interviews and in the food journalism we studied. To the extent that foodie discourse promotes consciousness of the ramifications of food choices, it tends to be much more concerned with environmental issues than with issues of fair working conditions, workers' health, or economic inequality, and its primary focus is on identifying eco-food choices that are high-quality, authentic, exotic, and ultimately delicious.

An alternative frame of political eating challenges the hegemony of consumerism, and views food as an opportunity to mobilize citizens for collective action (involving social movements or the state) to solve a variety of serious social and environmental problems associated with the food system. In our interviews with foodies, we identified a small minority of foodies that articulated a political-eating frame where the political issues (both social justice and sustainability issues) of citizens were a primary motivation and concern, and where classic consumer considerations such as price, convenience, and choice were of secondary importance. This political-eating frame was present for some of our foodie interviewees, but was very marginal in the mainstream gourmet foodscape we studied. In addition, a substantial minority of our interviewees, and a majority of the food discourse we studied, was predominantly apolitical—unconcerned with either the environmental or social justice issues associated with the food system, and instead primarily concerned with aesthetic matters of taste. This suggests that the current moment of foodie politics is important, but should not be overstated.

Where does our focus on foodie discourse and frames leave food as a material entity whose physical properties are a matter for both our health and our senses? How can we reconcile our perspective that quality is discursively created, with an obvious, but important, acknowledgment that some chefs are more skilled, and that some foods are fresher and more flavorful? While we approach the topic of food from a social constructionist perspective, we agree that there are ontological differences in foods' physical qualities, and that the chefs who prepare the dishes that foodies love have talent and expertise. We ourselves have foods that we love to eat, and in the course of researching this book, we became aware of many delicious dishes, ingredients, and ways of cooking. When evaluating food in our daily life, we jokingly pose the question, "Is this really worth the calories?" To answer the question, we primarily rely on our senses rather than on our reasoning. Although we are interested in analyzing foodie discourse, like most if not all foodies, we have much more than a cerebral interest in food.

We cannot deny this same connection to food among the foodies we interviewed or whose journalism we read. These foodies displayed an earnest passion for reading, writing, and talking about food, but they also clearly enjoyed the food itself—the sensual pleasures of eating and drinking delicious things. We also saw that evaluations of food were often based on sincere efforts to avoid being implicated in the industrial food system and its negative effects, such as the de-skilling of home cooks associated with the industrial production of prepared and pre-packaged foods. Foodies also evaluated foods based on a genuine desire to make intercultural connections and to expand their palates beyond traditional French highbrow classics, and to legitimate new kinds of foods and cuisines as sophisticated, worthy, and high-quality.

While food has an ontological and a biological reality that is connected to our cultural understandings, human tastes and determinations of food's aesthetic qualities must necessarily be social constructions. We can appreciate the physical reality of foods and the complex ecologies of food systems that exist beyond discourse, but we cannot deny the cultural filters that shape our understanding of what foods are delicious or disgusting, exciting or banal. Put differently, the boundaries between "good" and "bad" food are not based on enduring and objective truths about what is "truly" good and bad, but instead, these perceptions of worth are based on criteria that are socially agreed upon for a given place and time. In this case of foodies in the contemporary United States, we can identify their criteria through discourse—in the way they write and talk about good food. Describing the nature of these criteria is the primary empirical contribution of this book. We wish to underscore that to understand how people elevate certain foods and denigrate others, we have necessarily focused on talk about food (rather than the food itself), since it is only through an examination of discourse that the justifications for aesthetic evaluations can be observed.

If aesthetic values vary over time and space, how are we to understand the frames we observe? Are they simply food fashions that are in this year, but out the next? We cannot say with certainty how worthy food will be distinguished in the near or far future. However, we note that authenticity and exoticism enjoy a long-standing and broad positive appraisal in Western culture. These are not new ways of seeing and evaluating culture, but what is relatively new is their rise within the gourmet foodscape. Although greater historical work is needed in this field, we see authenticity and exoticism as having seeped into foodie discourse slowly since approximately the 1950s. Our data from the last several years show that authenticity and exoticism are the primary frames for evaluating food; however, we would hazard a guess that these frames have been predominant for the past couple of decades.

If we borrow from common parlance and think of fashion as "prevailing custom," then there is a basis for understanding authenticity and exoticism as food fashion. There is nothing in this brief definition of fashion that indicates duration of prevalence. Moreover, sociological analysis of fashion finds that people engage with fashion in part in order to generate social status, and our argument here is that a focus on authenticity and exoticism allows foodies to socially distinguish themselves through food. However, common usage of "fashion" most often indicates durations of months or a few years, as with clothes or hairstyles. In contrast, the positive evaluation of authenticity and exoticism in our culture has endured for over a century, and in food for decades.

And so we would not characterize the focus on authenticity and exoticism as food fashion or fads. Instead, fashion and fad apply better to particular foods or food preparation techniques that become popular with culinary trendsetters, and which may filter down to mainstream eaters (think fondue, or, more recently, foam). Instead, authenticity and exoticism, as keys to the logic of omnivorousness, are guiding aesthetic values for cultural consumption.

Our theoretical contribution in this book is not a causal explanation, but rather is an explanation in the sense that it aspires to tell us "what's really going on" with the omnivorous cultural consumption that characterizes foodie discourse.[78] We also hope to capitalize on the understanding we provide of the meanings behind omnivorous cultural preferences to make a statement about their normative implications. The normative ambiguity of omnivorousness has been relatively unexplored in the scholarly literature, yet we argue that this is a topic of pressing concern that can be understood through the ideological tension between democracy and distinction. The gourmet foodscape creates and reproduces moral ambiguities that are particularly evident in the trend of ethical consumption, and food politics more specifically. These ambiguities will only become more attenuated with a foodscape marked by heightened social and economic inequality at the national and global scale. Ethical food choices simultaneously allow for status signaling, and for publicizing (and potentially addressing) environmental and labor issues. Eating locally, seasonally, and with consideration of animal welfare is a key part of the foodie *Zeitgeist*, and this will be increasingly significant as the industrial food system generates further environmental stressors and creates additional ecological and health risks. At the same time eco-consumption and eco-eating has the benefit of drawing attention to the sustainability of the contemporary food system, the class and social justice issues of the food system have been woefully unexplored and underemphasized in foodie culture. If income inequality continues unabated, the conscientious and privileged green eater may increasingly serve as a kind of ideological device that gives foodies an air of moral superiority, while drawing public attention away from the gross inequality of food resources at the national and global scale. Whereas wealth and income inequality in the United States shrank through the middle decades of the 20th century, accompanied by an erosion of cultural hierarchy, wealth and income inequality in recent decades have sharply increased (Morgan and Cha 2007; Weeden et al. 2007). A truly democratic foodie culture would not only privilege good taste and deliciousness, but would resist the tendency to fetishize taste as the ultimate value, and incorporate both environmental concerns with social justice, taking into consideration not just the availability of locally-grown artistan products, but also the way that these foods remain on the menus of a relatively privileged few.

APPENDIX A
INTERVIEW QUESTIONS

Introductory issues: explanation of interview procedures, the objectives of the research, informed consent, confidentiality. Here the interviewer will make it clear that the research is conducted within the University of Toronto's Department of Sociology, and is not being commissioned by any private corporation.

1   To start with, can you tell me a bit about yourself and your living situation? [Prompts: Occupation? Education? Race/ethnicity? Age?]

2   How and when did you become interested in food?

3   What does the term foodie mean to you? Do you consider yourself a foodie? Who is the typical foodie? [Prompts: Age, social class, education.] Do you use any other term to describe your relationship to food? What terms do you like / dislike?

4   What kind of food media do you use? [Prompts: Magazines, television, cookbooks, newspapers.] How do you learn about new foods and food trends? [Prompts: Cookbooks, restaurants, websites.]

5   Where do you shop primarily for food? [Prompt: Do you shop at different places for different reasons? Why the places you have mentioned?]

6   What do you cook and eat? How often do you cook? Do you cook
     mainly for yourself or others? What is the most elaborate thing
     you might cook? What is an example of a 'simple' dish you might
     cook? Do you have a favorite cuisine?

7   The last time you went grocery shopping, did you look for or end
     up buying food based on an ethical concern of any sort? [Prompts:
     How important is environment, labor or fair-trade, local, organic,
     sustainability, others? For all or any of these, Tell me why that's
     important to you? If they don't say health by now, ask about
     health.]

8   What is important to you when you cook? What do you need to
     have access to when you cook? [Prompts: Quality of cooking
     implements, quality of ingredients, organic ingredients, local
     origin of ingredients, healthfulness of ingredients, technologies/
     equipment.] Do you usually follow recipes or improvise? [Prompt:
     classic dishes versus hybrid versus something newly found versus
     something cutting edge.] Where do you get ideas and/or recipes
     from?

9   How often do you eat out? Describe your favorite restaurant to me
     and tell me why you like it. Do you have a favourite chef or cook,
     and it doesn't have to be a restaurant you've been to? What are
     some of the more unusual meals you've enjoyed, and what did you
     like about them? [Prompts: Artistry versus shockingly unusual
     versus rarity versus authenticity.]

10   Now tell me about the kind of restaurant you avoid and have
     disliked in the past?

In case these don't come up by themselves, need to ask:

11   What is authentic food, and is authenticity important?

12   What is exotic food, and is exoticism important?

13   Has your taste in food changed over the years? If so, how? Why
     do you think it has?

14 The last question we have today is a demographic question: what income category does your household fall into: under 25k, 25–50k, 50–100k, 100–150k, 150k+

APPENDIX B
BASIC DEMOGRAPHICS OF INTERVIEWEES

Table A1 Basic demographics of interviewees

Interviewee Pseudonym	Age	Ethnicity	Highest Degree	Occupation or Industry of Employment	Household Income
Catherine Quilter	64	White	Masters	Entertainment Industry	Over 150,000
Chad Tucker	47	White	Masters	Librarian	50–100,000
David Teitelbaum	34	White	Bachelor	Journalist	Over 150,000
Dennis Nolan	37	White	Bachelor	Software Engineer	100–150,000
Faye Taggart	64	White	Masters	Landscape Designer	100–150,000
Fern Osborne	30	White	Masters	Publishing	Over 150,000
Fiona Callworth	54	White	Bachelor	Not employed	100–150,000
Florence Nagy	51	White	High School	Administrative Assistant	100–150,000
Fred Huntington	44	White	High School	Software Engineer	Over 150,000
Gillian Edelman	48	White	Masters	Journalist	Over 150,000
Harry Quinn	43	White	High School	Technical Support	100–150,000
Jessica Bowes	38	White	Bachelor	Journalist	Over 150,000
Karen Weiss	49	White	Bachelor	Homeopath	50–100,000
Katie Crawford	28	White	Masters	Journalist	50–100,000
Keith Lee	26	Mixed race white/Asian	Masters	Marketing	50–100,000
Kelly Jones	41	Black	Bachelor	Priest	100–150,000
Kevin D'Angelo	38	White	Bachelor	Technology	Over 150,000
Melissa Trent	58	White	Juris Doctor	Attorney	Over 150,000
Michelle Quinlan	37	White	Masters	Systems Analyst	100–150,000
Nancy Light	51	White	Bachelor	Marketing	Over 150,000
Nathalie Underhill	55	White	High School	Administrative Assistant	25–50,000
Nathaniel Snider	38	White	Doctorate	Engineer	100–150,000
Neil Taverna	25	White	Bachelor	Digital Media	50–100,000

Table A1 Basic demographics of interviewees *continued*

Interviewee Pseudonym	Age	Ethnicity	Highest Degree	Occupation or Industry of Employment	Household Income
Norman Arbus	56	White	Juris Doctor	Attorney	Over 150,000
Pedro Maradona	22	White Hispanic	Bachelor	Marketing	25–50,000
Sarah Driscoll	25	White	Masters	Student	Under 25,000
Ted Darby	56	White	Masters	Retired	Over 150,000
Theresa Callebaut	62	White	Bachelor	Administrative Assistant	Over 150,000
Timothy Bauer	68	White	Juris Doctor	Retired	Over 150,000
Trish Lincoln	31	White	Masters	Librarian	25–50,000

APPENDIX C
METHODS AND RESULTS

In this appendix we present a description of our method and the quantitative results for the framing of wealth and poverty in gourmet food writing.

Data and Methods

Unlike in news media and other forms of journalism where articles are indexed according to subject, we cannot target entertainment media articles that are about the topic of class inequality, poverty, or wealth. For this reason, we choose to sample from an entertainment medium, gourmet food writing, where we expect to find the topic of class inequality frequently encountered. This is because wealthy people with high cultural capital are often interested in gourmet food, but a good deal of contemporary gourmet food is derived from the "authentic" and "exotic" food of impoverished people, both within the United States and abroad (Johnston and Baumann 2007). In addition, a major component of gourmet food writing is a description of the social environments where food is produced and consumed, thereby providing a great deal of information about social contexts in addition to information about food itself.

Our data collection began with a broad reading of sources related to gourmet food, including gourmet food magazines, more general magazines that included articles on gourmet food, and newspaper columns and articles on gourmet food. From this reading we were able to identify that situations involving class inequality commonly appeared within gourmet food writing and that the extremes of both poverty and wealth were often present. This initial finding led us to generate a sample of gourmet food writing to serve as source for generating an objective description of how inequality was framed. Our sample is based on all 2004 issues of three of the most popular gourmet food magazines published in the United States: *Gourmet*, *Saveur*, and *Food & Wine*. Because we were interested in how food production and consumption were contextualized, we selected only those articles with at least one full page of text. Our resulting sample consists of 102 articles.

The first step in our data collection was an identification of the elements of frames found in prior research on the framing of poverty in news media. In order to verify whether the frames found in that research would be found here as well, we coded first for causes of poverty and wealth, and then for who was portrayed as poor and wealthy. To meet the threshold of poverty, we considered any instance when the terms "poverty" or "poor" were used, when identities typically associated with poverty were mentioned such as bike messengers, when conditions of disrepair or underdevelopment are mentioned, or when material hardship or deprivation is mentioned. In general, the threshold for identifying instances of poverty was set low, and any doubtful cases were coded as instances of poverty. For wealth, we considered any instance when the terms wealthy, rich, or other synonyms were used, when distinctly high prices were mentioned such as a $500 bottle of vinegar, when mention was made of high-status professions (e.g., surgeons, politicians, financiers), elite associations (e.g., celebrities or royalty), or institutions such as Ivy League universities, or mention of material conditions obviously and greatly in excess of an American middle-class lifestyle, such as yacht ownership or living in a home described as a "mansion." As with poverty, doubtful cases were coded as instances of wealth.

Results

How well do the frames identified in news media apply to an entertainment medium? Tables 1 and 2 provide the results of a quantitative assessment of the use of particular frames of poverty and wealth found in news media.

There are several main trends apparent in these results. First, for both poverty and wealth no cause is given or implied; neither structural nor individual causes are common. Second, poverty and wealth remain predominantly vague and abstract rather than conditions associated with identifiable groups and individuals. Third, in those cases when poverty is associated with people, there are no clear trends regarding who those people are, and there is only a slight tendency to associate wealth with European and American whites.

Table A2 Frames of poverty in gourmet food writing

Total Articles	102	
References to Poverty	31	
Articles in Sample with at least one Reference to Poverty	28% (29)	
Nature of Cause		
Cause of poverty is personal	0% (0)	
Cause of poverty is structural	10% (3)	
Cause of poverty is event	6% (2)	
No cause given or implied	84% (26)	
Who is Poor		
Poverty is a characteristic of the environment	77% (24)	
Poverty is a characteristic of people	23% (7)	
Poor are unemployed		0% (0)
Poor are employed		43% (3)
Employment status not indicated		57% (4)
Race of poor is indicated or inferrable due to geography	35% (11)	
Poor are African-American or African	0% (0)	

Table A3 Frames of wealth in gourmet food writing

Total Articles	102	
References to Wealth	59	
Articles in Sample with at least one Reference to Wealth	45% (46)	
Nature of Cause		
Cause of wealth is personal	8% (5)	
Cause of wealth is structural	3% (2)	
Cause of wealth is inheritance	12% (7)	
No cause given or implied	76% (45)	
Who is Wealthy		
Wealth is a characteristic of the environment	59% (35)	
Wealth is a characteristic of people	41% (24)	
Wealthy are unemployed		0% (0)
Wealthy are employed		33% (8)
Employment status not indicated		67% (16)
Race of wealthy is indicated or inferrable due to geography	39% (23)	
Wealthy are European or Euro-Americans	27% (16)	

ENDNOTES

1 One of our favorites is the "brown sugar icing" in a community cookbook put together by the Blackfoot Ladies Community Club, which is centered in the rural region west of Lloydminster, Alberta, Canada. We use it on a cocoa snack cake we found in *Fine Cooking*. Brown Sugar Icing: ½ cup margarine (we substitute butter); 1 cup firmly packed brown sugar; 1 teaspoon vanilla; ¼ cup milk, 1¼ cups icing sugar. Boil margarine, brown sugar, vanilla and milk for 1 minute (no more, and no less). Sift in icing sugar, beating until smooth. Pour over cake while icing is still hot. This recipe was contributed by Marj Neudorf.

2 While everyday eating habits were evolving and broadening with changing immigration patterns since well before the turn of the century (Gabaccia 1998), we emphasize that our project examines changes in *gourmet* food practice, rather than changes in general consumption patterns.

3 As with most historical trends, pinpointing an exact date for the "de-sacralization" of haute cuisine is problematic since an emphasis on "authentic" and non-formal food experiences emerged in the 1940s and 1950s with the writing of M. K. Fisher and Elizabeth David. The opening of the Four Seasons restaurant should not be interpreted as the catalyzing event of de-sacralization, since underlying forces challenging haute cuisine's hegemony emerged in earlier decades.

4 This is not to say that the influence of French cuisine as the technical "gold-standard" for professional chefs has been eradicated. Janer (2005) argues that Western culinary art presents French cooking techniques as rational, modern, and the basis of professional culinary knowledge, while ethnic foods are seen as pre-modern novelties, selectively added like spices without fundamentally changing the canon. In addition, we acknowledge that Julia Child's work won wider admiration for French cuisine, and so in an important sense increased respect for French cuisine. However, this respect grew among a broader, less elite base, and so helped, in relative terms, to weaken the association between French cuisine and elites.

5 This has also been labeled the "New American food revolution" (Reed 2003), a trend with considerable diversity (even within the state of California), which we do not wish to trivialize or homogenize.

6 The term "ethnic" is used in this work with awareness that it perpetuates the assumed
   centrality of the Euro-American perspective, and is used without scare quotes to
   enhance readability.

7 This is not to deny the long-standing existence of independent, ethnic grocers who
   catered to a gourmet clientele beyond their ethnic base, such as Balducci's in New York.

8 The USDA recommends that Americans eat between five and nine servings of fruits
   and vegetables daily, yet researchers find that only 21% of men and 30% of women eat
   fruits or vegetables or both five or more times per day (Blanck et al. 2008).

9 There is considerable debate about the extent to which obesity has reached "epidemic"
   proportions—especially since the term "epidemic" is traditionally used to describe
   diseases spread by contagion. For a critical account, see Guthman and DuPuis (2006).

10 Chef2Chef's celebrity chef consulting service helps firms find the right chef to endorse
   their product or event. See http://topchefs.chef2chef.net/personal-celebrity-chefs.php

11 The high costs of certification and the declining price premium for organics—as a
   result of the growing number of suppliers—has pushed (and kept) many small
   suppliers out of the market (Guthman 2004; Pollan 2006). Most of the world's largest
   food processing corporations are now involved in some dimension of organic food,
   and continue to acquire many of the original organic food companies, as well as
   develop their own organic brands (Rural Advancement Foundation International-
   USA 2003: 19). Corporate-organics are primarily distributed using the same global
   commodity chains as conventional agricultural products (Raynolds 2004), distributing
   produce from farms in California, and increasingly from China (Sanders 2006), to
   disparate market niches ranging from Whole Foods Market to WalMart. In sum,
   most organic products originate on large-scale industrial farms and processing
   facilities, travel long distances, and are sold from supermarket shelves—all in direct
   contrast to the original goals of the organics movement.

12 Cox's (2006) journalistic investigation into WFM found that there are no WFMs
   "located in zip codes with average 2003 household incomes at or below $31,000—the
   approximate income earned by a full-time employee earning the average Whole Foods
   wage," and that "half of the zip codes with Whole Foods stores lie above $72,000 in
   average income," and one-quarter have incomes over $100,000.

13 The connection between class and specialty or "quality" food is not unique to Whole
   Foods. See Guthman's description of these connections in the case of California
   organics (2003), and the connections made between gentrification, a high-wage
   economy, and class differentiation.

14 In recent years, food scholarship has thrived as an interdisciplinary academic realm
   but has been largely isolated from debates within the sociology of culture. Important
   exceptions to the trend include Alan Warde's work in the UK (e.g., Warde and
   Tomlinson 1995; Warde and Martens 2000), as well as Erickson (1996). A key
   finding of Erickson's is that knowledge of better restaurants is highly correlated
   with class position, while knowledge of chain restaurants is not. This finding is
   compatible with the thrust of our argument that knowledge of "quality" food is
   linked to class.

15 There is a significant popular literature on omnivorous themes (without employing
   the sociological nomenclature). See Seabrook's (2000) *Nobrow* and Brooks's (2000)
   work on "bobos" (bourgeois bohemians), which both comment on the declining
   distance between "high" and "low" culture, and observe the emergence of new forms
   of cultural, attainment that are (paradoxically) acquisitive, but scornful of obvious
   luxury consumption (e.g., valuing a professional kitchen with marble counter-tops
   and a $25,000 professional range over a Rolls-Royce).

16 We do not directly address the question of the cause of the shift from a snobbish cultural hierarchy to an omnivorous cultural hierarchy. Our work builds on prior research that has established that this shift has occurred and refines our knowledge about the nature of omnivorousness. An explanation of the historical changes that have made omnivorous cultural consumption the predominant high-status cultural consumption strategy is beyond the scope of this book.

17 The French social philosopher, Gilles Lipovetsky, makes a similar point in regards to the democratization of fashion (1994).

18 Interview data come from 30 in-depth interviews, between half an hour and one full hour in length, from 11 different states in the United States, conducted between January and July of 2008. We determined that in-depth, open-ended interviews was the best method for investigating how individuals draw symbolic boundaries between worthy and unworthy food, and especially for uncovering the discursive mechanisms for justifying why certain foods are worthy or unworthy (see, e.g., Lamont 1992, 2000). The open-ended nature of the questions allowed respondents to reveal the justifications for the symbolic boundaries they perceived. The interviews were structured according to an interview guide that asked 14 open-ended questions (see Appendix A). Overall, the interviews provided a picture of personal food preferences with special attention paid to the reasons behind respondents' evaluations of particular foods and particular cuisines. The questions about likes and dislikes in restaurants provided insight into respondents' opinions about various modes of food production and consumption, and the questions about authenticity and exoticism allowed us to compare respondents' answers directly with expert discourse. Respondents were initially identified through personal contacts (1 respondent) or recommendations from personal contacts (2 respondents), and further respondents were identified through snowball sampling, where interviewees referred us to other interviewees (27 respondents). To be eligible for inclusion, we asked respondents to give us the contact information of individuals whom they thought of as having particularly strong interests in eating good food or gourmet food, and who were not directly involved in the food industry. We also sought to diversify our sample geographically and prompted respondents to provide contacts for individuals living in states that were not yet represented or not heavily represented in our sample. Our sample is predominantly affluent, highly-educated, professionally-employed, and ethnically-white. Despite our best efforts, we were unable to obtain recommendations for an ethnically-diverse range of respondents, with 3 of the 30 interviewees describing their ethnicity or race as something other than "white." We were, however, able to contact nearly equal numbers of men and women. Our sample clearly does not represent the general population, but it does correspond reasonably well to the demographic characteristics of the common cultural depiction of foodies as relatively affluent and educated. In addition, it corresponds well to the demographic outline of the cultural omnivore as depicted in recent sociological literature. See Appendix B for a table of the main demographic characteristics of our sample.

19 This is not to say that pre-literate cultures lack cuisine (understood as an established culinary canon of cooking techniques and that represents a particular culture), but that *gastronomy* is distinguished by the element of public writing in the constitution of food practices and mores. For those who perceive this distinction as a diminishment of food culture in pre-literate societies, we would note that the term "gastronomy" allows us to make an empirical distinction, rather than a normative evaluation.

20 Discourse analysis allows for multiple qualitative methods of data collection; "texts" are not simply printed words, but include other materials such as visual sources, spoken words, ethnographic field notes, and artifacts that are collected in order to

better understand a discourse and its underlying ideological conflicts (Grant et al., 1998; Lutz and Collins 1993).

21 Many social movement scholars (e.g., Ferree and Merrill 2000: 455–456) have emphasized a value-neutral interpretation of ideologies that strips the concept of its critical roots to avoid the epistemologically problematic presumption that one can identify "true" causes of oppression. With Fegan (1996) and McLellan (1995), we suggest that a critical perspective on ideology remains key to understanding domination and inequality in socio-cultural arenas. For clarity of language and in keeping with mainstream sociological scholarship, we refer to "democracy" and "distinction" as ideologies, but acknowledge that these terms invoke normative ideals that may, or may not, involve an ideological *process* where power inequities are obscured. Our interest is not to distinguish ideology from "truth," but to identify how ideological processes naturalize and legitimize "ideas in pursuit of dominant interests," which are not imposed in a crude, top-down fashion, but involve a negotiation between individual subjects and dominant cultural constructions (Fegan 1996: 184).

22 We do not believe that democratic ideologies are the singular *cause* of omnivorous cultural patterns, an idealistic line of argumentation that we reject. The rise of omnivorousness is undoubtedly a multi-causal phenomenon with both ideational and structural underpinnings (e.g., migration patterns, post-war wealth, inter-class mobility), a discussion of which is beyond the scope of this book. See Peterson (1997a: 85–86) for a historical account of the decline of the highbrow snob.

23 Lamont's study (1992) is a rich explication of how cultural boundaries differ in two different national contexts, France and the US. While we do not want to diminish the important variations found in multiple national settings, liberal democracy, more generally, forces ideologies of status and distinction to operate at a covert level. In this book, our focus is on the US with its distinctive populist political culture, but we would suggest that this dialectical tension between democracy and distinction is present in varying degrees in other national contexts where an increasingly global democratic ideology makes it less acceptable for elites to present themselves as obviously superior to "common" people.

24 We use the term "faux populism" to make a distinction from populist traditions and histories which employ rhetoric *and* policies that serve the interests of middle- and low-income people. We recognize the conceptual ambiguity around the term populism, and understand that some use the term "populist" to refer to politicians who suggest inclusion with working-class people while introducing policies that exacerbate income inequality (e.g., Ronald Reagan and Margaret Thatcher).

25 When Pete Wells was named the editor of the *New York Times* Dining and Wine section in 2006, he was asked, "How about the restaurant criticism? Will the ultrapowerful, magisterial critic continue to be the model?", and his response spoke to the shift away from all-knowing food authority: "The paper's already getting away from having formal reviews as the only form of criticism. Bruni's less regimented blog is a way of doing that. The reviews now are great, but the world is changing quickly" (New "Times" Dining Editor Speaks, 20 Sept. 2006). While blogs written by established food critics add a more casual, accessible element to food writing, they also multiply the channels through which elite food criticism can reach readers.

26 Among *Gourmet* readers, the average head-of-household income is just over $132,000 (Mendelsohn Media Research 2005).

27 First released in 1994, *Saveur* was awarded three National Magazine Awards within its initial five years in circulation (Ambrozas 2003: 173).

28 Interestingly, when the Food Network debuted, it offered shows such as "Getting Healthy" and "Eating Lite," but prominent celebrity chefs were conspicuously absent from its early programming (Slatalla 2000).

29 While we can assume that most of the Food Network viewers have some interest in food, it is worth noting that an estimated 10% do not like to cook (*American Demographics* 2001).

30 Travel programs frequently center on a performance of multiculturalism, as " 'plausibly live' instantiations of fusion cooking appear to reference the ability of the United States to incorporate difference into a very literal, delicious, melting pot" (Miller 2007: 134).

31 Critiques of prepared foods and processed foods were ubiquitous in our interviews. While some of this critique reflects an obvious display of cultural capital, it is important to acknowledge that this critique is also a response to the centrality of processed foods in a corporate-dominated American foodscape, and represents an attempt to re-value culinary skills.

32 Some of our interviewees avidly watched a variety of shows on the Food Network, others occasionally watched some of the network's shows, and still others disavowed the network entirely. Within our sample, the general trend was that those who demonstrated the most knowledge about food and the most restrictive standards for evaluating worthy food were the least likely to watch the Food Network and the most likely to criticize its shows as debasing standards for good food. In the words of one interviewee, "Most of the stuff [on the Food Network], you know, the Rachael Rays and whatnot of the world, I mean I'm way past that" (Timothy). In the words of another interviewee, "Well, Rachael Ray and Paula Deen and Sandra Lee are not [laughs], are not people in the food world that I connect to. I'm not interested in convenient processed foods and how they can help me get my dinner on the table faster" (Sarah). While Rachael Ray (*30 minute meals*) and Sandra Lee (*Semi-homemade Food*) received the most scrutiny, even shows like the *Iron Chef* were critiqued for their focus on entertainment versus pure food aesthetics. In Ted's words: "You know, it used to be that when you watched the *Iron Chef*, they made interesting things. And then they turned the *Iron Chef* into a reality TV show. I think it's appealing to a lower, you know, a more common denominator than just foodies anymore."

33 See MacCannell (1973) for a discussion of inauthentic tourist settings that does not acknowledge that authenticity is socially constructed. As Erik Cohen (1988) notes, such a discussion is untenable because it cannot account for why places become more or, usually, less authentic over time.

34 Building on this link between food's place of origin and its authenticity, the European Union's Protected Geographical Status framework protects and authenticates foods that are produced in their original region. German cheesemakers, for example, can no longer legally sell "Parmesan." If this legal framework comes to be accepted within the World Trade Organization, Kraft Parmesan cheese sold in the United States would have to re-name itself.

35 In point of fact, most of the organic food consumed by Americans is grown and distributed through transnational agribusiness—an agricultural model far removed from the agrarian ideal of simple family farms, and reliant on complex, long-distance, large-scale distribution systems (Guthman 2004, 1998). However, on the subject of organic or natural production, foodie discourse focuses on individual farmers and small-scale producers that invoke images of a 'simple' rural life, rather than the complexities of globalized commodity chains endemic to supermarket shopping.

36 The Slow Food international movement was founded in 1989 as a critique of the pace of modern life in the post-industrial West, a pace that promotes a neglect of

traditional food practices and encourages the consumption of food that is neither delicious nor ecologically sustainable (www.slowfood.com).

37 First-world chefs (usually men) are written up as cerebral, artistic, and trained, while third-world peoples preparing food (often women) are often unnamed, and described in very different terms: Instinctual, intuitive, 'un-schooled,' and often naïve.

38 We were surprised to find very few uses of the term "fusion cuisine" in our study of gourmet food writing and discourse. We interpret this finding in two ways: (1) as indicative of a broad acceptance of authenticity as characterized in part as a dialog between innovation and tradition; (2) as evidence that "fusion food" was seen as a fad whose time has passed.

39 Heldke describes food adventurers as "those people for whom eating is an expedition into the unknown, a pursuit of the strange," the often Euro-American, Christian-raised eaters "who believe that we have no culture of our own," and who "long to spice up our diets (literally) with the flavors of exotic cuisines" (2003: xxi).

40 Some scholars understand Orientalism as one particular form of exoticism, distinguished by its geographic specificity (Santaolalla 2000). In our analysis, we understand the exotic frame in foodie discourse as centrally related to Orientalism.

41 Using the term geo-political "core," we are referring not only to economic centrality, but the center of political, geographic, and cultural power in the global economy. While the United States is clearly central to this geo-political "core" (although the status of its economic and military hegemony is vigorously contested), the global economy has produced multiple nodes of power in the global economy that are geographically dispersed (e.g., Singapore, Bangalore), while rendering swathes of the traditional core of the United States relatively peripheral (e.g., the rust belt cities, or the emptied-out towns of the rural United States).

42 While our understanding of exoticism explicitly takes the vantage point of the Euro-American food adventurer, it is important to recognize that other perspectives of exoticism exist, particularly in a global context of cross-cultural consumption (e.g., Japanese staples like sushi and kobe beef are consumed in India's finest restaurants). (On the topic of inter-cultural exoticism see Kadi 1996; Narayan 1997: 183–184, 187.)

43 The reader is reminded that French fries can be framed as gourmet food through claims of authenticity (e.g., hand-cut, made from heritage potatoes), even if they cannot be framed as exotic.

44 Although both authentic and exotic foods are frequently rare, the discourse that justifies these foods as worthy specifies other qualities—like the fact that the foods are hand-made, or come from a highly specific geographic location. Omnivorous logic must refer to these other qualities to valorize cultural objects because of the need to manage the tension between democracy and distinction, and satisfy contemporary norms that sanction overt snobbery suggesting that culture is good only when it is expensive or beyond the reach of the average person.

45 For a presentation of our quantitative findings on the geographic locations of gourmet food writing, see Johnston and Baumann (2007).

46 In this example we are told that the baby goat's head arrives at the table with the top of the skull sawed off for easy removal to allow access to the brains. Although the food writer finds this particular dish unappetizing, it sends a clear message that high-status eating needs to contemplate breaking boundaries.

47 The most famous culinary proponent of high-end offal is Fergus Henderson, British restaurateur (founder of St John restaurant) and author of the bestselling cookbook, *The Whole Beast: Nose to Tail Eating* (New York: Ecco/HarperCollins, 2004).

48 How do foodies of color frame exoticism in food? We would note that we are providing a reading of the dominant form of foodie discourse, one that is to a large degree a construction of the mass media. As the field of media studies has established, niche marketing notwithstanding, the creators of the mainstream mass media in the contemporary United States are predominantly white and produce content that both reflects and reinforces the dominant discourses of the American public sphere. Thus, while some foodies, and particularly foodies of color, can challenge the exoticism frame in foodie discourse, this frame is nonetheless dominant in foodie discourse.

49 Our analysis of gourmet food journalism in this chapter is primarily based on a close and systematic reading of 2008 January through June issues of *Gourmet, Bon Appétit,* and *Saveur,* and on the food and dining columns in the *New York Times* and *San Francisco Chronicle* over the same period. We examined the framing of food politics in other years (2004, 2006, 2009) as well, though less systematically. We incorporate examples from these other years when appropriate.

50 This is not to say that there have not been individuals that move between the countercuisine and gourmet worlds—individuals who were both interested in food politics and gourmet food. The most notable is Ruth Reichl, who in her memoirs recounts her journey from the Berkeley counterculture to the esteemed position of food editor at the *New York Times* (and who is currently the editor of *Gourmet* magazine) (Reichl 1999; Reichl 2002). Our point here is not that individuals did not possess multiple concerns about food, but that at an institutional level in the post-war period, political and gourmet concerns occupied relatively distinct realms—on the one hand, the youth-based countercuisine which drew from the emerging environmental movement and peace movement, and on the other hand, the older world of *Gourmet* magazine, fine dining establishments, and culinary personalities like Lucius Beebe.

51 Gourmet culture continued to emerge in the 1960s and 1970s, of course. It was not a static, monolithic pursuit of French food but became more omnivorous in its preferences (see Johnston and Baumann 2007). Food politics emerged alongside American gourmet culture, operating on a simultaneous but separate track that would eventually merge with contemporary foodie-ism.

52 The website of Sam Kass's private chef firm, Inevitable Table, has the bold statement: "We know we can improve our health, our families, and our communities by providing clean, simple, quality food" (http://www.inevitabletable.com/).

53 For a lengthier discussion on the distinction between the ideologies of consumerism and citizenship, and the contradictions involved in the hybrid concept of "citizen-consumers," see Johnston 2008: 241–244.

54 The meaning of citizenship has been a hotly debated historical question, and one that determines the vision of public life under debate (Beiner 2006). While political philosophers have traditionally understood citizenship as membership in a state or political community (e.g., Marshall 1992 [1950]), here we deliberately broaden the meaning of citizenship beyond the state-container of formal politics to encompass citizenship's political-economic, political-ecological, and cultural dimensions

55 Our use of the term "eco" is deliberately vague, and intended to mirror its discursive usage in foodie sources. This phrase is frequently and vaguely used in foodie discourse as a shorthand adjective to connote products that are responsible for promoting sustainability, even though the precise environmental implications of these products, and of affluent consumer consumption habits more generally, are left unspecified and unexplored.

56 Ethical consumption has been fueled by a growing "unease with abundance," where a life of luxury goods is not summarily equated with personal or moral satisfaction (Hilton 2003: 298; Soper 2007). It is important to emphasize that practices of ethical

consumption cover a wide swath of activities and commodities—fair-trade coffee, anti-sweatshop clothing, organic food at big box grocery stores—some of which are much more deeply engaged with citizenship concerns than others and have more of a social movement, collective-action dimension.

57 Approaches emphasizing the manipulation of consumers are most often associated with the Frankfurt School and post-war critiques of the advertising industry (e.g., Marcuse 1964; Packard 1957), but today, such approaches are often viewed as overly pessimistic and old-fashioned because they underestimate consumer agency, and overstate the importance of selling (or manipulating) consumers (Micheletti 2003: 70; Schudson 1991, 1984). Against Frankfurt pessimism, more optimistic accounts focus on consumers' abilities to influence the commercial environment to construct meaningful lifestyles and identities (e.g., Fiske 1989; Abercrombie 1994). Further, the business literature on the topic emphasizes how consumer demand fuels the growth of socially responsible corporations promoting social justice and environmental sustainability (Cairncross 1992).

58 Szasz refers to these strategies as "inverted quarantine," which means to assemble "a personal commodity bubble for one's body" (2007: 97). Like a conventional quarantine, the goal of inverted quarantine is to provide protection from pathology. Unlike a traditional quarantine which confines threats to an isolated area (e.g., a tuberculosis sanitarium), the inverted quarantine sees threats anywhere and everywhere. The inverted quarantine objective is to build small safe zones within a larger polluted industrial landscape.

59 More typical issues covered in these historic magazines include exposés on cultural history (e.g. "Fancy the Rose," June 1952, p. 16), tips on hosting a culinary event (e.g. "Luau In Your Own Backyard," Sept. 1952, p. 8), and enticing tales of exotic cuisine (e.g. "Foods of the Phillipines," Oct. 1980, p. 50). Notably, when food writers explore the Los Angeles Farmers' Market in the August 1980 issue, the story is framed in terms of nostalgia for childhood experiences, with no mention of the ethical issues that are consistently associated with farmers' markets in current issues.

60 Gourmet.com. The Gourmet Q+A: Michael Pollan. Jan. 8, 2008. (<http://www.gourmet.com/foodpolitics/2008/01/michael_pollan_QA>)

61 For example, of the 16 issues we systematically examined in 2008, one-quarter of them contained no substantive references to food politics. Among those that did, some included only an occasional textbox featuring an "eco" product, or featuring a seasonal recipe. When a substantial food politics feature piece is included, it is typically the only in-depth coverage of food politics in the issue.

62 In our reading of gourmet food sources, we observed that slightly more space was given to the contradictions surrounding organic food versus local eating. This reflects the heightened public scrutiny of corporate organic food (which has been criticized for veering from the sustainability practices of early, small-scale organic practices) whereas local eating has become the new orthodoxy of progressive eating (Johnston, Biro and MacKendrick 2009; Born and Purcell 2006; DuPuis and Goodman 2005).

63 For example, the federal government currently does very little to support sustainable food projects. The New York Times reported that farm subsidies in 2008 were $7.5 billion, compared with only $15 million in federal funds for organic and local foods (New York Times, 22 March 2009, p. BU1).

64 A blog site devoted to "ethicurean" issues defines the term as follows: "eth·i·cu·re·an n. (also adj.) Someone who seeks out tasty things that are also sustainable, organic, local, and/or ethical—SOLE food, for short." "The Ethicurean. Chew the Right Thing." Accessed October 23, 2008. (www.ethicurean.com)

65 For a discussion of the meanings surrounding the term "foodie", refer to Chapter 1.

66 The following discussion is based on our quantitative study of framing in gourmet food writing. See Appendix C for a presentation of the quantitative method and results.

67 We could locate no systematic research on which socio-demographic groups are portrayed as wealthy in the media or on the causes of wealth. However, Kendall's (2005) study of the framing of class in the media suggests that wealth is associated with whites, although she does not address this question explicitly.

68 It is worth mentioning that our reading of the presentation of wealthy—even extremely wealthy—environments in food writing is that these descriptions are not intended to be ironic or satirical.

69 Our use of "classless" here refers to the well-documented phenomenon of low class awareness and high tolerance for wealth and income inequality among the American public. See the conclusion to this chapter for further discussion and references to the sociological literature on this topic.

70 Within our sample, we found the romanticization of poverty frame to be less common in the newspapers than in the magazines. This may be due to the fact that the newspaper food sections tend to focus on home cooking and urban dining, and rarely include the "travel" stories to rural or foreign places that are prevalent in magazines.

71 One exception to this trend, albeit a contradictory one, can be found in *Gourmet*'s portrayal of Craig Sams, the founder of the organic chocolate company, Green & Black's (now owned by food industry giant, Cadbury Schweppes). The article obliquely implies that rural poverty is a problem by claiming that "everyone seems to have profited" from Green & Black's growth, including the cocoa farmers who now have concrete rather than dirt floors. At the same time, the article includes a quote from Sams admitting that "cacao will never make these farmers rich", and who argues for the development potential of tourism (*Gourmet*, August 2008, p. 61).

72 The origins of kitsch have a longer history; in the late 1960s, Susan Sontag noted that the classic American distinctions between highbrow and lowbrow cultural forms were becoming less meaningful, while the rise of "kitsch" and "camp" cultural forms introduced by Andy Warhol allowed a playful inversion and appropriation process that destabilized the boundaries between the snobbish world of "quality" Art and Culture, and the lowbrow world of commercial culture and mass production (1966: 297, 302).

73 Kendall (2005: 30) observes a similar frame in her study of the framing of the wealthy in the media. She labels this the "consensus frame."

74 As explained in our introduction, we argue that the cultural mode of snobbish "gourmets" has been replaced by an omnivorousness mode of "foodie" consumption. However, we use the term "gourmet" in instances where it is more linguistically appropriate, and to convey a meaning beyond mainstream, ordinary food (i.e., gourmet magazines, gourmet food specialty stores).

75 As explained in the introductory chapter, our use of the term "foodie" reflects exactly this recognition of omnivorous preferences as the term stands in contrast to the more conventional term of a "gourmet." "Gourmet" carries connotations of snobbism, and foodies clearly eschew snobbery.

76 It should be noted that some foodies defend the occasional fast-food indulgence as acceptable since it occurs in a larger consumption pattern focused on high-quality food, and also helps distinguish the reader from traditional food snobs (Serious Eats 2009).

77 See Warde et al. (2008) for support for this claim of the unacceptability of overt snobbery among omnivores in the UK.

78 We borrow this distinction between causal explanation and translational explanation from Abbott (2004: ch.7).

REFERENCES

"A Phrase Right Out of History (and 99 More)." 2006. *Chicago Sun-Times*, November 29, 40.

Abarca, Meredith. 2004. "Authentic or Not, It's Original." *Food & Foodways* 12: 1–25.

Abbott, Andrew. 2004. *Methods of Discovery*. New York: W.W. Norton & Company.

Abercrombie, Nicholas. 1994. "Authority and Consumer Society." Pp. 43–57 in *The Authority of the Consumer*, edited by R. Keat, N. Whiteley, and N. Abercrombie. New York: Routledge.

Adams, Mark. 1996. "How to Win a Food Fight." *Mediaweek*, May 6, 34.

Adema, Pauline. 2000. "Vicarious Consumption: Food, Television and the Ambiguity of Modernity." *Journal of American and Comparative Cultures* 23(3): 113–124.

Alford, Jeffrey. 2004. "Too Perfect by Half." *Globe & Mail*. November 27, D27.

Alford, Jeffrey and Naomi Duguid. 1998. *Seductions of Rice: A Cookbook*. New York: Artisan Publishers.

———. 2000. *Hot Sour Salty Sweet: A Culinary Journey Through Southeast Asia*. New York: Artisan Publishers.

Altheide, David L. 1997. "The News Media, the Problem Frame, and the Production of Fear." *The Sociological Quarterly* 38: 646–668.

Ambrozas, Diana. 2003. "Serious Feast: Vancouver Foodies in Globalized Consumer Society." *Dissertation Abstracts International* 66(6)A: 2406-A-2407-A.

———. 2005. "Kitchen Salivations: Vancouver Foodies Read Cooking Magazines." Presentation at the 2005 Joint Meetings of the Agriculture, Food and Human Values Society and Association for the Study of Food and Society. Portland, OR. June 10, 2005.

American Demographics. 2001. "Apron Envy—Information about Food Network Viewers—Brief Article—Statistical Data Included." July 1, 2001. Retrieved March 5, 2009 (http://findarticles.com/p/articles/mi_m4021/is_2001_July_1/ai_76574314)

American Dietetic Association (ADA). 2006. "Position of the American Dietetic Association: Food Insecurity and Hunger in the United States." *Journal of the American Dietetic Association* 106(3): 446–458.

Andrée, Peter. 2006. "And Miles to go before I eat . . . Local Limitations." *Alternatives Journal* 32(3): 19–21.

Appadurai, Arjun (ed.). 1986. *The Social Life of Things: Commodities in Cultural Perspective.* New York: Cambridge University Press.

——. 1988. "How to Make a National Cuisine: Cookbooks in Contemporary India." *Comparative Studies in Society and History* 30(1): 3–24.

Araghi, Farshad. 2000. "The Great Global Enclosure of Our Times: Peasants and the Agrarian Question at the End of the Twentieth Century." Pp. 145–160 in *Hungry for Profit: The Agribusiness Threat to Farmers, Food, and the Environment,* edited by F. Magdoff, J. Bellamy Foster, and F. Buttel. New York: Monthly Review Press.

Arnott, Nancy. 2003a. *The U.S. Market for Ethnic Foods,* Volume 1: *The U.S. Market for Hispanic Foods.* New York: Packaged Facts.

Arnott, Nancy. 2003b. *The U.S. Market for Ethnic Foods,* Volume 2: *The U.S. Market for Asian Foods.* New York: Packaged Facts.

Arnott, Nancy. 2003c. *The U.S. Market for Ethnic Foods,* Volume 3: *The U.S. Market for Emerging Ethnic Foods.* New York: Packaged Facts.

Arnould, E. J. 2007. "Should Consumer Citizens escape the Market?" *The Annals of the American Academy of Political and Social Science* 611(1): 193–204.

Barndt, Deborah. 2007. *Tangled Routes: Women, Work and Globalization on the Tomato Trail.* 2nd ed. Lanham, MD: Rowman & Littlefield.

Batterberry, Michael and Ariane Batterberry. 1999. *On the Town in New York: The Landmark History of Eating, Drinking, and Entertainments from the American Revolution to the Food Revolution.* New York: Routledge.

Beamish, Thomas D., Harvey Molotch, and Richard Flacks. 1995. "Who Supports the Troops? Vietnam, the Gulf War, and the Making of Collective Memory." *Social Problems* 42(3): 344–360.

Beck, Ulrich. 2002. "The Cosmopolitan Society and its Enemies." *Theory, Culture & Society* 19(1–2): 17–44.

——. 2006. *The Cosmopolitan Vision,* translated by Ciaran Cronin. Cambridge, UK: Polity.

Beckett, Katherine. 1996. "Culture and the Politics of Signification: The Case of Child Sexual Abuse." *Social Problems* 43(1): 57–76.

Beem, Edgar Allan. 2007. "Feast for the Eyes: The Award-winning Design Team is Always on the Lookout for Ways to Surprise Readers, and Itself." *Adweek,* March 5, SR8.

Beiner, R. 2006. "Multiculturalism and Citizenship: A Critical Response to Iris Marion Young." *Educational Philosophy and Theory* 38(1): 25–37.

Belasco, Warren. 1989. *Appetite for Change. How the Counterculture Took on the Food Industry, 1966–1988.* New York: Pantheon Books.

——. 2002. "Food Matters: Perspectives on an Emerging Field." Pp. 2–23 in *Food Nations: Selling Taste in Consumer Societies,* edited by W. Belasco and P. Scranton. New York: Routledge.

——. 2005. "Food and the Counterculture: A Story of Bread and Politics." Pp. 217–234 in *The Cultural Politics of Food and Eating,* edited by J. Watson and M. Caldwell. Malden, MA: Blackwell.

Bello, Walden. 2008. "Manufacturing a Food Crisis." *The Nation.* June 2. Retrieved March 31, 2009.
(http://www.thenation.com/doc/20080602/bello)

Benford, Robert D. and David A. Snow. 2000. "Framing Processes and Social Movements: An Overview and Assessment." *Annual Review of Sociology* 26: 611–639.

Benson, Rodney and Abigail Saguy. 2006. "Constructing Social Problems in an Age of Globalization: A French-American Comparison." *American Sociological Review* 70: 233–259.

Bentley, Amy. 1998. "From Culinary Other to Mainstream America: Meanings and Uses of Southwestern Cuisine." *Southern Folklore* 55(3): 238–252.

——. 2005. "Men on Atkins: Dieting, Meat and Masculinity." In *The Atkins Diet and Philosophy*, edited by L. Heldke, K. Mommer, and C. Pineo. Chicago: Open Court.

Best, Joel. 1999. *Random Violence: How We Talk about New Crimes and New Victims.* Berkeley, CA: University of California Press.

Binder, Amy. 1993. "Constructing Racial Rhetoric: Media Depictions of Harm in Heavy Metal and Rap Music." *American Sociological Review* 58: 753–767.

Binkley, Sam. 2007. *Getting Loose: Lifestyle Consumption in the 1970s.* Durham, NC: Duke University Press.

Bittman, Mark. 2007. *How to Cook Everything Vegetarian.* Hoboken, NJ: John Wiley & Sons Incorporated.

Blanck, H. M., C. Gillespie, J. E. Kimmons, J. D. Seymour, and M. K. Serdula. 2008. "Trends in Fruit and Vegetable Consumption among U.S. Men and Women, 1994–2005." *Preventing Chronic Disease* 5(2). Accessed March 18, 2009 (http://www.cdc.gov/pcd/issues/2008/ apr/07_0049.htm)

Bobo, Lawrence. 1991. "Social Responsibility, Individualism, and Redistributive Policies." *Sociological Forum* 6(1): 71–92.

Born, Branden and Mark Purcell. 2006. "Avoiding the Local Trap: Scale and Food Systems in Planning Research." *Journal of Planning Education and Research* 26: 195–207.

Bourdieu, Pierre. 1984. *Distinction: A Social Critique of the Judgment of Taste*, translated by R. Nice. Cambridge, MA: Harvard University Press.

——. 1993. *The Field of Cultural Production.* New York: Columbia University Press.

Brantlinger, Ellen. 1993. *The Politics of Social Class in Secondary School: Views of Affluent and Impoverished Youth.* New York: Teachers College Press.

Brooks, David. 2000. *Bobos in Paradise: The New Upper Class and How They Got There.* New York: Touchstone.

Brown, Doug. 2004. "Haute Cuisine." *American Journalism Review* 26(1): 50–55.

Bryson, Bethany. 1996. " 'Anything But Heavy Metal': Symbolic Exclusion and Musical Dislikes." *American Sociological Review* 61: 884–899.

Buford, Bill. 2007. "Extreme Chocolate." *The New Yorker*, October 29, p. 68.

Burros, Marian. 2009. "Newest White House Chef Knows the Obamas' Taste," *New York Times*, January 28 (http://www.nytimes.com/2009/01/29/us/politics/29cook.html)

Cairncross, Frances. 1992. *Costing the Earth: The Challenge for Governments, the Opportunities for Business.* Boston, MA: Harvard Business School Press.

Capella, Joseph N. and Kathleen Jamieson. 1996. "New Frames, Political Cynicism, and Media Cynicism." *Annals of the American Academy of Political and Social Science* 546: 71–84.

Carroll, William. 1992. "Introduction: Social Movements and Counter-Hegemony in a Canadian Context." Pp. 1–21 in *Organizing Dissent. Contemporary Social Movements in Theory and Practice*, edited by W. Carroll. Toronto: Garamond Press.

——. 2004. "Subverting Dominant Discourses: Critical Discourse Analysis." Pp. 225–231 in *Critical Strategies for Social Research*, edited by W. Carroll. Toronto: Canadian Scholars' Press.

Case, Tony. 2007. "Great Taste." *Mediaweek*, March 5, SR2.

CCD [Center for Culinary Development]. 2007. *Spices and Seasonings. Culinary Trend Mapping Report* 4(2). New York: Packaged Facts.

CDC. [Centers for Disease Control and Prevention]. 2005. "Fruit and Vegetable
    Consumption Among Adults—United States, 2005." *MMWR Weekly* 56(10):
    213–217. Retrieved
    (http://www.cdc.gov/mmwr/preview/mmwrhtml/mm5610a2.htm)
Centers, Richard. 1949. *The Psychology of Social Classes*. New York: Russell & Russell.
CFSC [Community Food Security Coalition]. 2008. *What Is Community Food Security?*
    Retrieved December 2008
    (http://www.foodsecurity.org/views_cfs_faq.html)
Chan, Andrew. 2003. " 'La Grande Bouffe': Cooking Shows as Pornography."
    Gastronomica 3(4): 47.
Chan, Tak Win and John H. Goldthorpe. 2007. "Class and Status. The Conceptual
    Distinction and its Empirical Relevance." *American Sociological Review* 72: 512–532.
Chowhound. 2008. "Chowhound Manifesto." Retrieved December 5, 2008
    (http://chowhound.chow.com/manifesto)
Civitello, Linda. 2007. *Cuisine and Culture: A History of Food and People*. 2nd ed. Hoboken,
    NJ: John Wiley & Sons.
Clawson, Rosalee A. and Rakuya Trice. 2000. "Poverty as We Know It: Media Portrayals
    of the Poor." *Public Opinion Quarterly* 64(1): 53–64.
Cobe, Patricia. 2006. "Foodservice Buyer World Flavors." *Restaurant Business* 105(6): 59–67.
Cohen, Andy. 2001. "Look Who's Cooking Now." *Sales & Marketing Management*
    153(12): 30–35.
Cohen, Erik. 1988. "Authenticity and Commoditization in Tourism." *Annals of Tourism
    Research* 15: 371–386.
Collins, Clayton. 2007. "It's a Starbucks World. (We Only Sip in It.)" *Christian Science
    Monitor*. Retrieved December 17, 2007
    (http://features.csmonitor.com/books/2007/12/17/its-a-starbucks-world-we-only-
    sip-in-it/)
Colman, Michelle Sinclair. 2008. *Foodie Babies Wear Bibs*. Illustrated by Nathalie Dion.
    Berkeley, CA: Tricycle Press.
Community Food Service Coalition. See CFSC.
Conrad, Peter. 2001. "Genetic Optimism: Framing Genes and Mental Illness in the
    News." *Culture, Medicine, and Psychiatry* 25: 225–247.
Cook, John, Deborah A. Frank, Carol Berkowitz, Maureen M. Black, Patrick H. Casey,
    Diana B. Cutts, Alan F. Meyers, Nieves Zaldivar, Anne Skalicky, Suzette Levenson,
    Tim Heeren, and Mark Nord. 2004. "Food Insecurity is associated with Adverse Health
    Outcomes among Human Infants and Toddlers." *Journal of Nutrition* 134: 1432–1438.
Cox, Stan. 2006. "Natural Food, Unnatural Prices." Alternet. Posted Jan. 25, 2006.
    Accessed June 24, 2009
    (http://www.alternet.org/story/31260/)
Curtin, Deane and Lisa Heldke. 1992. "Introduction." In *Cooking, Eating, Thinking:
    Transformative Philosophies of Food*, edited by Deane Curtin and Lisa Heldke.
    Bloomington, IN: Indiana University Press.
Danford, Natalie. 2005. "Video made the Cookbook Star: How the Food Network
    conquered the Category." *Publishers Weekly* 252(12) (March 21): 24(2). Available online:
    (http://www.publishersweekly.com/article/CA51/583.html)
Daponte, Beth Osborne and Shannon Bade. 2006. "How the Private Food Assistance
    Network Evolved: Interactions between Public and Private Responses to Hunger."
    Nonprofit and Voluntary Sector Quarterly 35(4): 668–690.
David, Elizabeth. 1998a [1950]. *A Book of Mediterranean Food*. 2nd ed. London: Penguin.
——. 1998b [1954]. *Italian Food*. Revised edition. London: Penguin.

——. 1998c [1951]. *French Provincial Cooking*. London: Penguin.

Davis, Mitchell. 2004. "Power Meal: Craig Claiborne's Last Supper for the *New York Times*." *Gastronomica* 4(3): 60.

Denitto, Emily. 2008. "Cooking classes preparing young chefs." *New York Times*, March 9, WE1.

Desrochers, Pierre and Hiroko Shimzu. 2008 (October). "Yes We Have No Bananas: A Critique of the Food Miles Perspective." Mercatus Policy Series Policy Primer, No. 8. Arlington, VA: Mercatus Center at George Mason University.

DiMaggio, Paul. 1982. "Cultural Entrepreneurship in Nineteenth Century Boston, Part I: The Creation of an Organizational Base for High Culture in America." *Media, Culture and Society* 4: 33–50.

——. 1992. "Cultural Boundaries and Structural Change: The Extension of the High Culture Model to Theatre, Opera and the Dance, 1900–1940." Pp. 21–57 in *Cultivating Differences: Symbolic Boundaries and the Making of Inequality*, edited by Michelle Lamont and Marcel Fournier. Chicago: University of Chicago Press.

DiMaggio, Paul and Toqir Mukhtar. 2004. "Arts Participation as Cultural Capital in the United States, 1982–2002: Signs of Decline?" *Poetics: Journal of Empirical Research on Culture, the Media and the Arts* 32: 169–194.

Dryzek, John S. 2005. *The Politics of the Earth: Environmental Discourses*. Oxford: Oxford University Press.

DuPuis, E. Melanie and David Goodman. 2005. "Should We Go 'Home' to Eat?: Toward a Reflexive Politics of Localism." *Journal of Rural Studies* 21(3): 359–371.

Eaton, Emily. 2008. "From feeding the Locals to selling the Locale: Adapting Local Sustainable Food Projects in Niagara to Neocommunitarianism and Neoliberalism." *Geoforum* 39: 994–1006.

eGullet. 2008. "Let's Kill 'Foodie'." Egullet Forums, Food Traditions and Culture. [Chris Hennes, 12:12 p.m.]. Message posted Jan. 24, to (http//forums.egullet.org/index.php?showtopic=112235)

Elias, Norbert. 2000. *The Civilizing Process: Sociogenetic and Psychogenetic Investigations*. Oxford: Blackwell Publishers.

Emmison, Michael. 2003. "Social Class and Cultural Mobility: Reconfiguring the Omnivore Thesis." *Journal of Sociology* 39: 211–230.

Entman, Robert M. 1993. "Framing: Toward Clarification of a Fractured Paradigm." *Journal of Communication* 43(4): 51–58.

——. 2004. *Projections of Power: Framing News, Public Opinion, and U.S. Foreign Policy*. Chicago: University of Chicago Press.

Erickson, Bonnie H. 1996. "Culture, Class and Connections." *American Journal of Sociology* 102: 217–251.

——. 2007. "The Crisis in Culture and Inequality." Pp.343–362 in *Engaging Art: The Next Great Transformation of America's Cultural Life*, edited by William Ivey and Steven J. Tepper. New York: Routledge.

Fairchild, Barbara. 2004. "Letter from the Editor. Reality Bites." *Bon Appétit* 49(1): 18.

Fairclough, Norman. 1992. *Discourse and Social Change*. Cambridge, MA: Polity Press.

Fairclough, Norman and R. Wodak. 1997. "Critical Discourse Analysis." Pp. 258–284 in *Discourse as Social Interaction*. Volume 1, edited by T. A. van Dijk. London: Sage.

Farmer, Anne. 2008. "35 lucky, and hungry, diners eat and walk with Calvin Trillin." *New York Times Online*. Retrieved October 5, 2008 (http://www.nytimes.com/2008/10/06/nyregion/06trillin.html?_r=2&scp=3&sq=calvin%20trillin&st=cse&oref=slogin)

Fegan, Eileen. 1996. " 'Ideology' After 'Discourse': A Reconceptualization for Feminist Analyses of Law." *Journal of Law and Society* 23(2): 173–197.

Ferguson, Priscilla Parkhurst. 1998. "A Cultural Field in the Making: Gastronomy in 19th Century France." *The American Journal of Sociology* 104(3): 597–641.

——. 2004. *Accounting for Taste: The Triumph of French Cuisine.* Chicago: University of Chicago Press.

——. 2005. "Eating Orders: Markets, Menus, and Meals." *Journal of Modern History* 77 (September): 275–300.

Ferguson, Priscilla Parkhurst and Sharon Zukin. 1995. "What's Cooking?" *Theory and Society* 24: 193–195.

Ferree, Myra Marx and David Merrill. 2000. "Hot Movements, Cold Cognition: Thinking about Social Movements in Gendered Frames." *Contemporary Sociology* 29(3): 454–462.

Ferry, Jane. 2003. *Food in Film: A Culinary Performance of Communication.* New York: Routledge.

Feuillet, Alice. 2007. "Real Foodies Don't Eat Lean Cuisine," *Pax Americana: Culture, Politics, and Ineffectual Debate.* Retrieved March 6, 2009 (http://paxamericana.wordpress.com/2007/09/21/real-foodies-don't-eat-lean-cuisine/)

Fine, Gary Alan. 1996. *Kitchens: The Culture of Restaurant Work.* Berkeley, CA: University of California Press.

——. 2003. "Crafting Authenticity: The Validation of Identity in Self-Taught Art." *Theory and Society* 33(2): 153–180.

Fischler, Claude. 1990. *L' Homnivore. Le Goût, La Cuisine et Le Corps.* Paris: Éditions Odile Jacob.

Fisher, Timothy C. G. and Stephen B. Preece. 2003. "Evolution, Extinction, or Status Quo: Canadian Performing Arts Audiences in the 1990s." *Poetics: Journal of Empirical Research on Culture, the Media and the Arts* 31: 69–86.

Fiske, John. 1989. *Reading the Popular.* London: Routledge.

Fold, Niels and Bill Pritchard (eds.). 2005. *Cross-Continental Food Chains.* London: Routledge.

Food Network. 2007. "About Food Network.com." Retrieved Sept. 5, 2007 (http://www.foodnetwork.com/food/about_us/)

Food Network Addict. 2008. "Questioning Gordon Elliott's Motives—Why I'm Not Happy with Big Daddy's House." [Jacob at 6:00p.m.]. Article posted September 1, to (http://foodnetworkaddict.blogspot.com/2008/09/questioning-gordon-elliotts-motives-why.html)

Frank, Thomas. 2000. *One Market Under God: Extreme Capitalism, Market Populism and the End of Economic Democracy.* New York: Doubleday.

Fromartz, Samuel. 2006. *Organic Inc. Natural Foods and How They Grew.* Toronto: Harcourt Inc.

Fussell, Betty. 2005. *Masters of American Cookery: M. F. K. Fisher, James Beard, Craig Claiborne, Julia Child.* Lincoln, NE: University of Nebraska Press.

Gabaccia, Donna. 1998. *We Are What We Eat: Ethnic Food and the Making of Americans.* Cambridge, MA: Harvard University Press.

Gabriel, Yiannis and Tim Lang. 2006 [1995]. *The Unmanageable Consumer: Contemporary Consumption and its Fragmentations.* 2nd edition. London: Sage Publications.

Gallagher, Mario. 2008. "Brother, Can You Spare an Apple?" *Huffington Post.* Posted September 9, 2008. Retrieved (http://www.huffingtonpost.com/mari-gallagher/brother-can-you-spare-an_b_124762.html)

Gamson, William A. 1989. "News as Framing: Comments on Graber." *American Behavioral Scientist* 33(2): 157–161.

Gamson, William A. and Andre Modigliani. 1989. "Media Discourse and Public Opinion on Nuclear Power: A Constructionist Approach." *American Journal of Sociology* 95(1): 1–37.

Gans, Herbert. 1995. *The War Against the Poor: The Underclass and Anti-Poverty Policy.* New York: Basic Books.

———. 1999. *Popular Culture and High Culture: An Analysis and Evaluation of Taste*, revised and updated. New York: Basic Books.

Garber, Amy. 2003. "Upscale Chef Bayless to Weigh in for BK." *Nation's Restaurant News.* Sept. 29, 2003. (http://findarticles.com/p/articles/mi_m3190/is_39_37/ai_108550259)

Gibson, Campbell and Kay Jung. 2002. "Historical Census Statistics on Population Totals By Race, 1790 to 1990, and By Hispanic Origin, 1970 to 1990, For The United States, Regions, Divisions, and States." U.S. Census Bureau, Working Paper Series No. 56. Retrieved March 13, 2009 (http://www.census.gov/population/www/documentation/twps0056/twps0056.html)

Gilens, Martin. 1996. "Race and Poverty in America: Public Misperceptions and the American News Media." *Public Opinion Quarterly* 60: 515–541.

———. 1999. *Why Americans Hate Welfare: Race, Media, and the Politics of Anti-Poverty Policy.* Chicago: University of Chicago Press.

Goffman, Erving. 1974. *Frame Analysis: An Essay on the Organization of Experience.* New York: Harper & Row.

Goodman, D. and M. Goodman. 2001. "Sustaining Foods: Organic Consumption and the Socio-Ecological Imaginary." Pp. 97–119 in *Exploring Sustainable Consumption: Environmental Policy and the Social Sciences*, edited by Maurie J. Cohen and Joseph Murphy. Amsterdam: Pergamon.

Goody, Jack. 1982. *Cooking, Cuisine and Class. A Study in Comparative Sociology.* Cambridge: Cambridge University Press.

Gottdiener, Mark (ed.). 2000. *New Forms of Consumption. Consumers, Culture, and Commodification.* New York: Rowman & Littlefield Publishers Inc.

Gould, Carol. 2004. *Globalizing Democracy and Human Rights.* Cambridge, UK: Cambridge University Press.

Gramsci, Antonio. 1971. *Selections from the Prison Notebooks.* New York: International Publishers.

Granastein, Lisa. 1999. "Galloping Gourmet." *Mediaweek*, August 9, 50.

Grant, David, Tom Keenoy, and Clifford Oswick. 1998. "Organizational Discourse: Of Diversity, Dichotomy and Multi-Disciplinarity." Pp. 1–14 in *Discourse and Organization*, edited by David Grant, Tom Keenoy and Clifford Oswick. London: Sage Publications.

Gray, Steven. 2006. "Boss Talk: Natural Competitor; How Whole Foods CEO Mackey Intends to Stop Growth Slippage." *Wall Street Journal*, December 4, 2006, B.1.

Grazian, David. 2003. *Blue Chicago: The Search for Authenticity in Urban Blues Clubs.* Chicago: University of Chicago Press.

Grieco, Elizabeth M., and Rachel C. Cassidy. 2001. "Overview of Race and Hispanic Origin, Census 2000 Brief." U.S. Department of Commerce. Retrieved on March 13, 2009 (http://www.census.gov/prod/2001pubs/c2kbr01–1.pdf)

Guest, Avery M. 1974. "Class Consciousness and American Political Attitudes." *Social Forces* 52(4): 496–510.

Guthman, Julie. 1998. "Regulating Meaning, Appropriating Nature: The Codification of California Organic Agriculture." *Antipode* 30(2): 135–154.

——. 2003. "Fast Food / Organic Food: Reflexive Tastes and the Making of 'Yuppie Chow'." *Social and Cultural Geography* 4(1): 45–58.

——. 2004. *Agrarian Dreams. The Paradox of Organic Farming in California.* Berkeley, CA: University of California Press.

——. 2007. "Commentary on Teaching Food: Why I am fed up with Michael Pollan et al." *Agriculture and Human Values* 24: 261–264.

——. 2008a. "Bringing Good Food to Others: Investigating the Subjects of Alternative Food Practice." *Cultural Geographies* 15: 431–447.

——. 2008b. " 'If They Only Knew': Color Blindness and Universalism in California Alternative Food Institutions." *The Professional Geographer* 60(3): 387–397.

Guthman, Julie and Melanie DuPuis. 2006. "Embodying Neoliberalism: Economy, Culture, and the Politics of Fat." *Environment and Planning D: Society and Space* 24: 427–448.

Haer, John L. 1957. "An Empirical Study of Social Class Awareness." *Social Forces* 36(2): 117–121.

Hall, Stewart. 2001. "Cultural Studies." Pp. 88–100 in *The New Social Theory Reader*, edited by Steven Seidman and Jeffrey Alexander. New York: Routledge.

Halweil, Brian. 2005. "The Rise of Food Democracy." *UN Chronicle* 42(1): 71–73.

Hamm, Liza and Michelle Tauber. 2007. "All the Dish!" *People.* Retrieved May 14, 2007. (http://www.people.com/people/archive/article/0,,20062211,00.html)

Hannerz, Ulf. 1996. "Cosmopolitans and Locals in World Culture." Pp. 102–124 in his *Transnational Connections: Culture, People, Places*, London: Routledge.

Harrison, Christy. 2009. "White House Chef Wars." Gourmet online. Posted Jan. 15, 2009 (http://www.gourmet.com/foodpolitics/2009/01/white-house-chef-wars)

Hauck-Lawson, Annie and Jonathon Deutsch (eds.). 2009. *Gastropolis: Food and New York City.* New York: Columbia University Press.

Heldke, Lisa. 2003. *Exotic Appetites. Ruminations of a Food Adventurer.* New York: Routledge.

——. 2005. "But Is it Authentic: Culinary Travel and the Search for the Genuine Article." Pp. 385–394 in *The Taste Culture Reader: Experiencing Food and Drink*, edited by Carolyn Korsmeyer. New York: Berg.

Hesser, A. 1998. "Under the toque: 'Here's Emeril!' Where's the Chef?" *New York Times*, November 4.

Hilton, Matthew. 2003. *Consumerism in Twentieth-Century Britain: The Search for a Historical Movement.* New York: Cambridge University Press.

Hochschild, Jennifer. 1981. *What's Fair? American Beliefs about Distributive Justice.* Cambridge, MA: Harvard University Press.

Hodge, Robert W. and Donald J. Treiman. 1968. "Class Identification in the United States." *American Journal of Sociology* 73(5): 535–547.

hooks, bell. 1992. "Eating the Other: Desire and Resistance." In her *Black Looks: Race and Representation.* Boston, MA: South End Press.

Huggan, Graham. 2000. "Exoticism, Ethnicity, and the Multicultural Fallacy." Pp. 91–96 in *New Exoticisms: Changing Patterns in the Construction of Otherness*, edited by Isabel Santaolalla. Amsterdam: Rodopi.

Hughes, Holly (ed.). 2008. *Best Food Writing 2008.* Emeryville, CA: Marlow & Company.

Inness, Sherri (ed.). 2001. *Kitchen Culture in America: Popular Representations of Food, Gender, and Race.* Philadelphia: University of Pennsylvania Press, 2001.

International Trade Administration. 1998. "International Visitors (Inbound) and
    U.S. Residents (Outbound) (1988–1997)." Item #: f-1997–06–001. Retrieved
    March 13, 2009
    (http://tinet.ita.doc.gov/view/f-1997–06–001/index.html)
———. 2001. "Select Destinations Visited by U.S. Resident Travelers 2000–1999." Item #:
    f-2000–08–001. Retrieved March 13, 2009
    (http://tinet.ita.doc.gov/view/f-2000–08–001/index.html)
Iyengar, Shento. 1990. "Framing Responsibility for Political Issues: The Case of Poverty."
    Political Behavior 12(1): 19–40.
Jackman, Mary R. and Robert W. Jackman. 1983. *Class Awareness in the United States.*
    Berkeley: University of California Press.
Jacobs, Jay. 2002. "James Beard, An American Icon: The Later Years." Pp. 241–276 in
    Endless Feasts. Sixty Years of Food Writing from Gourmet, edited by Ruth Reichl.
    New York: Modern Library.
James, Allison. 2005. "Identity and the Global Stew." Pp. 372–384 in *The Taste Culture
    Reader: Experiencing Food and Drink*, edited by Carolyn Korsmeyer. New York: Berg.
James, Peter. 2002. "Starbucks' Growth Still Hot; Gift Card Jolts Chain's Sales." *Nation's
    Restaurant News* 36(6): 1–2.
Janer, Zilkia. 2005. "Cooking Eurocentrism: Towards a Critical History of French
    Cuisine." Presentation on June 11, 2005, at the Joint Meetings of the Agriculture,
    Food and Human Values Society and Association for the Study of Food and Society.
    Portland, OR.
Johnston, Josée. 2007. "Counter-hegemony or Bourgeois Piggery? Food Politics and the
    Case of FoodShare." Pp. 93–119 in *The Fight over Food: Producers, Consumers, and
    Activists Challenge the Global Food System*, edited by Wynne Wright and Gerrad
    Middendorf. University Park, PA: Rural Sociological Society's Rural Studies Series
    and Pennsylvania State Press.
———. 2008. "The Citizen-Consumer Hybrid: Ideological Tensions and the Case of Whole
    Foods Market." *Theory and Society* 37: 229–270.
Johnston, Josée and Shyon Baumann. 2007. "Democracy versus Distinction: A Study
    of Omnivorousness in Gourmet Food Writing." *American Journal of Sociology*
    113: 165–204.
Johnston, Josée, Andrew Biro, and Norah MacKendrick. 2009. "Lost in the Supermarket:
    The Corporate Organic Foodscape and the Struggle for Food Democracy." *Antipode:
    A Radical Journal of Geography* 41(3): 509–532.
Kadi, Joanna. 1996. *Thinking Class.* Boston, MA: South End Press.
Kamp, David. 2006. *The United States of Arugula. How We Became a Gourmet Nation.*
    New York: Broadway Books.
Keeling Bond, Jennifer, Dawn Thilmany, and Craig Bond. 2006. "Direct Marketing of
    Fresh Produce: Understanding Consumer Purchasing Decisions." *Choices* 21(4): 1–6.
Kellner, Douglas. 1983. "Critical Theory, Commodities and Consumer Society." *Theory,
    Culture and Society* 1(3): 64–84.
Kendall, Diana. 2005. *Framing Class: Media Representations of Wealth and Poverty.* New
    York: Rowman & Littlefield.
Ketchum, Cheri. 2005. "The Essence of Cooking Shows: How the Food Network
    Constructs Consumer Fantasies." *Journal of Communication Inquiry* 29(3): 217–234.
King, P. 2004. "Menu Trends. On-site Sales Drivers Ethnic." *Nation's Restaurant News*
    38(29): 18.
Kluegel, James R. and Eliot R. Smith. 1986. *Beliefs About Inequality.* New York: Aldine
    de Gruyter.

Kollmeyer, Christopher J. 2004. "How the News Media Portray the Economy." *Social Problems* 51(3): 432–452.

Korsmeyer, Carolyn (ed.). 2005. *The Taste Culture Reader: Experiencing Food and Drink.* New York: Berg.

Kruse, Nancy. 2007. "Surveyed Chefs Say Seasonality, Diversity and Updated Tradition Are Hot Culinary Trends." *Nation's Restaurant News*, July 23, 50.

Kuh, Patric. 2001. *The Last Days of Haute Cuisine.* New York: Viking.

Lamont, Michèle. 1992. *Money, Morals, and Manners: The Culture of the French and the American Upper-Middle Class.* Chicago: University of Chicago Press.

——. 2000. *Morality and the Boundaries of Race, Class, and Immigration.* Cambridge, MA and New York: Harvard University Press and Russell Sage Foundation.

Lamont, Michèle and Sada Aksartova. 2002. "Ordinary Cosmopolitanisms: Strategies for Bridging Racial Boundaries among Working-Class Men." *Theory, Culture & Society* 19(4): 1–25.

Lang, Joan. 2007. *Emerging Food Concept Trends in Foodservice.* New York: Packaged Facts.

Lappé, Frances Moore. 1971. *Diet for a Small Planet.* New York: Ballantine Books.

Lefebvre, Henri. 2002. *The Critique of Everyday Life*, Vol. II: *Foundations for a Sociology of the Everyday*, translated by John Moore. New York: Verso.

Levenstein, Harvey. 1989. "Two Hundred Years of French Food in America." *Journal of Gastronomy* 5(Spring): 67–89.

——. 1993. *Paradox of Plenty. A Social History of Eating in Modern America.* New York: Oxford University Press.

Levine, Ed. 2007. "Turkey Talk 2007 with Gourmet's Ruth Reichl." *Serious Eats*, November 13, 2007 (http://www.seriouseats.com/2007/11/thanksgiving-turkey-talk-with-gourmet-magazines-ruth-reichl.html)

Levine, Lawrence W. 1988. *Highbrow/Lowbrow: The Emergence of Cultural Hierarchy in America.* Cambridge, MA: Harvard University Press.

Levy, Paul and Ann Bar. 1984. *The Official Foodie Handbook (Be Modern—Worship Food).* New York: Timbre Books.

Lipovetsky, Gille. 1994. *The Empire of Fashion: Dressing Modern Democracy*, translated by Catherine Porter. Princeton, NJ: Princeton University Press.

LocalHarvest Inc. 2008. "Community Supported Agriculture." Retrieved November 26, 2008 (http://www.localharvest.org/csa/)

Long, Lucy M. (ed.). 2004. *Culinary Tourism: Exploring the Other Through Food.* Lexington: University of Kentucky Press.

Longley, Katerina Olijnyk. 2000. "Fabricating Otherness: Dimidenko and Exoticism." Pp. 21–40 in *New Exoticisms: Changing Patterns in the Construction of Otherness*, edited by Isabel Santaolalla, Amsterdam: Rodopi.

López Sintas, Jordi and Ercilia García Álvarez. 2004. "Omnivore Versus Univore Consumption and its Symbolic Properties: Evidence from Spaniards' Performing Arts Attendance." *Poetics: Journal of Empirical Research on Culture, the Media and the Arts* 32: 463–483.

Lotter, Dan. 2005. "Sizing up Organic Farming in Mexico." Rodale Institute. Retrieved on March 20, 2009 (http://newfarm.rodaleinstitute.org/international/pan-am_don/feb05/mx_organic/index.shtml)

Lovegren, Sylvia. 1995. *Fashionable Food: Seven Decades of Food Fads.* Chicago: University of Chicago Press.

Lutz, Catherine A. and Jane L. Collins. 1993. *Reading National Geographic*. Chicago: University of Chicago Press.

MacCannell, Dean. 1973. "Staged Authenticity: Arrangements of Social Space in Tourist Settings." *American Journal of Sociology* 79: 589–603.

Malone, Nolan, Kaari F. Baluja, Joseph M. Costanzo, and Cynthia J. Davis. 2003. "The Foreign-Born Population: 2000, Census 2000 Brief." U.S. Department of Commerce. Retrieved March 13, 2009 (http://www.census.gov/prod/2003pubs/c2kbr-34.pdf)

Marcuse, Herbert. 1964. *One-Dimensional Man*. Boston, MA: Beacon Press.

Marshall, T. H. 1992 (1950). "Citizenship and Social Class." Pp. 3–51 in *Citizenship and Social Class*, edited by T. Bottomore. London: Pluto Press.

McLellan, David. 1995. *Ideology*. 2nd edn. Milton Keynes, Bucks: Open University Press.

McMichael, Philip. 2000. "Global Food Politics." Pp. 125–143 in *Hungry for Profit: The Agribusiness Threat to Farmers, Food, and the Environment*, edited by Fred Magdoff, John Bellamy Foster, and Frederick H. Buttel. New York: Monthly Review Press.

McNamee, Thomas. 2007. *Alice Waters & Chez Panisse: The Romantic, Impractical, Often Eccentric, Ultimately Brilliant Making of a Food Revolution*. New York: Penguin Group.

Meister, Mark. 2000. "Cultural Feeding, Good Life Science, and the TV Food Network." *Mass Communication and Society* 4(2): 165–182.

Mendelsohn Media Research. 2005. "2005 Mendelsohn Affluent Survey." Retrieved August 30, 2006 (www.mmrsurveys.com/data/2005mendelsohnaffluentsurvey.htm)

Mennell, Stephen. 1996 [1985]. *All Manners of Food. Eating and Taste in England and France from the Middle Ages to the Present*. New York: Basil Blackwell.

Micheletti, Michele. 2003. *Political Virtue and Shopping. Individuals, Consumerism and Collective Action*. New York: Palgrave Macmillan.

Micheletti, Michele, Andreas Føllesdal, and Dietlind Stolle (eds.). 2004. *Politics, Products, and Markets: Exploring Political Consumerism Past and Present*. New Brunswick, NJ: Transaction Publishers.

Miller, Toby. 2007. *Cultural Citizenship: Cosmopolitanism, Consumerism, and Television in a Neoliberal Age*. Philadelphia, PA: Temple University Press.

Mitchell, Don. 2002. "Cultural Landscapes: The Dialectical Landscape? Recent Landscape Research in Human Geography." *Progress in Human Geography* 26(3): 381–389.

Mintz, Sidney. 1985. *Sweetness and Power: The Place of Sugar in Modern History*. New York: Viking.

——. 1996. *Tasting Food, Tasting Freedom: Excursions into Eating, Culture and the Past*. Boston, MA: Beacon Press.

——. 2002. "Food and Eating: Some Persisting Questions." Pp. 24–33 in *Food Nations: Selling Taste in Consumer Societies*, edited by W. Belasco and P. Scranton. New York: Routledge.

Molz, Jennie Germain. 2007. "Eating Difference: The Cosmopolitan Mobilities of Culinary Tourism." *Space and Culture* 10(1): 77–93.

Morgan, Stephen L. and Youngjoo Cha. 2007. "Rent and the Evolution of Inequality in Late Industrial United States." *American Behavioral Scientist* 50: 677–701.

Moskin, Julia. 2006. "Food For the People, Whipped Up by the People." *New York Times*, December 27, F3.

Myers, Ella. 2008. "Resisting Foucauldian Ethics: Associative Politics and the Limits of the Care of the Self." *Contemporary Political Theory* 7(2): 125–146.

Narayan, Uma. 1997. *Dislocating Cultures*. New York: Routledge.

National Restaurant Association. 2007. "Americans Embracing Culinary Tourism, According to New National Restaurant Association/Travel Industry Association Research." *National Restaurant Association News Release*, February 15. Retrieved July 4, 2007 (http://www.restaurant.org/pressroom/pressrelease.cfm?ID=1381)

——. 2008. "Restaurant Industry Fact Sheet." Retrieved November 26, 2008 (http://www.restaurant.org/pdfs/research/2008forecast_factbook.pdf)

Ness, Carol. 2006. "Whole Foods, Taking Flak, Thinks Local." *San Francisco Chronicle*, July 26, F1.

Nestle, Marion. 2003. *Food Politics: How the Food Industry Influences Nutrition and Health*. Berkeley: University of California Press.

"New 'Times' Dining Editor Speaks." 2006. *New York Magazine*. Retrieved September 20, 2006 (http://nymag.com/daily/food/2006/09/new_dining_editor_to_take_rein_1.html)

Nichols, Lawrence T. 1997. "Social Problems as Landmark Narratives: Bank of Boston, Mass Media, and 'Money Laundering'." *Social Problems* 44(3): 324–341.

Nyeleni Declaration. 2007. Accessed December 2008 (http://www.nyeleni2007.org/spip.php?article290)

Oliver, Pamela and Hank Johnston. 1999. "What a Good Idea! Ideology and Frames in Social Movement Research." *Mobilization* 5(1): 37–54.

Packard, Vance. 1957. *The Hidden Persuaders*. New York: D. McKay Co.

Parasecoli, Fabio. 2005. "Feeding Hard Bodies: Food and Masculinities in Men's Fitness Magazines." *Food & Foodways* 13(1–2): 17–37.

——. 2007. "Bootylicious: Food and the Female Body in Contemporary Pop Culture." *Women's Studies Quarterly* 35(1–2): 110–125.

——. 2008. *Bite Me: Food in Popular Culture*. New York: Berg.

Paschel, J. 2006. "4 Hot Food Trends." *Hartbeat: Taking the Pulse of the Marketplace*. The Hartman Group. Retrieved September 4, 2007 (http://www.hartman-group.com/products/HB/2006_08_02.html)

Penfold, Steve. 2008. *The Donut: A Canadian History*. Toronto: University of Toronto Press.

Peterson, Richard. 1997a. "The Rise and Fall of Highbrow Snobbery as a Status Marker." *Poetics: Journal of Empirical Research on Culture, the Media and the Arts* 25: 75–92.

——. 1997b. *Creating Country Music: Fabricating Authenticity*. Chicago: University of Chicago Press.

——. 2005. "Problems in Comparative Research: The Example of Omnivorousness." *Poetics: Journal of Empirical Research on Culture, the Media and the Arts* 33: 257–282.

Peterson, Richard A. and Roger M. Kern. 1996. "Changing Highbrow Taste: From Snob to Omnivore." *American Sociological Review* 61(5): 900–907.

Peterson, Richard A. and Albert Simkus. 1992. "How Musical Taste Groups Mark Occupational Status Groups." Pp. 152–168 in *Cultivating Differences: Symbolic Boundaries and the Making of Inequality*, edited by Michele Lamong and Marcel Fournier. Chicago: University of Chicago Press.

Phillips, Nelson and Cynthia Hardy. 2002. *Discourse Analysis*. Thousand Oaks, CA: Sage Publications.

Pollan, Michael. 2001. *The Botany of Desire: A Plant's-Eye View of the World*. New York: Random House.

——. 2006. *The Omnivore's Dilemma: A Natural History of Four Meals*. New York: Penguin.

Porjes, Susan. 2005 (September). *The U.S. Market for Gourmet and Specialty Foods and Beverages: Market, Product and Trends*. New York: Packaged Facts.

——. 2007a (May). *Fresh and Local Foods in the U.S.* New York: Packaged Facts.

——. 2007b (January). *Conscientious Consumerism and Corporate Responsibility: The Market and Trends for Ethical Products in Food and Beverage, Personal Care and Household Items.* New York: Packaged Facts.

ProfessorBainbridgeOnWine.com. 2008. "The Case Against Rachael Ray." Retrieved May 29, 2008 (http://www.professorbainbridgeonwine.com/wineandfood/comments/the_case_against_rachael_ray/)

Purcell, Denise. 2008. "Specialty Food for the Powerful Twenty-Somethings." *Specialty Food Magazine.* Retrieved December 5, 2008 (http://www.specialtyfood.com/do/news/ViewNewsArticle?id=2334)

Racialicious. 2008. "Is the Food Network the Whitest of Cable Stations?" February 6. [Jae Ran Kim at 12:54 p.m.]. Article posted (http://www.racialicious.com/2008/02/06/is-the-food-network-the-whitest-of-the-cable-stations/)

RAFI [Rural Advancement Foundation International-USA]. 2003. *Who Owns Organic? The Global Status, Prospects and Challenges of a Changing Organic Market.* Retrieved May 15, 2006 (http://www.rafiusa.org/pubs/OrganicReport.pdf.)

Raja, Samina, C. Ma and P. Yadav. 2008. "Beyond Food Deserts: Measuring and Mapping Racial Disparities in Neighborhood Food Environments." *Journal of Planning Education and Research* 27(4): 469–482.

Ram, Uri. 2007. "Liquid Identities: Mecca Cola versus Coca-Cola." *European Journal of Cultural Studies* 10(4): 465–484.

Ray, Krishnendu. 2004. *The Migrant's Table: Meals and Memories in Bengali-American Households.* Philadelphia, PA: Temple University Press.

Raynolds, Laura T. 2004. "The Globalization of Organic Agro-food Networks." *World Development* 32(5): 725–743.

Raynolds, Laura T., Douglas Murray, and John Wilkinson (eds). 2007. *Fair Trade: The Challenges of Transforming Globalization.* New York: Routledge.

Reed, Julia. 2003. "Food for Thought." *New York Times Magazine*, December 14.

Reichl, Ruth. 1999. *Tender at the Bone.* New York: Random House.

——. 2002. *Comfort Me with Apples.* New York: Random House.

——. 2005. *Garlic and Sapphires. The Secret Life of a Critic in Disguise.* New York: Penguin Books.

Ritzer, George. 2000. *McDonaldization of Society.* Thousand Oaks, CA: Pine Forge Press.

Roberts, Martin. 2000. "Transnational Geographic: Perspectives on Baraka." Pp. 97–114 in *New Exoticisms: Changing Patterns in the Construction of Otherness*, edited by Isabel Santaolalla. Amsterdam: Rodopi.

Root, Deborah. 1996. *Cannibal Culture: Art, Appropriation, & the Commodification of Difference.* Boulder, CO: Westview Press.

Roseberry, William. 1994. "The Language of Contention." Pp. 355–365 in *Everyday Forms of State Formation. Revolution and the Negotiation of Rule in Modern Mexico*, edited by Gilbert M. Joseph and Daniel Nugent. Durham, NC: Duke University Press.

Rosset, Peter. 2006. *Food is Different: Why We Must Get the WTO Out of Agriculture.* Black Point, NS, Canada: Fernwood / Zed Books.

Rousseau, George S. and Roy Porter. 1990. *Exoticism in the Enlightenment.* Manchester: Manchester University Press.

Rural Advancement Foundation International-USA. See RAFI.

Said, Edward. 1978. *Orientalism*. New York: Vintage.

Salkin, Allen. 2007. "Sharp Bites." *New York Times*, February 4, 9.

Sanders, Richard. 2006. "A Market Road to Sustainable Agriculture? Ecological Agriculture, Green Food and Organic Agriculture in China." *Development and Change* 37(1): 201–226.

Santaolalla, Isabel (ed.). 2000. "Introduction: What Is 'New' In 'New' Exoticisms?" Pp. 9–20 in *New Exoticisms: Changing Patterns in the Construction of Otherness*, edited by Isabel Santaolalla. Amsterdam: Rodopi.

Scammell, Margaret. 2000. "The Internet and Civic Engagement: The Age of the Citizen-consumer." *Political Communication* 17(4): 351–355.

Schlosser, Eric. 2001. *Fast Food Nations: The Dark Side of the All-American Meal*. New York: Houghton Mifflin Harcourt.

School Library Journal. 2008. "SLJ Talks to Chef Alice Waters about Healthy School Lunches," Debra Lau Whelan, 6/4/2008. Retrieved March 18, 2009 (http://www.schoollibraryjournal.com/article/CA6567284.html?nid=2413&rid=1717931564)

Schor, Juliet. 1998. *The Overspent American: Upscaling, Downshifting, and the New Consumer*. New York: Basic Books.

Schudson, Michael. 1984. *Advertising: The Uneasy Persuasion*. New York: Basic Books.

——. 1991. "Delectable Materialism: Were the Critics of Consumer Culture Wrong All Along?" *The American Prospect*. Retrieved September 1, 2007 (http://www.prospect.org/cs/articles?article=delectable_materialism_were_the_critics_of_consumer_culture_wrong_all_along)

——. 2007. "Citizens, Consumers, and the Good Society." *The Annals of the American Academy of Political and Social Science* 611(1): 236–249.

Seabrook, John. 2001. *Nobrow: The Culture of Marketing—The Marketing of Culture*. New York: Knopf.

Sen, Indrani. 2009. "Green Giant." *Saveur* 119 (April): 45–46.

Serious Eats A. 2008. February 28. "Who's a Foodie Here?" [PumpkinBear at 4:20 p.m.]. Message posted (http://www.seriouseats.com/talk/2008/02/whos-a-foodie-here.html)

Serious Eats B. 2008. February 28. "Who's a Foodie Here?" [aungieinphx at 5:20 p.m.]. Message posted (http://www.seriouseats.com/talk/2008/02/whos-a-foodie-here.html)

Serious Eats C. 2008. February 28. "Who's a Foodie Here?" [ride&cook at 5:25 p.m.]. Message posted (http://www.seriouseats.com/talk/2008/02/whos-a-foodie-here.html)

Serious Eats D. 2008. July 17. "A Real Foodie Or Not?" [embolini9 at 4:15 p.m.]. Message posted (http://www.seriouseats.com/talk/2008/07/a-real-foodie-or-not.html#comments)

Serious Eats E. 2008. February 29. "Who's a Foodie Here?" [Zapatista at 12:55 p.m.]. Message posted (http://www.seriouseats.com/talk/2008/02/whos-a-foodie-here.html)

Serious Eats. 2009. April 15. "Disgruntled Foodie." *Serious Eats* (http://www.seriouseats.com/talk/2009/04/disgruntled-foodie.html)

Shaffer, Joan. 2008. "Number of Farmers' Markets Continues to Rise in U.S." *Agricultural Marketing Service*. United States Department of Agriculture. Retrieved November 26, 2008 (http://www.ams.usda.gov/AMSv1.0/getfiledDocName=STELPRDC5072472&acct=frmrdirmkt)

Shapiro, Laura. 2007. *Julia Child*. New York: Penguin Books.

Shaw, D., Newholm, T. and Dickinson, R. 2006. "Consumption as Voting: An Exploration of Consumer Empowerment." *European Journal of Marketing*. Special Issue: *Consumer Empowerment* 40(9–10): 1049–1067.

Shoukas, Denise. 2008. "Taking the 'Fancy' out of 'Fancy' Food." *Specialty Food Magazine*, July. Retrieved December 5, 2008 (http://www.specialtyfood.com/do/news/ViewNewsArticle?id=2705)

Simmel, Georg. 1957 [1904]. "Fashion." *American Journal of Sociology* 62: 541–558.

Sklair, Leslie. 2001. *The Transnational Capitalist Class*. Malden, MA: Blackwell Publishers.

Slashfood. 2006 Feb. 10. "What Is a Foodie, Anyway?" [Nicole Weston at 3:27 p.m.]. Message posted (http://www.slashfood.com/2006/02/10/what-is-a-foodie-anyway/)

Slatalla, Michelle. 2000. "Mixed Media; Joined by Hip: Food and TV." *New York Times*, September 6, F1.

Slater, Don. 1997. *Consumer Culture and Modernity*. Oxford: Policy Press.

Slocum, Rachel. 2004. "Consumer Citizens and the Cities for Climate Protection Campaign." *Environment and Planning A* 36(5): 763–782

———. 2006. "Anti-racist Practice and the Work of Community Food Organizations." *Antipode* 38(2): 327–349.

———.2007. "Whiteness, Space and Alternative Food Practice." *Geoforum* 38: 520–533.

Sloan, Elizabeth A. 2007a. "Top 10 Food Trends." *Food Technology* 61(4): 23–39.

———. 2007b. "Market Trends: The Experts Speak Out." *Food Technology* 9(7): 59–65.

———. 2008. "Dissecting Demographics." *Food Technology* 8(8): 55–60.

Smith, Alison and J. B. MacKinnon. 2007. *Plenty: One Man, One Woman, and a Raucous Year of Eating Locally*. New York: Crown Publishers.

Smith, Dorothy. 1987. *The Everyday World as Problematic: A Feminist Sociology*. Toronto: University of Toronto Press.

Smith, Jackie, John D. McCarthy, Clark McPhail, and Boguslaw Augustyn. 2001. "From Protest to Agenda Building: Description Bias in Media Coverage of Protest Events in Washington, D.C." *Social Forces* 79(4): 1397–1423.

Smith, Mick. 1997. "Against the Enclosure of the Ethical Commons: Radical Environmentalism as an 'Ethics of Place'." *Environmental Ethics* 18: 339–353.

Smith, Philip. 2001. *Cultural Theory. An Introduction*. Malden, MA: Blackwell Publishers.

Smith, Sherwood Badger. 2006. "The New Face of the Natural Products Consumer." *Natural Foods Merchandiser* 27(8): 17.

Snow, David and Robert Benford. 1988. "Ideology, Frame Resonance, and Participant Mobilization." *International Social Movement Research* 1: 197–218.

Sontag, Susan. 1966. *Against Interpretation and Other Essays*. New York: Farrar, Straus & Giroux.

Soper, Kate. 2004. "Rethinking the Good Life: Consumer as Citizen." *Capitalism, Nature, Socialism* 15(3): 111–116.

———. 2007. "Re-thinking the 'Good Life': The Citizenship Dimension of Consumer Disaffection with Consumerism." *Journal of Consumer Culture* 7(2): 205–229.

Staller, Karen M. 2003. "Constructing the Runaway Youth Problem: Boy Adventurers to Girl Prostitutes, 1960–1978." *Journal of Communication* 53(2): 330–346.

Stern, Frederick Martin. 1952. *Capitalism in America: A Classless Society*. Toronto: Rinehart & Co.

Stuber, Jenny. 2006. "Talk of Class: The Discursive Repertoires of White Working- and Upper-Middle-Class College Students." *Journal of Contemporary Ethnography* 35(3): 285–318.

Stuff, J. E., P. H. Casey, C., Connell, C. M. Champagne, J. M. Gossett, D. Harsha, B. J. McCabe Sellers, J. M. Robbins, P. M. Simpson, K. L. Szeto, J. L. Weber, and M. L. Bogle. 2007. "Household Food Insecurity and Obesity, Chronic Disease, and Chronic Disease Risk Factors." *Journal of Hunger and Environmental Nutrition* 1(2): 43–62.

Szasz, Andrew. 2007. *Shopping our Way to Safety*. Minneapolis: University of Minnesota Press.

Tanyeri, Dana. 2006. "10 Food Innovations." *Restaurant Business* 105(9): 22–28.

Taylor, Charles. 1992. *The Ethics of Authenticity*. Cambridge, MA: Harvard University Press.

Tedeschi, Bob. 2007. "E-Commerce report: readers are key ingredient as virtual kitchen heats up." *New York Times*, June 25, C6.

The Daily Beast. 2008 Nov. 14. "Why Foodies Give Me Indigestion." [B38293 at 1:54 p.m.]. Message posted (http://www.thedailybeast.com/blogs-and-stories/ 2008-11-14/foodies-make-me-sick/)

The Frugal Foodie. 2006. Dec. 8. "Friday Food Politics: The Economist vs. Ethical Food Edition." [John V at 11:29 p.m.]. Message posted (http://frugalfoodie.blogspot.com/search/label/Food%20Politics)

The L Magazine. 2008. Jan. 10. "Cracking the New York Times Most-Emailed-Article Code." [Edith at 3:27 p.m.]. Message posted (http://www.thelmagazine.com/lmag_blog/blog/post__07100805.cfm)

Thilmany, Dawn, Craig A. Bond, and Jennifer K. Bond. 2008. "Going Local: Exploring Consumer Behaviour and Motivations for Direct Food Purchases." *American Journal of Agricultural Economics* 90: 1303–1309.

Titus, Jordan J. 2004. "Boy Trouble: Rhetorical Framing of Boys' Underachievement." *Discourse: Studies in the Cultural Politics of Education* 25(2): 145–169.

Travel Industry Association of America. 2007. Feb. 2. "Comprehensive Culinary Travel Survey Provides Insights on Food and Wine Travelers." *Travel Industry Association of America News Release*. Retrieved July 4, 2007 (http://www.tia.org/pressmedia/pressrec.asp?Item=750)

Trilling, Lionel. 1972. *Sincerity and Authenticity*. Cambridge, MA: Harvard University Press.

Vander Stichele, Alexander and Rudi Laermans. 2006. "Cultural Participation in Flanders: Testing the Cultural Omnivore Thesis with Population Data." *Poetics: Journal of Empirical Research on Culture, the Media and the Arts* 34: 45–64.

van Eijck, Koen. 2001. "Social Differentiation in Musical Taste Patterns." *Social Forces* 79: 1163–1184.

van Eijck, Koen and Bartine Bargeman. 2004. "The Changing Impact of Social Background on Lifestyle: 'Culturalization' instead of Individualization?" *Poetics: Journal of Empirical Research on Culture, the Media and Arts* 32: 6439–6461.

Vasterman, Peter L. M. 2005. "Media Hype: Self-Reinforcing News Waves, Journalistic Standards and the Construction of Social Problems." *European Journal of Communication* 20(4): 508–530.

Veblen, Thorstein. 1994 [1899]. *Theory of the Leisure Class*. New York: Penguin Classics.

Warde, Alan. 1997. *Consumption, Food and Taste: Culinary Antinomies and Commodity Culture*. London: Sage Publications.

——. 2008. "Does Taste Still Serve Power?" *Sociologica: Italian Online Sociological Review* 3.

Warde, Alan and Lydia Martens. 2000. *Eating Out: Social Differentiation, Consumption and Pleasure*. Cambridge, UK: Cambridge University Press.

Warde, Alan and M. Tomlinson. 1995. "Taste among the British Middle Classes, 1968–88." Pp. 241–256 in *Social Change and the Middle Classes*, edited by T. Butler and M. Savage. London: UCL Press.

Warde, Alan, David Wright, and Modesto Gayo-Cal. 2008. "The Omnivorous Orientation in the UK." *Poetics* 36(2–3): 148–165.

We Are Never Full. 2008. Jan. 18. "News Shocker! Diversity Finally Comes to Food Network!" [Amy]. Article posted (http://www.weareneverfull.com/news-shocker-diversity-finally-comes-to-food-network/)

Weeden, Kim A. and David B. Grusky. 2005. "The Case for a New Class Map." *American Journal of Sociology* 111(1): 141–212.

Weeden, Kim A., Young-Mi Kim, Matthew Di Carlo, and David B. Grusky. 2007. "Social Class and Earnings Inequality." *American Behavioral Scientist* 50: 702–736.

Williams-Forson, Psyche A. 2006. *Building Houses out of Chicken Legs: Black Women, Food and Power*. Chapel Hill: University of North Carolina Press.

Wilk, Richard. 2002. "Food and Nationalism: The Origins of 'Belizean Food' ". Pp. 67–89 in *Food Nations: Selling Taste in Consumer Societies*, edited by W. Belasco and P. Scranton. New York: Routledge.

——. 2006. *Home Cooking in the Global Village: Caribbean Food from Buccaneers to Ecotourists*. New York: Berg.

Wood, Roy. 1995. *The Sociology of the Meal*. Edinburgh: University of Edinburgh Press.

Wray, Tom. 2007. "Eastern Inspiration." *National Provisioner* 221(5): 80–84.

Wright, Erik Olin. 1997. *Class Counts: Comparative Studies in Class Analysis*. Cambridge, UK: Cambridge University Press.

Wright, Wynne and Gerad Middendorf (eds.). 2008. *The Fight Over Food: Producers, Consumers, and Activists Challenge the Global Food System*. Philadelphia: Pennsylvania State University Press.

Zagat. 2008. "Company Overview." Retrieved December 5, 2008 (http://www.zagat.com/about/)

Zavisca, Jane. 2005. "The Status of Cultural Omnivorism: A Case Study of Reading in Russia." *Social Forces* 84(2): 1233–1255.

Zelman, Kathleen. 2008. "Top 10 Food Trends for 2008." *Medicinenet*, 17 January 2008. Retrieved December 5, 2008 (www.medicinenet.com/script/main/art.asp?articlekey=86520)

Zukin, Sharon. 1991. *Landscapes of Power: From Detroit to Disneyworld*. Berkeley: University of California Press.

——. 2004. *Point of Purchase: How Shopping Changed American Culture*. New York: Routledge.

——. 2008. "Consuming Authenticity: From Outposts of Difference to Means of Exclusion." *Cultural Studies* 22(5): 724–748.

Zukin, Sharon and Jennifer Smith Maguire. 2004. "Consumers and Consumption." *Annual Review of Sociology* 30: 173–197.

INDEX